FLOWERS for ALL SEASONS

A Guide to Colorful Trees, Shrubs and Vines

Jeff and Marilyn Cox, Authors of *The Perennial Garden*

Rodale Press, Emmaus, Pennsylvania

To the Devas

Printed in the United States of America

Book design by Linda Jacopetti.

Illustrations by Pamela Carroll.

Photographs by Candace Billman, Richard Brown, David Cavagnaro, Marilyn Cox, Brian Davis, Derek Fell, T. L. Gettings, Heather Hafleigh, J. Michael Kanouff, Alison Miksch, Joanne Pavia, Rodale Press Photography Department, Margaret Skrovanek, Marilyn Stouffer, M. Hamilton Whitman.

Library of Congress Cataloging-in-Publication Data

Cox, Jeff, 1940-
    Flowers for all seasons : a guide to colorful trees, shrubs, and vines / Jeff and Marilyn Cox.
        p.   cm.

    Includes index.
    ISBN 0-87857-726-2
    1. Flowering woody plants.   2. Flowers.
    3. Landscape gardening.   I. Cox, Marilyn,
    1951-   . II. Title.
    SB435.C794   1987
    S35.9—dc19   87-20444
                          CIP
ISBN 0-87857-726-2   hardcover

2   4   6   8   10   9   7   5   3   hardcover

Contents

Acknowledgments

We'd like to thank all those unsung horticultural heroes whose work has given us the plants we celebrate in this book. They are a large cadre of dedicated souls spread through the centuries—people who have cared for beauty and have chosen their plants for that divine quality.

We'd especially like to thank the photographers who worked on this book. We chanced to meet David Cavagnaro at our local organic gardening club, and he turned out to be one of the finest photographic artists in the country. We feel lucky that his work is so well represented in this book. We found photographer Heather Hafleigh through Larry Korn, a longtime friend who also helped us with the charts. Tom Gettings and his staff photographers gave us excellent photos, plus technical support and encouragement, for which we are very grateful. We want to especially thank Rose Reichl, who kept tabs on the thousands of photos from which the final 79 were selected, and who sleuthed out many hard-to-find plant identifications.

Dr. Darrell Apps at Longwood Gardens, M. Hamilton Whitman at Ladew Topiary Gardens, Morris Cecil of Hearst Castle, Hadley Osborne at Filoli, and Victor Yool at Berkeley Hort all helped and supported our work, and they deserve our thanks.

We'd like to thank Anne Halpin, Suzanne Nelson, and Ellen Cohen for their editing, and Barb Emert and Dorothy Smickley for all their help and hard work. To the art staff go special thanks for their efforts to make the book beautiful.

Introduction

Through 14 years and three houses, we've never been without fresh flowers. They may be the last blossoms on an African violet, or droopy daisies in a Ball jar. Most often they're a fresh bouquet of cut flowers on the kitchen table—ones we've grown, or a two-dollar special from the flower shop, or whatever we can find growing wild. But always, something has been blooming to brighten the indoors.

The earth "household" is also never without flowers. When half the world is locked in frost, the other half is blooming under the solstitial sun. Even in the dead of the Northern winter, rare and brave plants manage to flower. The most thrilling sights in the winter woods are the tiny red strands of the filbert flowers dangling in the frozen air, and the strange, yellow zigzags of the witch-hazel's flowers adorning the bush in the dreariest, darkest part of the year.

Here in northern California, where the climate borders on the semitropical, nature has a whole crop of wild winter bloomers that it arrays for the season. These winter flowers may not be spectacular, but they are constant and cheerful, and easily maintain the tradition of flowers for all seasons.

I want our house and property to be submerged by waves of flowers that follow one another through the cycling years. The vines will climb the walls, the flowering trees will leap up to cover the roof, and the shrubs will lead whole beds of perennials and annuals in the great dance of life and joy.

In our previous book, *The Perennial Garden* (Rodale Press, 1985), we described guidelines for using herbaceous perennial flowers in beds and borders. Herbaceous perennials are plants that die back to the roots each year, putting up new, green growth and blossoms for the new growing season. In this book we will concentrate on the woody perennial flowers—trees, shrubs, and vines that may be evergreen or deciduous, but whose woody stems, branches, and trunks stay alive, if asleep, during the dormant season. These permanent, flowering woody plants form the foundation of the garden. We will, of course, discuss the use of flowering herbaceous perennials, biennials, annuals, and ground covers along with these woody plants, but the focus will be on plants that form the skeletal structure on which nature hangs her annual, fresh green growth. The gardens we will be describing throughout these pages are mixed gardens—ones where many types of blooming plants join together in an artistic arrangement to provide flowers and beautiful colors through all the seasons.

We start in the first chapter by discussing how to use different kinds of flowering woody plants in artful arrangements in the yard. Chapter 2 offers a month-by-month rundown of what can be blooming in the garden throughout the year, from trees, shrubs, and vines to perennials, annuals, and bulbs (and even indoor bloomers). Each month has a Featured Flower of the Month, in which we

"We want our house and property to be submerged under waves of flowers that follow one another through the cycling years."

call a special plant to your attention. In Chapter 3 we give photographic examples of superb flowers in all seasons. The fourth chapter of the book is given to charts of flowering trees, shrubs, and vines. These charts represent a selection process that reduced tens of thousands of species and cultivars to the 300 or so that we think consistently star in the garden. We believe these charts will be of the greatest help to gardeners trying to sort through the huge number of cultivated flowering plants offered in catalogs and nurseries.

Our main interest is to help you turn your beautiful dreams into reality by helping you make the best selection of permanent plants. These trees and shrubs will become old friends as they bloom through the years. Out of bloom, they provide green masses of foliage and strong lines in their stems as back-

drops for the herbaceous flowers.

Look at the beautiful displays of flowers you know. Part of the beauty is invariably the setting: a green lawn between masses of trees and shrubs; a shady spot formed by large canopies of rhododendrons. Beds of perennials look best held in the strong arms of their woody brethren. In this book, our focus is on the garden and landscape in which the perennials are set. A garden reveals the hand of man in nature's appearance, delighting those who view it with a comforting sense that a benign intelligence has planned such beauty for their enjoyment.

We too can create gardens that will grow in beauty, even after we're gone. To do this, we need first to please our own sensibilities. The greatest gardens, after all, are the ones that please us most.

Chapter 1

Creating Combinations of Flowering Plants

When we arrange flowers in a vase, we're looking to harmonize and balance color, shape, line, mass, texture, tension, and in some cases, fragrance. Once arranged, the flowers don't change except to fall apart.

When we arrange flowers in a garden, we start with those same formal concerns on paper, but then must translate them into horticultural ones.

We work with living plants. Plants produce the flowers that elicit the praise. Behind the full-blown facade of the spring bower lies the gardener's talent for growing things in the right places, and a forebearance of muddy clothes, thorns in fingers, and shirts glued to one's sweaty back from several hours of weeding.

The gardener has to plan for the fact that his plants bloom at different times. Each plant has a different lifespan—from less than a growing season for some annuals to more than several human lifetimes for some trees. A garden structured with long-lasting woody plants will have a certain appearance when young, quite another when it matures years later, and yet another when overmature and ready to be thinned out. These are the kinds of elements the gardener has to deal with in order to effectively solve the formal artistic concerns of flower arranging as applied to a living garden.

For their part, the plants seem to solve the problems of harmonizing form, color, mass, line, and texture quite easily—almost as a by-product of their primary concerns of reproducing and getting enough nutrients, water, and sunlight. The gardener's job, then, is to take care of all these primary concerns for the plant, so that it may turn its attention to creating a refined display and achieving its full potential.

When the gardener fulfills her part of the bargain, the plants fulfill theirs. It's always thrilling to notice how well the plants can balance masses, intertwine forms for great aesthetic effect, and dangle flowers casually yet perfectly. Can nature make a mistake? If we see a mistake, the flaw may be in our vision rather than in creation.

The word "casually" is key here. Personally, we feel that overly formal gardens are suffocating. It's as if the gardener is saying to the plants: "I know better than you how you should look. I have human expectations, and you're going to fit them." The gardener rules with an iron conception and a busy hand restraining the floppy exuberance of much of nature's growth. Plants in such for-

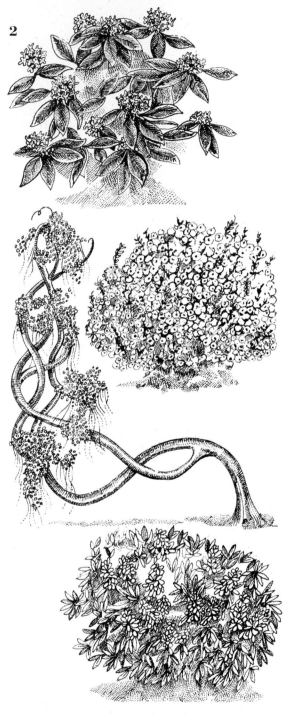

Plant features to be harmonized in the garden, besides color, include form, shown by the winter daphne, at top; mass, shown by New Zealand tea tree's bushy appearance; line, given by the sinuous trunks of a wisteria, and texture, such as boxleaf hebe's regular rows of leaves.

mal arrangements bear the treatment rather sullenly. Very strict gardens may be amazing, but they are not joyful.

The casual, even unplanned, achievement of beautiful effects is the true mark of a functioning person-plant partnership. Our part is to think out the initial arrangement of plants, put the stock in the ground, care for it, and allow it to grow as it will.

When our minds and the natural mind are in harmony, joyful beauty results. Who could have known that the trumpet vine would find its way to such a perfect spot atop the garden shed? Who could have ever planned for the birds that chitter among the thicket of rambling rose canes above the doorway? In the best gardens, the work may be hard, but the effect is natural and easy.

So, we feel that it is extremely important not to plan out every turn of the vine, every inch of the garden. Creating good combinations of flowering plants starts simply—perhaps with a favorite plant that you must have in the garden—and moves by guidelines to an overall plan. We leave the fine details to nature.

Site Considerations

The best site for an assortment of flowering plants is the one with the most varied conditions. We'd love to find an acre with a low, marshy spot and a pond, a sunny sward, a wooded grove, a rock outcropping, a stream, and a dappled glade. That way we could have some of all the flowering plants, for each plant likes different conditions.

Most likely you, like us, will start with something less, and that cuts into your choices for what to plant. And thank goodness it does, because the world is awash with planting stock and we have to start limiting ourselves somewhere.

We start with what we have, with what's given to us by nature as amended by mankind. It may be a flat field of weeds without a tree in sight, or a hillside that falls to a wet slough littered with rubber tires, or just a regular suburban yard. Whatever it is, it can be transformed into a place of beauty by someone's love and effort. Once that land was part of the North American wilderness, and nature had a plan for it. Or perhaps it was eastern hardwood forest, tallgrass prairie, or coastal marsh. It had a native vegetation, and any gardener is wise to begin to plan the garden by considering what naturally does well there.

If you need help identifying the trees, shrubs, and flowers that are growing naturally on your site, use a good basic guide like the *Shrubs, Ground Covers,* or *Perennials* volumes in the Taylor's Guides series (Houghton Mifflin, 1987). For trees, *The Tree Identification Book* (Quill, 1958) is a good place to start. There may also be a native plant society in your area that can assist you. Then, once you know what's growing, check the plant's preferred growing requirements. If there's a stand of mountain laurel—shrubs that favor semishaded, moist, humusy conditions—that's your clue that any plants you bring to the site should be suited to those conditions. By figuring out what thrives naturally in that spot, you can better understand all the characteristics of the site, and make enlightened plant selections.

For the first year after moving to our California house, we made no drastic alterations in the landscape. We wanted to see a full cycle of the seasons before deciding how to landscape the property. "Look before you leap" is a good approach for everyone who is thinking about landscaping a new property. Designing gardens that include permanent woody plants takes a lot of observation, and a good plan.

What's Already There?

The land to be beautified may already have large trees, shrubs, and other shade-throwing structures, giving you definite areas of sun, partial shade, and full shade. Preserve the best of what's there. I never remove mature trees and shrubs unless they're ugly, diseased, or too close to other trees. If they throw shade, plant shade-loving flowering plants. Starting with a bare area means you have to consider structural plantings that will throw pools of shade when they reach full size in a few years. At this point, however, you are simply assessing what's on the site, and how that limits and defines the kind of garden you can make.

Planning for Pathways

The circulation of human beings through the future garden must now be considered. Where paths are already established on the property, keep them. Few habits die harder than taking the well-worn path. If there are no paths, walk the property and visualize how you want it to be when it's complete. What route will you take? How will the path curve to hide parts of the garden? What's the most interesting path? Walkways based on the fanciful idea that a nice path will meander through a lawn are simply impediments to passage, and you'll soon see the grass worn bare where feet have ignored the meander to go straight to their destination. When planning paths, know the next destination, and get there by a realistic route, if not a straight one. If your paths take people out into the garden, remember to bring them back to the house. Nothing is more anticlimactic than walking into a garden, reaching the end of the path at a point farthest away from the house, then having to retrace your steps over the same route. Avoid that disappointment by making your paths a loop, laid out the way a golf course is laid out, discrete areas side by side, always swinging back to the starting point.

Creating Interesting Vantage Points

Have you noticed how paths are laid out in parks that feature nature walks? Numbered posts signal the hiker that something of interest is at hand, and the guidebook explains what that is. We don't want numbered posts and guidebooks in our gardens, but we want the rest of the idea: that certain spots encourage the walker to stop, be still, and see what's there. Maybe that's the spot to place a bench. Or perhaps the path widens so that the walker can step back and observe a beautiful association of plants. It's from such vantage points that visitors will see sculpture that we've placed in the garden for their enjoyment (and ours). All this presupposes the ability to interrupt a view with a barrier, whether hedge, shrub, house, or fence.

Major Changes

It may be that you want to change the natural condition of a site. For instance, a soggy half acre, unfit for much except Joe-pye weed and water grasses, might be beautified by channeling the surface water to a pond, and raising the level of the rest of the site for better drainage. Then several kinds of plants could be used, and instead of the monotonous bog, several types of ecosystems would be established: water, waterside, bog, moist soil, and perhaps dry soil if a mound is made.

Changing the natural conditions of a site is usually a radical job, involving heavy equipment and the importing of boulders and other materials. Most such man-made landscapes look phony, like a caricature of a landscape. Unless your site is a bog, you might do better working with what nature provides.

Practical Considerations

Consider whether your potential garden site has any natural features you can use to the garden's advantage: a large rock or group of rocks; a small stream; a large old tree; a raised portion where a wall might be built. It's at these natural features that garden planning starts. Man-made features, such as a fence, pool, outbuilding, or stone wall also provide starting points for garden design.

Whether your site has features or is flat and featureless, it will probably include the most important feature of all—the house. Your gardens, in the end, will be created to surround your home with beauty and make outdoor living delightful.

In planning, remember that the gardens that take the most maintenance work should be closest to the house and toolshed; the more natural and easy to maintain gardens should be farther from the house.

When selecting sites for plantings, look through the main windows of the house to make sure you're not going to plant large specimens smack in the middle of the picture window view. In other cases, you may want to look into a small garden from, for instance, a kitchen window, to admire the lilies while you peel the potatoes.

Poetic Considerations

When choosing a site, use your heart as well as your brain. Try to feel how the land will respond to your efforts. Follow a hunch.

There's an artistry to siting gardens that takes many things into account—some practical, some poetic. By poetic, we mean being able to visualize a plant—say, a mock orange—growing in a bare spot. You can see the bush, 15 feet tall and as wide across, arrayed with its white blooms, looking beautiful. In effect,

A path winds back into a garden of herbaceous perennials and trees, revealing new treasures at every turn.

you're seeing a potential future. You can choose to make it actual, or set aside that vision and imagine another.

It is at that level of choosing sites that the gardener begins to have real fun. The same kind of enjoyment is to be had fitting the right plant to the given site. You'll know the right plant—it's the one that will grow well and flower beautifully. It will be happy.

Selecting Plant Materials

Have you ever noticed how the woods are built? Near the ground are herbaceous plants that will disappear with the frosts. Next there is a shrubby layer of woody-stemmed plants that tops out at about eye level. Above this towers the canopy of the trees, whose trunks and branches are draped with vines and creepers.

By horticultural analogy, many gardens in the eastern United States are designed with low beds and borders of herbaceous plants interspersed with medium-sized shrubbery, and surrounded by tall flowering trees. Trees can be used as support for flowering vines. Thus, a careful grouping of cultivated plants can reproduce the arrangement of the wild woods, but now with plants selected for their beautiful flowers. The rest of this section will help you construct a garden by thinking in terms of large trees, medium shrubs, and possible vines and ground covers.

The Return of the Natives

Every region has native flowering vines, trees, and shrubs, as well as perennial types of flowers. These plants have many "built-in" advantages: they tolerate the local climate; few pests and diseases bother them; and they often need less water (where periodic drought is a feature of the climate). As a group, they are preeminently suited to your garden, as long as you give them the conditions of soil, moisture, and sun that they like. When North America was wilderness, your native plants were there, doing fine, with no one to fuss over them. Plant breeders have since given us varieties of these natives with larger flowers in vast arrays of colors. Natives are the old reliables—trouble-free, familiar, and predictable. Whether in the plains, the Rockies, the eastern hills or on the Pacific Coast, arrangements of native vegetation give us clues to stable arrangements of cultivated varieties.

Trees

Trees are our sturdy protectors, deeply alive, creating a gentle, shady, moist, green world for us away from the burning sun. When the trees flower, the effect can be spectacular. I remember a large old apple tree a few miles from my father's house exploding with bloom. The scent of the apple blossoms hung in the warm May air. The tree hummed with myriad bees working the flowers. For me, it became the archetypal image of spring, and showed me that a well-pruned apple tree can be the centerpiece of any fine landscape design.

Most flowering trees need full sun to make good bloom. Think of the fruit trees you've seen. Where they intercept adequate light, they produce profuse bloom. Where they're shaded, just a few sparse blossoms appear. The same is true for most other flowering trees, except natural understory trees such as the dogwoods that erupt into bloom before the canopy trees open their leaves.

You're not going to be able to have a forest of perfect specimens. Planted close enough for their canopies to crowd each other, ornamental trees will only bloom on their sunlit tops, visible more to pigeons than to people on the ground. Planted alone as specimens in order to achieve full bloom, on the other hand, ornamental trees will produce a polka dot landscape—not very artistic or satisfactory.

Pleasing Arrangements

One very good solution to this problem is to plan to use trees in groups of two or three. Where they grow together, they produce a canopy under which you can plant low-light shrubs, such as rhododendrons, or herbaceous plants like hostas and ferns. Each of the trees in such an association will have a large side exposed to the sun or bright light, allowing for bloom from top to bottom. Trees may be chosen for continual bloom (for example, *Amelanchier grandiflora* blooms in April, *Cornus alternifolia* in May to June, and *Stewartia pseudocamellia* in June and July) or for an association of three that bloom together with careful color harmony, such as the whites and pinks of May-blooming dogwoods, crabapples, and English hawthorn. In addition to these compatible groupings, give a few very special and beautiful specimens, such as beauty bush or buddleia, a solitary space, in full sun and full view.

It's best to use trees of different genera in these associations. That is, mix a flowering white crabapple (*Malus floribunda*) with a pink weeping cherry (*Prunus subhirtella* var. *pendula*), rather than two crabapples or

At top, a natural woods scene with tall canopy trees, understory brush, and native herbaceous ground covers. Below, similar structure given by crabapples, shrubs, and ground cover.

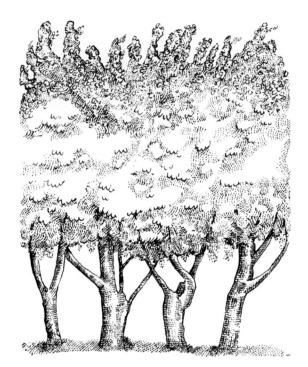

Crabapple trees spaced too closely only get sun on their tops, and consequently, bloom best only on top. Spaced evenly to intercept sun, the typical "orchard" arrangement is dull and uninteresting.

Three trees, a crabapple on the left, a weeping cherry in the background, and an evergreen magnolia, create a shady area beneath them for a rhododendron, hostas, and ferns.

two cherries in the same association. By contrasting different genera, the look and feel of the trees are contrasted too. Some trees are grove trees, meaning they do well in the company of their kind, but flowering fruit trees tend to repel others of their kind if grown too close together.

Groups of trees may be freestanding or designed to touch other groups of trees. This creates the backdrop against which flowering shrubs and herbaceous plants are set.

As you can see from the illustration on page 10, when a property is planted in groups of trees with select specimen trees set off by themselves, there is a mixture of open lawn or meadow, woods edge, and woods. This arrangement gives most of the possible conditions for light and shade, providing accommodations for all kinds of plants with differing requirements. It provides for areas where paths can wind, and hides one area from another to entice visitors to the garden and lure them around corners into undiscovered territory.

When deciding where to plant trees, consider the lateral view of the property as well as the aerial view. Rolling hills create dells where tender trees may be protected from prevailing winds.

Trees will shield the property from a road or highway. They give shade, coolness, and protection from wind; provide a sound barrier; and have a beneficial visual effect on buildings by softening their contours. Most importantly, they screen off the outdoor living spaces from neighbors and thus provide highly prized privacy. Consider how to take advantage of these benefits when siting your trees.

When you plant trees, you're usually

A mix of specimens and groups of trees arranged to the edges of a central lawn provides the most varied habitats for a large yard.

planting saplings 20 or 30 feet apart, with the idea that someday they will grow to make a mature association. For the first 5 years, you have mostly open area with a few small trees. There will be lots of sunlight reaching the ground. From 5 to 10 years, you will have increasing amounts of shade as the trees grow toward maturity. By 10 to 15 years, they will usually touch, forming a canopy.

This situation occurs almost every time someone landscapes a garden. It means that you do not plant a finished landscape. The garden is ever changing, always growing, and this changing means that plants have to be moved, divided, pruned, and eliminated or added. For instance, in the first five years, when the trees are saplings, you may choose to plant the open area between them with tall, sun-loving perennials. Between five and ten years, as the shade thrown by the trees deepens, the sun-loving perennials can be moved to other, sunnier gardens, while the space between the trees may be planted to shade-loving shrubs and perennials. When the canopy is fully closed, it may be your plan to eliminate the shrubbery in the center area between the trees and create a cool outdoor living area with a stone pavement.

Another way to handle the large distances between saplings is to interplant the slow-maturing varieties with quick-growing kinds. These trees can be removed when the slower ones mature. The trouble is that, human nature being what it is, people forget to remove the "weed" trees and a jumble of dense tree growth results.

A catalpa is one of these weed trees, with pretty, pinkish-white flowers in the summer and long, beanlike seedpods in the fall. Other fast-maturing flowering trees include the acacia, which erupts into bright yellow bloom in the middle of the winter in Zone 9; the *Paulownia tomentosa,* or empress tree, with its light lilac trumpets appearing in spring in Zone 7; and *Robinia pseudoacacia,* or

black locust, with its fragrant pea-shaped flowers in May in Zone 3. By the time they are ready to come out, these so-called weed trees will be enormous and require specialized help to remove.

Combinations with Year-Round Beauty

Trees that attract bees in the spring, such as cultivars of *Malus, Prunus,* and *Sorbus,* usually attract birds in the fall. Flowering trees also attract people. Apples, plums, peaches, cherries, apricots, loquats, jujubes, serviceberries, almonds, citrus, and many others please the eye and nose in one season and the mouth in another.

Flowering trees often look best associated with evergreens for a dark, contrasting background to their floral displays. Groups of trees can and should include the evergreens, for they are the permanent features of the garden in which deciduous plants wax and wane. Coniferous plants provide the deepest, darkest backgrounds, while broad-leaved evergreens often provide associated bloom. The combination of rhododendron, dark pine such as Serbian spruce, and dogwood provides lots of foliage that will persist through the winter months and give a splash of color in spring.

For summer-blooming trees, you can choose hot-colored types like *Lagerstroemia indica,* the crape myrtle, which blooms in July in Zone 7. Or subtler trees like *Franklinia alatamaha,* a Georgia native with silky white flower petals that cup a spray of golden stamens in August. The leaves of both crape myrtle and franklinia also color up beautifully in the fall—an added bonus. Good autumn color may not be such an important planning consideration in New England and the northern Middle Atlantic states where the native trees light up with fiery colors,

The three ages of the garden: young, with trees surrounded by sun-loving perennials and annuals; half-grown, with trees throwing partial shade onto perennials; and fully grown, with a pool of deep shade claimed by the owner.

An evergreen Serbian spruce, deciduous dogwood, and evergreen rhododendron make a threesome that remains interesting in the winter.

but is worth planning for in the Sun Belt and the West.

Other aesthetic characteristics of flowering trees are the quality of their leaves, their bark, and how they look in the winter when they lose their leaves. Dogwood, crape myrtle, magnolia, yellowwood, crabapple, cherry, and stewartia all have pleasing winter shapes. Pruning can refine their naturally attractive shapes.

Some Cultural Considerations

When considering trees for your landscape, realize that more of the tree lies below the soil than grows above it. The roots of a tree grow well beyond the dripline (the area on the ground that would be shaded if the sun were directly over the top of the tree), usually twice the diameter of the dripline, and sometimes three times. Roots can penetrate to 20 feet beneath the soil surface, too, making an enormous mass of wood and root around the tree.

Drought-tolerant plants may thrive where tree roots underlie the soil, but herbaceous plants that like moisture often have a hard time in such zones. Woody flowering shrubs are more suited to these areas, as they are used to competing with trees for nutrients and moisture, and they establish a root system that intertwines with the tree's roots. It's possible to grow shade-loving perennials under the trees, but it takes special effort, such as dug-out planting holes, deep soil behind a retaining wall, or containers, plus extra water during dry periods.

For the best water retention, good looks, weed control, and source of continuing fertility for your flowering tree and shrub associations, mulch everything under the driplines with lots of leaf mold, except directly around the trunk. Pulling mulch up against trunks may promote rot.

As this mulch continues to decay over the years, you'll find that it adds enough fertility and moisture-holding capacity to support more herbaceous perennials than before.

Mulching the area under woody plants means that no lawn will grow there—a definite plus for several reasons. Lawns need water in the summer drought periods, and watering trees, especially their trunks, promotes root rot and crown diseases. If you must water ornamental trees, place a soaker or drip hose in a circle at about the dripline, under the mulch, and water deeply and well until the soil is thoroughly wet.

Trees are naturally conical, domed, irregular, prostrate, rounded, spreading, vase-shaped, or weeping. Although some pruning

Tree roots extend well past the dripline of the outer leaves. Note that the middle tree will exhaust available nutrients and water first, as it has no open area for free root growth.

is necessary for a neat look and to accentuate the natural growth habit of the tree, trying to prune a conical tree into a rounded one is impossibly demanding.

Shrubs

Shrubs star in our gardens because we look them right in the eye. They present their foliage and flowers right in front of us. We don't rest our eyes on the treetops or on the ground covers at our feet, but on the middle distance—shrub territory. Shrubs range in size from very short heathers to medium-sized spiraea to large lilacs to huge, billowing smoke trees. Because of their importance in garden design, tens of thousands of shrubs have been cultivated over the years; with thousands available, gardeners have their pick of forms and colors.

Account for Mature Size

Shrubs in the garden often tend to get out of hand because not enough attention is paid to their eventual size. Bushes crowd into one another. Natural pathways are lost. Fungus and rot form under the shaded hedgerows of plantings gone wild. Too little light reaches the low flowering shrubs for them to bloom. Hedges meant to be kept low reach up to the trees.

To avoid the fate of the overgrown landscape, plant shrubs whose eventual size will

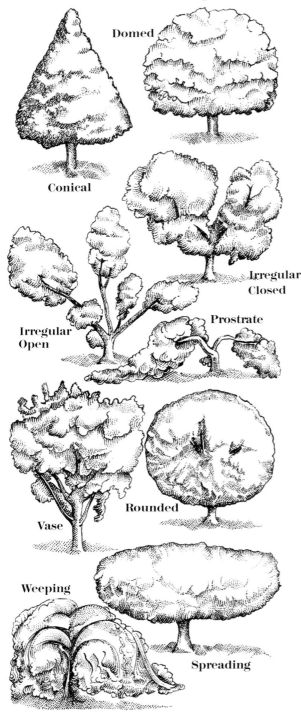

Conical

Domed

Irregular
Closed

Irregular
Open

Prostrate

Vase

Rounded

Weeping

Spreading

Types of Tree Shapes

allow them to coexist properly, growing only in wisdom, not in girth. To help guide you, the chart on Flowering Shrubs in Chapter 4 provides mature shrub sizes.

What constitutes a flowering woody shrub varies with the climatic zone. When we lived in Pennsylvania, our butterfly bush was a herbaceous perennial, hacked to the ground by winter's icy knives. Here in the more equable climate of Sonoma County, California, it's a woody shrub. Similarly, many salvias are herbaceous perennials in cold-winter regions but become woody shrubs where their stems are not subjected to killing temperatures. Many shrubs are classed as semi-evergreen, meaning that in the warm climates they are evergreen, but they drop some of their leaves where cold, not killing, conditions prevail. If you live in the north-eastern United States or southeastern Canada, many shrubs will be herbaceous and should be treated like perennials. In the Sun Belt states, treat them like the woody, permanent plants they are.

Seasonal Interest

Because most shrubs top out at about eye level, their foliage is often more noticeable than that of trees. Most shrubs only bloom for a short time—it's their leaves that one sees through the longest portion of the year. Therefore, carefully consider the leaf texture of the shrubs you plant. Some shrubs will have fine leaves, some large leaves, some coarse-looking leaves. An old landscaper's trick is to arrange a group of shrubs in a small yard so that the finest foliage is placed to the rear and coarser foliage to the front, giving a look of greater depth than the reverse arrangement.

Deciduous shrubs show the line of their bare branches in winter. Wise gardeners tuck

Foliage textures run from fine, as on the New Zealand tea tree at top, to medium, the camellia in the middle, to coarse, the hibiscus at bottom.

all this twigginess into spaces guarded in winter by coniferous shrubs or broad-leaved evergreens. I've seen the leaves of rhododendron happily holding up little puffs of snow after a storm caused by an approaching cold front. When the front passes and the skies clear and the temperatures drop, the rhododendron's leaves turn limp, dropping miniature flurries into the soft new snow below. Such effects may not rival a 60-foot horse-chestnut in full bloom, but in winter, we work with the little things.

One of the little things we can do to dress up our mixed gardens (ones in which trees, shrubs, vines, and herbaceous plants share space) in the winter is to choose varieties with naturally beautiful limbs and stems. The twisted, interesting wood of Harry Lauder's walking stick makes a big show on its own, and visitors to your property in winter will surely notice it. *Clethra alnifolia* is another shrubby plant—or small tree—with a pretty bodyline. *Kerria japonica* carries green stems through the winter, while *Cornus alba* 'Sibirica' has bright red bark.

Pruning for Beauty

Besides naturally pretty wood, we can create our own appealing woody forms with the pruning shears. This is often done with prized fruit trees, and a well-pruned cherry, for example, is a gorgeous sight. But creative pruning can be done even more easily with lesser-sized plants. Many shrubs can be pruned to reveal the naturally beautiful, woody growth. Because they are often at eye level, well-pruned shrubs are a real joy to walk among on a snowy winter's day when only woody structure—stark against the white snow—is visible. (In Chapter 5, there is a further discussion of artistic pruning.)

The point of good pruning is not to force the shrub or tree to some preconceived idea of what constitutes a pretty shape. We are

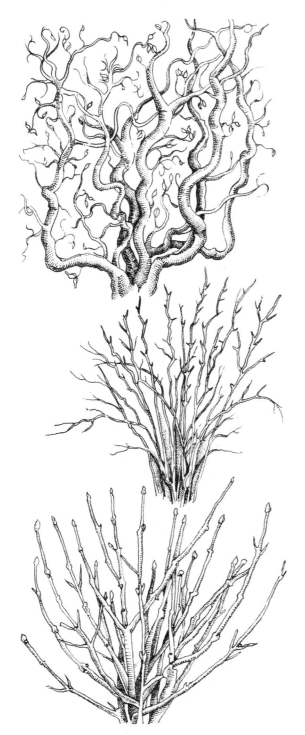

Shrubs with naturally striking branch shape or color include, top to bottom, Harry Lauder's walking stick, globeflower, and Siberian red-stemmed dogwood.

not yet intelligent enough for that, and should leave such strategic decisions to the plants. Our job is to remove what is not art, and reveal the art that's already there.

Shrub Functions

When confronted by a jumble of rank shrubs that reveals no obvious art at all, remember that form should follow function. The major shrub functions are listed below, and may be combined in any given planting. There are certainly other functions for shrubs—topiary, for instance—but the chief ones for most home landscapers are covered here.

Provide Background and Shade   The shrub blooms, and then is used as a background for other flowers or to cast pools of shade in which shade-loving perennials might be planted.

Contribute to a Group   What could be nicer than a wood's edge bordered by a well-chosen association of several shrubs? They look good together in flower; they look good together as an association of foliage types during the bulk of the growing season; they look good together in the fall when their leaves turn varying shades of color; and they look good together in the winter because of good positioning and a bit of artful pruning.

Create an Accent   Forsythias accent the landscape with a huge splash of yellow in the early spring. A red-flowered hibiscus can accent a planting of purple lantana. A shrub with unusual leaf shape or color can also function as an accent, as with the big leaves of oakleaf hydrangea among conifers, or the red leaves of the new growth of *Pieris* accenting the dense greens of broad-leaved evergreens. An accent shrub sets off the plants around it and provides an unexpected color or shape.

Serve as Specimen   When you want to call attention to a prized shrub, you set it apart as a specimen, or at least feature it in a group. Sun-loving specimens get the maxi-

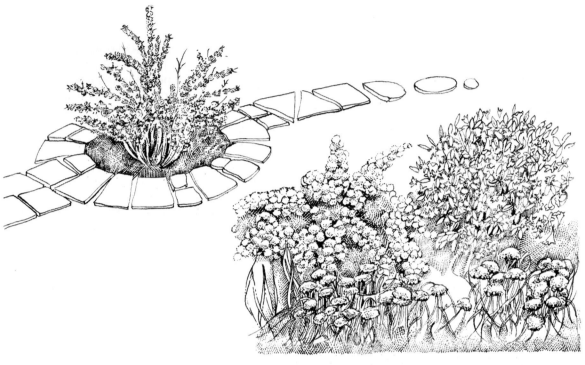

Major uses for shrubs: a butterfly bush used as a specimen in the center of a pathway, at top; spiraea and bush arbutus used as a backdrop for lower-growing perennials, forming a wall in a garden "room"; a lilac and a mock orange make a nice association that conceals a tool shed.

mum possible sunlight, since they grow alone and are not impinged upon by other plants. Create paths to encircle your specimen plants so they can be viewed from all angles.

Form a Hedge   Sometimes the shrub's function may be to screen off a neighbor's yard, or to act as a windscreen. In these cases, choose evergreens first, since they'll maintain their function in winter.

Hide Something   Shrubs are great for hiding the pump house or the garbage cans. Shrubs can also camouflage the long vertical lines of buildings when placed at the corners, and obscure long horizontal lines when massed a third of the way along a wall.

Serve as Walls for Garden "Rooms" Shrubs are commonly used to separate defined outdoor spaces. One side of a row of shrubs may be edged with perennials; the other side forms a wall of adjacent space, in which a collection of fragrant shrubs like white viburnum is featured. The shrubs will be the foundation around which you "decorate" each garden room.

Vines

Nature trims her trees and shrubs with vines. They festoon the somber evergreens. They glide protectively over porches and doorways, creating leafy bowers where there had been just bare wood. They whirl themselves lovingly, drunkenly around posts. They are for the delirious flower lover who would clothe her world in color and fragrance.

Of all the flowering plants, vines are the most mobile. Trees and shrubs stay where you put them. Perennials and annuals can be grown in containers and moved around, but their herbaceous habit keeps them close to the pot. Vines, on the other hand, can be trained up and away. They'll cover a pergola or arbor with their spreading arms. With vines, it's possible to throw a flash of brilliant red high into a tree, ring a second-story window with fiery trumpets, or cover a bank.

Earlier this season we discovered *Passiflora jamesonii,* an evergreen passion vine. The color of its flowers is remarkable. Often described as coral or salmon, it seems closer to carmine, with perhaps some scarlet mixed in. The quality of the color is luminescent, clear, jewellike.

This passion vine runs its tendrils out about 25 feet and opens showers of these treasured flowers all summer. We saw it growing along a rustic fence bordering a rush-rimmed pond. Its color drew our eyes immediately and invited scrutiny. We stopped the car and spent 15 minutes admiring it.

Passiflora jamesonii has a long, open look, so it's not for screening. It opens its flowers toward the sun, so it's not particularly suited to covering an arbor. It needs to be placed low—along a fence or as a ground cover—so that people can see its flowers full in the face. It makes a show-stopping display on the same large trellis with a blue passionflower and sprays of white *Mandevilla laxa.*

As we discovered with our passion vine, each vine has a personality and a function. How you use a vine and where you place it must take both of these features into account.

Vine "Personalities"

To give you an idea of the range of personalities or styles a vine may have, here are some possibilities.

Dainty   *Clematis alpina* 'Pamela Jackman', Alpine virgin's bower, is a dainty little vine with profusions of satiny blue bells, perfect for growing over a child's playhouse.

Striking   *Thunbergia gregorii,* the orange clock vine, is also small, but punches the eye with its pure orange note.

Lush   Most of the trumpet vines have a lush appearance when blooming well, as do vining roses.

Elegant   *Clematis montana* has a classical look, with classic white, starry flowers.

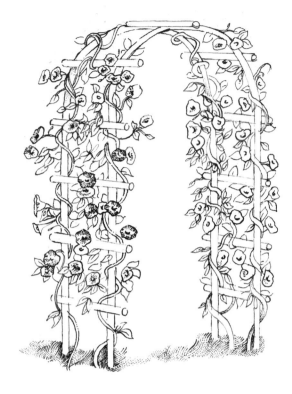

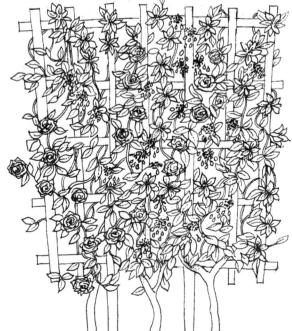

Trellising for vines can be as simple as growing a clematis into a tree, at top left. A morning-glory covers an arbor, at top right. At bottom, three vines associate on a trellis: a climbing rose, a climbing hydrangea vine (Schizophragma), and an autumn clematis. All three will need heavy yearly pruning and summer pinching to keep them confined to a trellis this small.

Vigorous   Given a few years, *Wisteria sinensis* reaches three stories high and just as wide to dominate whole vistas with its glorious clusters of concord grape blue flowers.

Vine Functions

Here are four of the basic functions vines can serve.

Decorative   Vines remain unsurpassed for dressing up a pillar or post, decorating a fruit tree, or enhancing a fence.

Provide Shade   Vines are commonly grown on arbors and trellises to shade the area underneath. How pretty an arbor or trellis looks when the dappled sunlight that filters through the overhead vines carries beams of color from the petals of the back-lit flowers.

Hide Something   Fast-growing vines can turn an eyesore of an outbuilding into a mound of floral beauty in a couple of seasons. Vines also soften the edges and corners of buildings, and are especially effective trailing their arabesques from above a doorway or an entranceway. We've all seen honeysuckle hiding an ugly chain link fence.

Enhance a Plant Group   A shrub and perennials may be paired, but lack an essential third color. A vine chosen to bloom with the shrub and the perennials can be placed to add that color in just the right spot. Or, weave three vines of varying, but related, flower colors together on a trellis for a spectacular effect.

Some Points on Culture

Most vines will need pruning. Otherwise they build up accumulations of dead wood and look sparse and ratty. Old, unpruned vines can also devour their trellises and fences and end up as an ungainly heap of foliage and twisting arms. The necessity of pruning has its advantages though. Vines, by their nature, will obligingly fill odd spaces, and fit snugly when pruned to that shape.

Pruning also keeps vines from overrunning their hosts when grown among the branches of a tree. And of course, pruning is essential for the production of future flower buds on many vines.

Because most vines will rapidly grow to 15 to 20 feet, they will outgrow a small trellis fairly quickly, or become a bunched ball of tangled vines seeking room to grow at the top of the trellis. From this observation, we learn the importance of providing adequate trellising for vigorous vines—sometimes covering a whole wall with supports for a single vine—and regular pruning to keep growth looking good and to promote flowering over the whole length of the vine.

Most vines originated in tropical regions, and many of the best flowering varieties need winter protection. They can be planted in pots or boxes, allowing you to move them outside during the warm months. Angel-wing jasmine, *Jasminum nitidum,* produces starry blossoms all summer with a delicate fragrance that must be enjoyed up close. Put it near your favorite garden seat. (For more on growing vines, see the discussion under July in Chapter 2.)

Using Vines in the Garden

Perennial or annual flowers can also be used with a vine in an association. *Wisteria sinensis* trained as a standard, that is, to a tree form with a single trunk, growing out of a pool of *Aubrieta deltoidea,* purple rock cress, will take the viewer's breath away. The lilac in the wisteria's panicles is reflected in the purple rock cress's melange of lilac, purple, rose, and red blossoms.

Ornamental vines are evergreen, semievergreen or deciduous, giving the vine grower possibilities for mixing evergreen and deciduous vines so that a screening or shading effect is maintained even in winter.

Given their pliable nature, it would

be possible to construct a landscape of vines; the "trees" would be vigorous vines trained as standards, with low-growing vines at their bases and trailing vines forming a ground cover.

Herbaceous Flowering Plants

When people think of flower gardens, they usually think first of masses of perennials and biennials, decorative annuals, and the yearly explosion of spring bulbs. All these types of plants are herbaceous, meaning their young growth is soft and juicy, not woody. Many die back each year.

Within this broad category of herbaceous plants, each group has its own specific life cycle. Perennials' roots persist through the winter, sending up new leaves, stems, and flowering parts each year. Biennials have a two-year cycle. The first year they sprout from seeds and make a strong root that persists through the winter. In the second season, the root sends up a flower stalk, sets seed, and the whole plant dies. Annuals are "born" in flats in spring and die with the frosts in fall. Bulbs are perennials—some kinds, like the daffodils, faithfully return each spring for many decades. They are usually quick about their business, displaying sheets of color before most of the earth's "household" is awake, then withering away before July.

As a general rule, bulbs bloom earliest, followed by the early perennials. Perennials, biennials, and early annuals show prettily in midsummer, while late perennials and annuals bloom heavily right to frost.

Perennials

These flowers are this season's dress, the clothing of the flower garden. The best flower beds and borders result from the artistic juxtaposition of various colors and shapes. Perennials range in size from the nearly microscopic miniature armeria (our well-established stand covers an area the size of a salad plate) to the 15 foot tall clumps of *Miscanthus sinensis* 'Giganteus'.

Although many mail-order catalogs carry perennials—some successfully specialize in these plants—we've always found excellent plants at our local nurseries, available in friends' backyards, or waiting to be rescued at properties soon to be bulldozed for new construction.

For flower lovers, perennial beds and borders assume a supreme importance in the home landscape. Beneath the trees, along a driveway, or as an island bed in an expanse of lawn, perennials bring vibrant life to the setting, pleasing us with mounds of luscious colors just beneath eye level.

Perennials are some of our dearest and oldest garden friends. If we could see back through time, we'd surely find ourselves as children exploring the baroque shapes of a bearded iris, or pulling off the waxy petals of a tulip. However we arrange the woody plants in our gardens, perennials will help to pull the scene together with color.

Biennials

These flowering plants are best thought of as two-stage annuals. They bloom in their second year, so don't waste garden space on them in their first year. If you're planting biennials from seed, plant them in an out-of-the-way nursery bed. We have a friend in Connecticut who starts little blue forget-me-nots in small pots each spring and sets them out in the early fall where she will want their cheery blooms the following spring. She always puts some in the aster and chrysanthemum beds because these perennials emerge late and cover the dying foliage of the forget-me-nots. You may also find some biennials at nurseries and plant sales as 1-year-old plants ready for setting out in the garden. Selection is often limited, however.

Annuals

These flower garden regulars are available as seed and as started plants. Growing your own annuals from seed gives you an enormous amount of plant stock to choose from, in every color and height desired. Started plants are usually limited to those varieties that sell well, but that category includes quite a number of good plants available at garden sales in the spring.

Annuals are for fun. They can be called upon to add a quick spot of color—harmony or contrasting accent—whenever the need arises. Let's say you have white and soft pink flowers and you decide a blue is needed as an accent. Annual love-in-a-mist could be planted in a small clump at the front of the bed to achieve the effect for this season, while you make a note to add blue perennial carpathian harebells which will replace the annual with a similar blue that returns faithfully in future years.

Annuals fill in the gaps in a newly planted garden whose woody plants and perennial clumps are still small. And finally, annuals can provide exceptional and unusual colors that may be hard to find—the soft, satiny, milky salmon daisies of *Dimorphotheca sinuata,* for instance, or the intense sapphire and amethyst markings of *Torenia fournieri.*

Annuals are useful, but too often misused. Whole beds of lemon yellow zinnias can make the eyeballs ache. We think annuals are best used sparingly, and then for specific purposes.

Bulbs

Unlike annuals, bulbs are best used en masse. We've had great success ordering from the catalogs of Dutch bulb companies, but there are many American suppliers, too. This fall we're realizing a dream of many years by beginning a collection of fritillaries, including two varieties of the tall imperial, the offbeat checkered fritillary, a white sport of the checkered species, plus three other species of this interesting genus. We found them all in just a handful of American plant catalogs.

Bulbs are the opening act in the flower garden, and the early-flowering kinds like chionodoxa, scilla, puschkinia, galanthus, and crocus have the stage to themselves. You can hardly have enough of them, as they appear against the immense sward of the browned and bleached early spring landscape. Later, when the grass has greened, come the daffodils, and when the leaves appear on the trees, it's tulip time. All the bulbs disappear by summer, and so most careful gardeners interplant their bulb beds with other perennials that emerge through the failing bulb foliage. Bulbs are usually planted in fall for bloom the following spring, and many springs thereafter.

Ground Covers

Any low-growing plant—not much more than a foot tall—can be considered a ground cover. These plants clothe the earth the way grass does, but, because they remain small, they never need the kind of maintenance that grass does. Ground covers function best when massed, so as to prevent weed growth. They are usually dense plants, sometimes evergreen, and often floriferous.

Several ground-hugging species of phlox are typical of the beauty and practicality of flowering ground covers. *Phlox divaricata* grows about 1 foot tall with pure blue stars for flowers. *Phlox stolonifera* also carries blue stars, but its foliage lies flat on the ground. *Phlox subulata* is well known to everyone as the mounds of shockingly bright colors called "pinks" that appear in lawns and rock gardens in May. The foliage is like moss and mats together to protect the soil from the sun.

As much as phlox likes the sunshine, *Vinca minor* likes the shade. It's an evergreen, even in the North, and carries familiar lavender-blue flowers singly along its trailing stems. In areas that suit it—generally humusy, woodsy conditions with lots of moisture—it will naturalize to carpet hundreds of square feet.

Ground covers add greatly to the palette that the horticultural artist works with. They add color in their blooming season and a neat, cheery, and tidy look to the floor of the garden during the rest of the year. One of the prettiest gardens we've ever seen is a small private garden in San Francisco, where the ground is covered with baby's tears. The soft mounds of tiny green leaves invite visitors to run a hand or bare foot over their surface. (For more on delightful, flowering ground covers to add to your garden, see September in Chapter 2.)

Most ground covers are shallow rooted, so droughty conditions prevailing under thirsty trees may make these hard to grow. The shallow-rooted ground covers will have to be given lots of water-retaining organic matter and frequent irrigation if they are to survive the summer months. Delicate ground-covering plants like myosotis, mertensia, and polemonium need plenty of water to thrive. *Vinca minor* and hostas can tolerate drier conditions.

Creativity in Garden Design

Dabs of flowering ground covers among the perennial beds, all set among flowering trees and shrubs—these are the ingredients of the garden we all strive to create.

Associations of all these plants can be made in small backyards as well as large estates. As the Japanese prove with their spare but powerful garden designs, the simple and the beautiful are often the same thing.

In the end, we want our landscape to embody these virtues: a sense of unused strength, a tender regard for life, a restful naturalness, a theme and purpose, and moderation.

This last—moderation—is especially important. Flowering plants must be used in moderation in a landscape that also includes evergreens and nonflowering plants like lawn grass. And plants themselves must be used in moderation. Not every vista needs to be green. Most landscaping is foliage, and most foliage is busy. When the landscape is entirely foliage, it is busy, busy, busy. That's neither moderate nor restful.

Water is often used to rescue a landscape from being nothing more than a tangle of leaves. It is level, slick, and liquid. It's responsive to physical forces, but not living forces—a perfect contrast to the living wood and leaf patterns of plants. It remains a great pacifier and unifier in the garden.

Water Gardening

A wonderful way to add dimension to your garden is to include a water feature. Whether it's a formal concrete pool, a kidney-shaped plastic pool, or a barrel garden, water gardens are delightful and different. They let you play with water plants like the gorgeous water lilies and lotuses, and with water's-edge plants like yellow and blue flags, cattails, and the brilliant cardinal flower. And they let you design the water's reflection as you would a painting.

One morning last summer our family came to the kitchen and looked out the window to find a bright yellow-white waterlily open upon the surface of a pool we'd created

Flowering trees form a backdrop for lilacs and roses, which themselves form a backdrop for herbaceous flowers at the front of the garden.

from half a wine barrel. The lily, ordinary among waterlilies but extraordinarily beautiful by itself, turned our simple tub of water into a dazzling pool. Watching its dancing light touch the silvery surface, it became easy to see why botanists chose *Nymphaea* for the name of its genus: the nymphs.

Ours is a hardy waterlily, *Nymphaea odorata,* that carries a sweet fragrance. Some other particularly nice white varieties of waterlilies include 'Virginiana', with softly ruffled petals, and the very double 'Gonnere'. Hardies also come in pink ('Hollandia' is exquisite), yellow ('Charlene Strawn' is a fine, long-season variety), red ('Gloriosa' lives up to its name), and the so-called changeables that shift colors through their three-day bloom period ('Paul Hariot' is a fine tub plant).

Hardies aren't that hardy. They must be lifted from their tubs where the water will freeze, and stored moist (packed in damp moss and moist compost) over winter—until late April in New York—when they can be set out again.

Tropical waterlilies—also genus *Nymphaea*—must be lifted and stored in a tub of water over winter in a sunspace or greenhouse where no freezes occur. These lilies come in the intense colors of the tropics, including blue varieties, and generally have much larger leaves, requiring a larger outdoor pool. There are day- and (how romantic!) night-blooming tropical lilies. Most are highly perfumed.

Lotuses are of the genus *Nelumbo*, require full sun and, like *Nymphaeas*, lots of fertilizer to produce the greatest number of blooms. Lotuses thrust their leaves and blooms well above the water.

Living vs. Nonliving Elements

Our view into any garden reveals that a portion of the field of view is living green tissue or wood. A nonliving portion includes water, rock, sand, flagstone, pebbles, cement, packed clay, and even mulches. These non-living areas are as important to the proper aesthetic presentation of flowering plants as yin is to yang or background is to foreground. Sky is a nonliving area, but it is an intangible backdrop beyond our manipulation. Sand and stone on the other hand can be moved, and therefore concern us directly.

Nonliving areas in the landscape relieve the onslaught of foliage. They introduce the element of scarcity into the picture, which adds beauty and value. Too much green and a person begins longing for a rock to sit on. Too much rock and one starts longing for an oasis. The proper balance between these elements is—as with most dynamic compositions—a little off center. Two-thirds greenery and one-third wood, rock, sand, or water might be right, or vice versa. A beautiful broad walkway may itself be enough nonliving area, because it takes up about a third of the field of view when standing in the walkway's center. An area of round, dark stones might contain ferns placed to take up a third of the field of view.

The Whole Picture

When designing gardens, we must look at the whole picture—everything we can see

In the top scene, the tableau is one-third green living things to two-thirds non-living. In the bottom picture, the ratio is reversed and green living things occupy two-thirds of the tableau.

on our own and neighboring properties, even the distant mountains. Our hand-created landscape can be subtly designed to harmonize with the local look of the land and the indigenous flora. The gray and silver foliage of many high desert shrubs can be echoed in passages in the garden—with centaurea, Russian olive, artemisias, and similar plants with gray-green leaves. A view of a dominant white church spire can be brought home with *Veronica spicata* 'Snow White'. The long elliptical shape of a lake can be repeated by a garden pond, or even an island bed of flowers.

Subtle repetition is a time-honored solution to many artistic design problems. This is especially true in painting, where artists compose their canvases by subtly repeating a shape, but varying its size, color, and shade, and turning it this way and that. When choosing flowers, observe that a bell is but a cup turned upside down.

Mixed Plantings, Sometimes Mixed Results

Few gardens, thankfully, are a monoculture of just one plant. Most are polycultures combining herbaceous and woody flowering plants. The plants have come from Japan, China, the Himalayan regions, the Caucasus, Eastern Europe, the Alps—all over the world—to associate together. In this part of California it's perfectly common to see *Pieris japonica* from Japan growing with *Choisya ternata* from Mexico and *Leptospermum scoparium*, the New Zealand tea tree. We are setting up plant groupings that have never occurred naturally, with unpredictable results. Some plants may be alternate hosts to their neighbors' insect pests, while others

The landscape designer has borrowed the shape of the mountain in placing the rocks, the gazebo, and the shrub. When the shrub reaches maturity, it will form the apex of the composition. Good designs bring the visual elements of nature home.

may have a natural repellent effect on the pests, alleviating the problem. Be prepared for Nature to respond to your carefully thought out groupings with some ideas of her own. Some of her ideas may be beneficial, some may not.

Guidelines from Nature

To achieve simplicity and stability in our mixtures of flowering plants, we need some principles to guide us through the absolute welter of flowering plant stock offered for sale these days. We can find these principles operating already in natural preserves, where soil is continually being renewed as leaves and branches fall and decay, and where all plants and animals are dependent on each other for such things as food, shelter, and pollination; the regeneration of the soil through proper shading and deciduous shedding of organic materials to form a duff; and the ecology, or the interdependencies, interworkings, and co-evolutions of all the life forms in an area.

The most stable natural systems are those whose members have evolved together. The more members, and the more diverse the members, the more stable the system. In climax ecosystems—those groupings of plants that naturally dominate a region when Nature is left to her own devices—there is an indescribable complexity of interrelatedness.

You might plan your mix of flowering plants on a feature of the local ecosystem. If you live on the salt marshes of New England, you would choose some of the little, salt-tolerant, seaside flowers like sea pinks, and flowering trees and shrubs like lilacs, clethra, myrtle, beach plum, and the rugosa rose. For inspiration on how to arrange them in your garden, look to the salt marshes with their inlets of water, their tall, waving grasses, and their hummocks and hills clothed in dark evergreens. If the shore is edged with huge flat rocks, perhaps that's the way to treat your rock garden.

Good Garden Design

The overall garden design is the strategy. Once you have that, you apply tactics. Tactical decisions involve specific siting of specific plants. Again, we need a couple of guiding principles to help us sort out the mass of plant materials: opposites and correspondences.

Opposites

Opposites give drama to the garden. A tall, dark, cylindrical evergreen situated by a short, spreading, light green deciduous tree is one example. Light against dark, tall and slender against short and squat, and fine foliage against broad leaves are other pairings of opposites. The more opposites you can fit into your selections, the better. The Hinoki cypress, a tall plant with very finely divided evergreen leaves, casts a dense shade for a contrasting low-growing, wide-leaved plant like *Viburnum davidii*.

Correspondences

Correspondences, or similarities, give thematic unity to the garden, and are most effective when they contain opposite elements as well. Let's envision walking down a gently turning garden path: on the right side is the feathery foliage of the mimosa, or silk tree, arching over our heads, its pink and white flowers glowing in the sun's backlighting. On the left side of the path, low down and in the shade, are the feathery fronds of the maidenhair fern, corresponding in an interesting and inexact way to the mimosa leaves. A visitor could walk down the path many times and never stop to consider the clever way in which these plants have been laid out to echo one another's foliage forms, yet the beauty will come through.

Another example of correspondences with opposite elements is seen in the straight, hanging, bluish-gray-green, beadlike segments of donkey tail sedum grown in a basket above a shrub that contains correspondences—a cotoneaster's beadlike berries, for instance—and opposites—the angular lines of cotoneaster's spreading arms. When you find plants that have a number of similarities and differences in forms and colors, try them together. They often produce the most satisfying combinations. Modern garden designs usually incorporate lots of curves and very few straight lines, although there were times when straight lines and very formal gardens were in vogue. Today we try to express our feeling for nature when designing a garden, and nature is partial to curves and freeform shapes.

Transitions

As we travel along the free form, curvilinear paths through the plantings, there will be places that mark a transition from one part of the landscape to another, perhaps from one garden "room" to another, or where a new vista opens up. At these junctions, plant specimen trees or distinctive shrubs—plants you want to emphasize. They will arrest the eye, hold the attention, and allow the mind to complete the enjoyment of the previous scene before moving on to the next. As you walk where paths will be, dream your deepest floral dreams, then bring them to life.

Keep an Open Center

At places where the prettiest scenes appear, keep the center of the picture open, not cluttered. Mass your plantings toward the edges and sides, building upward toward the trees. The open center allows placement of water, stone, paths, and patios. It gives visitors a place to stand or sit and view the scene. It creates a room whose space is defined by the walls and ceilings of foliage and flowers.

Maintain a Sense of Scale

Plants should be in scale to one another and to the whole garden in which they appear. Japanese maples are tiny, delicate trees that make good solitary specimens, while the sargent cherry explodes into a white cloud 60 feet high. Both trees are wonderful, but out of scale to each other and unsuitable companions. Plan realistically for the mature size of the plants, so that your garden will grow into a pleasing scale, and not be overcrowded and dominated by trees and bushes run amok.

Work with Landforms

Take advantage of slopes and other landforms to display the flowers of your trees, shrubs, perennials, and annuals. Steps leading up or down are slopes—albeit zigzag ones. Soften their contours with low flowering shrubs like potentilla along their edges.

Cultivate Your Sense of Design

The more highly developed and refined your sense of design, the more beautiful your garden will be. A method of design comprehension and appreciation that has helped me over the years is to look for natural forms that I like. Sometimes these are obvious—driftwood, spider webs, snail shells, and so forth. Sometimes they're not so obvi-

Water and stone form the flat, placid center of the scene. The edges build toward a crescendo of trees in the background.

ous. Sit quietly in your yard or in the woods on a sunny afternoon and let your visual focus go soft. Focus on nothing, but let your perception apprehend the whole picture. Now let the dark areas intensify in darkness, and the light areas intensify in brightness, which is easily done if you are not looking at things, but at the pattern of the whole picture. Always when I've been able to see this effect, the world begins to take on a shimmer, and from the overall patterns in the scene, a larger pattern emerges. These deep patterns are always beautiful and regular, like electron microscope photos of molecular rings. They serve as ways to organize our refinements to the garden, for we can always take in the whole garden scene and see immediately, by looking at these patterns, what's lacking or incomplete.

For instance, the pattern of the lights and darks may be interrupted by an awkward patch of color, and you'll take it out. Or you'll see a classic composition marred by an out-of-place plant, and remove it. You may see that the pattern has a hole that calls for a plant of a certain size and shape, then find and plant it.

It is precisely through such deeply perceived garden design that visitors will be able to see a larger pattern, or meaning, emerge from our plantings, will get the idea behind the garden, and will be thrilled at its intelligence, wit, and beauty, and at their own ability to perceive it.

Now that we've examined the principles and tactics for establishing a flowering garden, let's look at some plants that dominate the visual landscape during their seasons.

Chapter 2
Flowers Month by Month

We've tried to make this book useful for gardeners everywhere—north and south, east and west. And so in this chapter describing flowers month by month, when we talk about gardening during the height of June, we're talking about plants suitable to varied regions from Canada to Mexico. When we talk about what's blooming in January, we're limited to the southernmost USDA plant hardiness zones, Zones 8-10—regions warm enough to support flowering plants outdoors in the dead of winter. (To find your hardiness zone, look at the USDA Hardiness Zone Map on page 297.)

This chapter is thus a travelogue of sorts, beginning our journey in January, where we explore the flowers of Florida, the Gulf Coast, Texas, and the quaking coast of California. By March we've advanced to the mid-South and the first flowers of the warmer temperate regions.

Flowers that grace the northern tier of states share the spotlight in high summer, but then as fall comes and winter closes in, we retire again to the warm zones, where we find nature's color show more brilliant than ever. Here we also look at greenhouse plants for fresh flowers right through the cold months in the northern states.

In each of the months, we focus a spotlight on a special flowering plant or class of plants we're sure will please you. If you already grow some of them, see if you agree with our choices.

The purpose of this chapter is to familiarize you with the major kinds of flowering plants for ornamental gardens, especially ones that stand out for beauty, form, fall color, or other desirable quality. When creating your own flower gardens, use these month-by-month discussions to get a feel for the major plants that characterize fine gardens at different times of the year. Explore them further in the charts of flowering trees, shrubs, and vines in Chapter 4. This should help you make headway choosing plants for your specific situation and needs, which can be a surprisingly arduous and time-consuming task given the sheer amount of nursery material offered.

January (Midwinter)

As winter stamps most heavily on the North American continent, most regions sleep under ice and snow. Yet along the continent's fringes, from Delaware's southern shores to the tip of Florida, around the Gulf crescent to Texas, and up and down the Pacific Coast, flowers are blooming. And in protected, warm, sunny greenhouses and sunspaces throughout the ice-locked land, flowers are blooming. In every month, in every state, flowers are always blooming.

We'll not include Zone 10 in this discussion, for winter is but a cool and wet continuation of the constant growing season in this zone; and residents will select their winter bloomers from the local nurseries that specialize in tropical and subtropical plants.

Trees and Shrubs

In Zones 7 through 9, where the ground never freezes, or is easily kept thawed with mulch, many plants flower through the cold months. Here in coastal northern California, January is when the acacias suddenly burst into bloom. These exotic-looking trees and shrubs from Australia take a rather inconspicuous role in the landscape during most of the year, but in winter they seem to perk up; their gray-green to blue-green foliage glistens. Then one cold morning they explode in frothy sprays of bright yellow. The tree-sized *Acacia baileyana* and *A. dealbata* begin to bloom in January, while the more shrublike *A. podalyriifolia*, or pearl acacia, begins in November and continues through the winter to March.

When siting the acacias in the garden, move them to background positions. Mass them to one side, far back in the composition, and echo the mass with a smaller planting of acacias in another part of the garden. Come January, they will dominate the garden with their masses of color, and if regularly spaced, will give the unwelcome appearance of huge yellow polka dots.

A good flowering specimen tree for January is *Hamamelis mollis,* the Chinese witch-hazel, with its fragrant clusters of yellow streamers appearing directly from the stems. The Chinese witch-hazel and *H. ×intermedia,* a hybrid of Chinese and Japanese types, get lost near dominant bloomers like acacias. They carry sweet little blooms that charm us rather than wow us. Because of the color of their yellow petals and reddish-brown calyxes, they look best set off against a brick or stone wall, or against a dark mass of evergreens.

In Zone 9, you'll be able to grow the manzanitas—graceful shrubs with smooth, reddish-purple bark. One variety in particular, *Arctostaphylos edmundsii* 'Danville', the Little Sur manzanita, which grows only a foot or two tall but spreads broadly, begins its blooming in late December or January in the cool, wet conditions of the coast. It starts later in the colder zones inland and to the north, through the Willamette Valley to Portland, Oregon.

In areas where the ground doesn't freeze, consider the January-blooming *Rhododendron mucronulatum,* a deciduous form of the genus which grows to 4 or 5 feet and arrays its bare branches with magenta flowers in the dead of winter. 'Cornell Pink' is a cultivar with a more endurable color, although if any time of year is appropriate for bright magenta, January is probably it.

Fragrance, as well as colorful blossoms, characterizes the large, shrubby *Chimonanthus praecox.* Generally known as wintersweet, it covers its leafless branches with spicily fragrant, light yellow, inch-wide flowers beginning in December and lasting through the winter. In colder regions, bloom time may begin in January or February. It withstands winters down to about 15 to 20°F.

Folks along the Gulf Coast and the West Coast, including Zones 8 through 10 in California, Oregon, and Washington, have the good fortune to be able to grow camellias. Thousands of varieties of this wonderful plant bloom through January. The formal double *Camellia japonica* 'Pink Perfection' bears flowers with the appearance of fine porcelain, finely chiselled alabaster, or translucent wax. Japanese camellia flowers come in several other forms, each more beautiful than the next. Besides the formal double, the blooms come in single and semidouble forms, anemone-form, peony-form, and several rare, frilled styles. These large shrubs are evergreen, with leaves of polished, dark green that show off the flowers at their best. When the camellias finish blooming, their

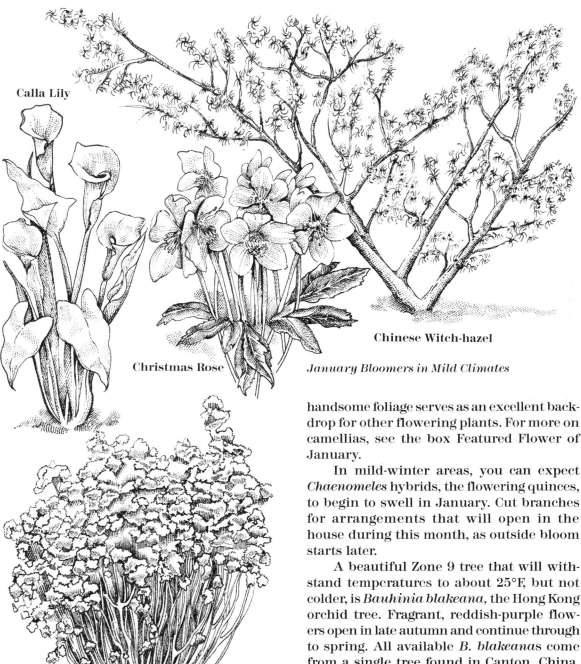

Calla Lily

Christmas Rose

Chinese Witch-hazel

January Bloomers in Mild Climates

Rhododendron Macronulatum

handsome foliage serves as an excellent backdrop for other flowering plants. For more on camellias, see the box Featured Flower of January.

In mild-winter areas, you can expect *Chaenomeles* hybrids, the flowering quinces, to begin to swell in January. Cut branches for arrangements that will open in the house during this month, as outside bloom starts later.

A beautiful Zone 9 tree that will withstand temperatures to about 25°F, but not colder, is *Bauhinia blakeana,* the Hong Kong orchid tree. Fragrant, reddish-purple flowers open in late autumn and continue through to spring. All available *B. blakeana*s come from a single tree found in Canton, China. *B. variegata,* the purple orchid tree, begins to bloom in January in the warmest parts of the zone, especially in central and southern California, reaching a peak in April. You may not want to put up with the large crop of beanlike, inedible fruit that drops from the tree after ripening.

A number of heaths, those low-growing, shrubby plants native to northern Europe, are commonly used in Zone 9 areas of the Pacific Coast, where they brighten up the winter garden. *Erica darleyensis*, which has many cultivars in shades of pink, rose, purple, and white, blooms right through the winter, November to May. *E. hyemalis* bears pinkish-coral, tubular flowers in great profusion through the winter, and is a striking, underused plant in the Zone 9 areas that come closest to its South African climate of origin. *E. lusitanica*, the Spanish heath, starts blooming in January with whitish-pink, sweet-smelling flowers. *E. mediterranea*, the Biscay heath native to the western coast of Europe from Spain to Ireland, produces a rosy lavender shower of flowers.

The tapestry of a heath garden is woven from the varied but related colors and textures of its little flowers and needly leaves. The hills of Scotland are justly renowned for their beauty because they are covered with heaths.

As we've said, northern gardeners can't expect much in the way of blooming color at this point in the year. But there are other plant features that can add dramatic color besides flowers. For an interesting display of highly colored twigs in winter, mass two types of shrubby dogwoods. Use *Cornus alba* 'Sibirica' for its bright red stems and *C. stolonifera* 'Flaviramea' for its distinctive bright yellow.

Noteworthy Flowers

Helleborus niger, the Christmas rose, is a hard-to-transplant evergreen perennial with greenish-white flowers that turn somewhat brownish-purple with age. It blooms in Zone 7, or even 6 in sheltered locations, in December and bravely faces the cold right through the winter.

Winter-blooming bergenia (*Bergenia crassifolia*) is a short evergreen with wide, dark green leaves and flowers ranging from rose to lavender. These are borne on stalks 1 foot above the leaves and provide good basic color to associate with the shorter, more intensely colored primulas, *Primula ×polyantha*, called the polyanthus primrose, is the common one found at most nurseries in fall. Polyanthus gives cheery summerlike colors and interesting lime green, crinkly foliage.

The perennial African daisies known as *Osteospermum* will be blooming in California. *O. fruticosum*, with its sprawling habit and lilac and white daisies, blooms heaviest during the winter, while *O. barberae* is a taller (2 to 3 feet) type with blue to purple flowers.

Calla lilies, *Zantedeschia aethiopica*, bloom in the cool, wet, mild conditions right along the West Coast. Bloom is delayed where frosts are frequent, and the tender rhizomes must be overwintered in a root cellar where the ground freezes.

Flowering vines for January outdoor gardens include the winter jasmine, *Jasminum nudiflorum*, which produces scentless, 1 inch long, yellow flowers beginning in January and going to March. This is the hardiest of the jasmines, growing to Zone 6, although it will only be blooming in January in the warm regions.

Cyclamens provide nice spots of January color among their dark green leaves. *Cyclamen atkinsii* comes in white, pink, and red varieties. *C. cilicium* has purplish marked flowers, *C. coum* is a deep, rosy red, and *C. persicum*, the common florist's cyclamen, comes in a wide variety of colors. Plant them outdoors where their small but pretty flowers may be easily seen, such as in a featured rock garden site. Where that's not possible, they make perfect potted plants for the cold but sunny plant room.

Annuals for the Zone 9 garden include snapdragons, calendulas, dimorphotheca daisies, the snapdragonlike toadflax, and sweet alyssum. In favored locations, pansies, stock, and Iceland poppies may put out some tentative flowers in January, but these don't really get going in most Zone 9 areas until February.

Colorful Fruits and Berries

Besides flowers, persistent fruit and berries can give color. The plants that have this trait include the familiar barberry (*Berberis* spp.), but we have yanked too many of the thorny things from their strongholds in the stony soil to ever want to plant them.

Red chokeberry, either *Aronia arbutifolia* or *A. melanocarpa,* provides handsome winter fruit without barberry's problems. So does the tree called green hawthorn (*Crataegus viridis* 'Winter King') with its dainty, clustered, white flowers in spring and elegant red berries glazed with ice the following January. *Viburnum opulus,* the European cranberry, carries large red fruit through the winter. This plant reaches 15 feet and more, although there is a dwarf form, 'Compactum', which keeps itself within 4- to 5-foot bounds. *V. trilobum,* the American cranberry bush, has fruit similar to *V. opulus,* and its berries are edible. Residents of Zones 8 and 9 will enjoy the sprays of red berries of heavenly bamboo, *Nandina domestica,* this month. Although it's not a true bamboo, it gives that effect, and should be massed to produce good bloom.

More rough and weedy-looking, but quite showy with January berries, are two old standbys, one western and one eastern. The western staple is *Pyracantha coccinea,* the firethorn, with its red to orange beads spilling out in profusion from the leafy stems. The eastern one is *Cotoneaster salicifolius* 'Autumn Fire', or one of the many other cultivars of this useful shrub with its bright red berries and interesting branching and foliage.

Elaeagnus umbellata, the autumn olive, covers itself with small, but fragrant, yellow flowers in May and June. These are replaced in September by silvery fruits that turn scarlet as they hang through January. These fruits are one of the birds' favorites. This hardy plant survives all the way to the northerly reaches of Zone 2.

Other plants that produce colorful berries for winter include holly, dogwood, juniper, Virginia creeper, staghorn sumac, cotoneaster, mountain ash or rowan, skimmia, the white-berried snowberry, and the pink-berried snowberry cultivar, 'Mother of Pearl'. While berries may not be flowers, they give an appearance as close to flowers as most of us will get in the January garden outdoors.

Flowers Indoors

This brings us to the possibility of a January garden indoors. In the warm, humid greenhouse, thousands of flowering tropical plants can be successfully grown, but most sunspaces have an atmosphere closer to a cool, dry, mountain morning, which narrows the choice of plants. Although a few indoor sunspaces may have growing beds, most growing is done in pots and containers. Some of the plants suited to indoor growing actually flower best when potbound.

Some indoor sunspaces may be functioning solar greenhouses. These usually get fairly cold—to the low 40s—on winter nights, relying for heat on the warmth stored in the walls or other thermal mass. Gardenias would not do well here, but a flowering cactus would. *Hermannia verticillata,* whose sweet-scented little yellow bells on trailing stems give it the common name of honey bells, requires cool winter nights, with temperatures around 35 to 50°F.

On the other hand, the sunspace may be

a well-lighted part of the house with a sky-light in the ceiling and lots of glass on a south or southeastern wall. Areas like these usually have some kind of drape or device for closing off the expanse of glass from the house interior on cold nights. The climate here is the same as that of the rest of the house: relatively dry and cool, but not cold, at night. It would be suited to a *Buddleia asiatica,* the winter flowering lilac, in a large container. This plant is a thrilling sight in the dark days of winter as it throws up slender white racemes. As a bonus, it's wonderfully fragrant. Another very fragrant plant that likes a house climate and lots of sun is *Cestrum nocturnum,* night-blooming jasmine. It reliably flowers in midwinter, filling the house with a rich and exotic aroma sometime after 8 P.M. Its fragrance perfumes your dreams,

then is gone by morning. Sunny house conditions also suit cymbidium orchids.

Then there are those rooms kept warm, humid and sunny—never going below 60°F. In these you can grow gardenias, exotic vines, orchids, and large, showy-flowered plants like *Dombeya wallichii.* This plant's rose-pink, pendulous umbels give off a honey scent during its winter flowering period.

Even though the sunspace may be just a windowsill on a south wall, it can still frame a hanging basket of succulent *Kalanchoe pumila,* with dainty gray-green leaves and sweet little pink flowers in winter. Polyanthus primroses will flower on the windowsill. (For an extensive source of January greenhouse plants, see the entry for Logee's Greenhouses in Mail-Order Sources for Ornamental Trees, Shrubs, and Vines on page 295.)

Three indoor plants to brighten winter: night-blooming jasmine; Kalanchoe pumila, *a colorful pot plant for a sunny windowsill; and honeybells, trailing its sweet flowers from a hanging pot.*

FEATURED FLOWER OF JANUARY: CAMELLIA

Perhaps it's the flowering presence in the darkness of the year that makes the camellia so revered. It has been called the most beautiful shrub, and certainly it ranks near the top of our list. And why not—its leathery leaves have fine, even teeth and its flowers are translucent and finely chiseled. Plus, it flowers just when you need it most.

Just because you live in a cold-winter area doesn't mean you have to forgo the pleasure of winter-blooming camellias. These lustrous, evergreen shrubs make perfect container plants if given a potting mix of finished compost, sand, and vermiculite, then kept well watered.

They are thrifty plants, with a compact habit and neat, glossy leaves. They won't need much pinching back in their pots as their roots determine their above-ground size. If they should grow spindly, cut back side shoots and create a leader, then nip back the tips over the whole plant in April, or whenever flowering finishes, to promote bushiness and budding the next fall.

When young, camellias are rather sun tender and need dappled shade, great drainage, lots of water, and a place where their roots can stay cool. When they reach 6 to 8 feet tall, move them to a sunnier location if you choose, but we find the prettiest specimens bloom brightly in light shade. They transplant very easily when small, without needing any pruning. Specimens over 8 feet tall still transplant easily but should be lightly tip pruned after moving to bring the tops and shorn roots into balance.

You'll notice that your camellias, whether outside or inside in tubs, drop a good number of unopened blossoms. A certain amount of this is normal for the plant, but excessive bud drop is possible if the plant is stressed; kept dry, then drenched, for instance, or kept moist, then allowed to dry; or exposed to a hard freeze at night, followed by warm sunshine, when the buds are swelling. *Camellia japonica* can take cold snaps down to near 0°F, but does best in Zones 8 through 10. Other species are usually less hardy.

Outstanding Camellias

The nicest camellias include the hybrid 'Inspiration', with semidouble, translucent pink blooms. It's as hardy as cultivars of the *Camellia japonica* species.

Camellia japonica comes in early, mid-, and late-season varieties. For January flowers, choose mid-season bloomers, including:

'Alba Plena': white blooms with the oriental formal double habit.
'Carter's Sunburst': sports pink, semidouble blooms.
'Chandler Elegans': rosy pink blooms with an anemone form.
'Debutante': flowers are pink with a peony form.
'Finlandia Red': shows off with red, semidouble flowers.
'Nunncio's Gem': flowers are white, formal double.
'Reg Ragland': red, semidouble blooms.
'Tomorrow': flowers are red, semidouble.

Several species camellias show interesting variations from the japonica form. *Camellia reticulata* grows tall and rangy, but puts forth the largest camellia flowers. 'Captain Rawes' is a very large, semidouble, rosy pink *reticulata* named after the old English sea captain who brought her home from China. It blooms in January in California, later in the Pacific Northwest.

Camellia sasanqua is a fall-flowering kind. It blooms furiously, dropping blossoms quickly, but persists in flowering for months. Winter rains usually end the flowering period. Sasanquas like life in a pot, and are a good choice for the sunspace. One of our favorites is 'Yuletide', a variety with single, little red flowers decorating the compact, green leaves. There are plenty of shades of cherished deep rose in this species. The deep rose red 'Shishi Gashira' is sometimes listed as a sasanqua, but is actually *Camellia hiemalis,* a species with fine-textured leaves and compact appearance.

In addition to the ones given above, there are many noteworthy hybrid camellias of mixed parentage. One is a fragrant variety, aptly named 'Fragrant Pink'.

(continued)

FEATURED FLOWER
OF JANUARY: CAMELLIA—*continued*

Single

Formal Double

Semidouble

Peony

Anemone

Types of Camellia Blossoms

February (Late Winter)

Many January bloomers will be even more floriferous in February, and quite a few other plants begin to join them in Zones 9 and 10. The finicky, but very handsome and heavily scented *Daphne odora* 'Marginata' can begin to bloom in February in the warmest zones, as will *D. mezereum*, the February daphne. In the colder regions, both daphnes begin in late March. *D. odora* is a tidy looking, 4- to 6-foot shrub with glossy, evergreen leaves and little bunches of red-outside, pink-inside flowers with a heavenly scent that's considered the most powerful aroma of any shrub. It takes careful siting to provide good drainage in a sandy, neutral soil of low fertility, giving the plant a cool, moist root run in a place that gets only morning sun. Shade daphne's roots by mulching it with compost made with ground limestone.

In coastal climates where spring comes early, the *Bauhinia variegata* that began blooming in January in the warmest zones now blooms in February, producing displays of pink to purple, 3-inch flowers. You can cut back the tips after flowering to remove the developing beans, but that becomes progressively harder to do as the plant throws up tall shoots. It can be trained to a single trunk.

February is brightened in Zone 9 by *Chamelaucium uncinatum*, sometimes called Geraldton waxflower. Its loose and open form is sheathed in bright green, needlelike foliage and brushed with small pink and rose flowers. This plant sprawls to an 8-foot diameter.

Two forms of *Euryops,* a genus of evergreen perennials from South Africa, will give Zone 9 and 10 gardeners yellow, daisylike flowers. *Euryops athanasiae* has very finely divided, whitish leaves and carries its flowers on long stems. *E. pectinatus* is a denser shrub, with grayish-green leaves and small yellow daisies on short stems. It puts on heavy bloom in February.

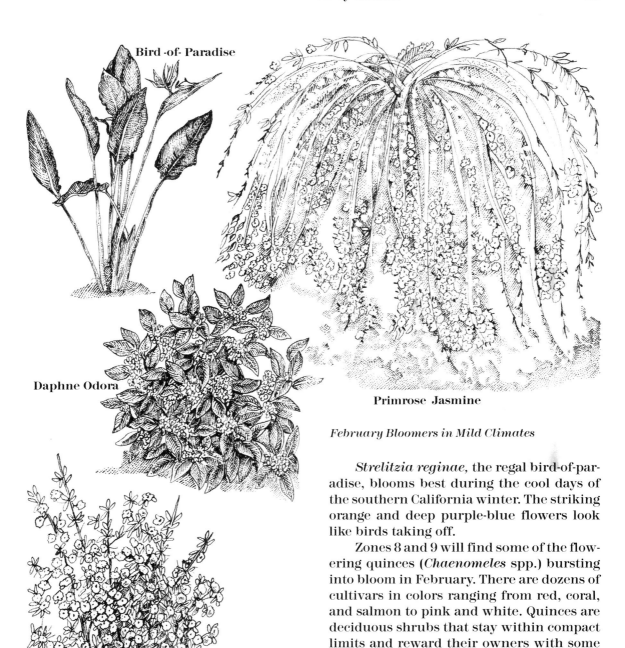

Bird -of- Paradise

Daphne Odora

Primrose Jasmine

Flowering Quince

February Bloomers in Mild Climates

Strelitzia reginae, the regal bird-of-paradise, blooms best during the cool days of the southern California winter. The striking orange and deep purple-blue flowers look like birds taking off.

Zones 8 and 9 will find some of the flowering quinces (*Chaenomeles* spp.) bursting into bloom in February. There are dozens of cultivars in colors ranging from red, coral, and salmon to pink and white. Quinces are deciduous shrubs that stay within compact limits and reward their owners with some of the earliest blooms available.

In the warmer zones, expect forsythia to react to February's intensifying sun by exploding into its familiar yellow showers. Forsythias, to be elegant, need yearly pruning and training, but this is too rarely done, giving the plant its reputation for careless sprawling.

Another plant that needs a yearly shearing to remain neat, but that provides good February bloom in Zones 8 to 10, is *Jasminum mesnyi*, the primrose jasmine. Its bright yellow, semidouble flowers are borne singly along the 6-foot stems. There's no scent, but it will produce flowers all winter where freezes don't occur, or start blooming in February where winter minimums reach 20°F.

While most shrubs and small trees stay locked up tight through the middle of the country, some specimens in those warm, favored locations may bloom this month. *Chimonanthus praecox*, wintersweet, for instance, may hang out its yellow flowers. *Erica carnea*, the spring heath, opens flowers as early as January. White, rosy purple, and pink forms are available. *E. carnea* 'Springwood White' may be the prettiest of all. This species is hardy to Zone 5. The *E. darleyensis* that started blooming last fall will continue its winter pageant of lilac-pink flowers.

Gardeners in Zone 4 should make sure to plant the small *Hamamelis vernalis*, spring witch-hazel, in a sheltered place, for it will surely be the first plant to bloom—no later than late February, and sometimes as early as January. Its secret is to hang out its streamer-like flowers in the sun, then roll them up at night when the temperatures plunge.

Lonicera fragrantissima, the winter honeysuckle, is the earliest blooming honeysuckle. It will produce the first of myriads of tiny, creamy white, richly fragrant flowers in February and continue blooming into April. Trained under a south-facing window, it perfumes the first warm breezes of the approaching spring. Carolina yellow jessamine (*Gelsemium sempervirens*), hardy to Zone 7, now begins to open small, fragrant, yellow trumpets. It's a wilding along roadsides and woods' edges in South Carolina.

Vines

In Zone 9, the vines begin to open a rich palette of colors: *Hardenbergia violacea*, the lilac vine; *Senecio confusus*, the Mexican flame vine; *Tecomaria capensis*, the cape honeysuckle; and *Solandra maxima*, the cup-of-gold vine. For Zone 10 or a warm greenhouse, there are the piercing scarlet flowers of *Manettia cordifolia*, the firecracker vine, that climbs to 6 feet, or hangs from a basket. The marvelous blue trumpet vine, also known as the clock vine (*Thunbergia grandiflora*), will sprinkle the greenhouse with its bits of sky at this time of year.

Flowers to Brighten February

Readers who live in Zones 9 and 10 will be familiar with the succulent ice plant, *Lampranthus* spp., that's used to hold dry banks in summer and gives out searing waves of op-art colors in February and March. Perhaps the extensive roadside and office building displays are enough, so that we don't need to bring it home. Instead, we might plant *Iris reticulata* and *Iris unguicularis*, two shy winter types that are no less beautiful for the rarity of such delicate flowers in the winter months.

In Zones 6 to 8, many plants begin to stir. Among perennials, *Helleborus niger* continues its bloom. Plant groups of *Eranthis hyemalis*, the winter aconite, around the base of the hellebore. Winter aconite has small, yellow, cuplike flowers. In sheltered locations from Zone 6 south, it blooms in February, while snow may still be on the ground.

A sheltered stone wall facing south and well-drained earth provide a chance for February bloom from several other types of flowers in Zone 6, especially in a mild year. In

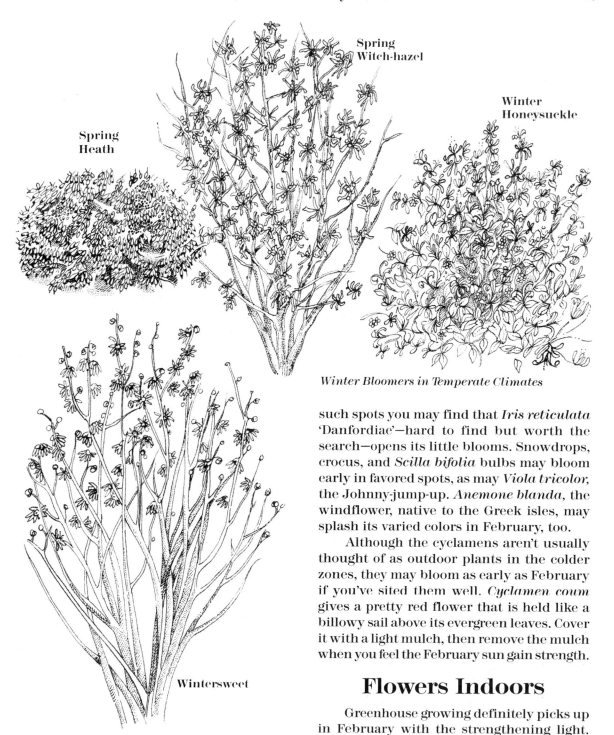

Spring
Witch-hazel

Winter
Honeysuckle

Spring
Heath

Winter Bloomers in Temperate Climates

Wintersweet

such spots you may find that *Iris reticulata* 'Danfordiae'—hard to find but worth the search—opens its little blooms. Snowdrops, crocus, and *Scilla bifolia* bulbs may bloom early in favored spots, as may *Viola tricolor*, the Johnny-jump-up. *Anemone blanda*, the windflower, native to the Greek isles, may splash its varied colors in February, too.

Although the cyclamens aren't usually thought of as outdoor plants in the colder zones, they may bloom as early as February if you've sited them well. *Cyclamen coum* gives a pretty red flower that is held like a billowy sail above its evergreen leaves. Cover it with a light mulch, then remove the mulch when you feel the February sun gain strength.

Flowers Indoors

Greenhouse growing definitely picks up in February with the strengthening light.

FEATURED FLOWER OF FEBRUARY: NEW ZEALAND TEA TREE

If you think of the trees and shrubs as dancing, the spreading oaks sweep into low bows, the Lombardy poplars leap straight upward, the willows curtsy, and the aspens do the shimmy. Continuing with the analogy, the New Zealand tea tree's angular branches seem to be doing a tango.

Leptospermum scoparium, actually a shrub, is called a tea tree because Captain James Cook, the great British navigator of the eighteenth century, used a tea brewed from its leaves to prevent scurvy, the disease that had been decimating ships' crews for hundreds of years. The tea provided vitamin C, which was missing from the seamen's diets.

This New Zealand tea tree has its lower foliage removed to show its dense branching habit.

Since its discovery, the shrub has been selected and bred to an assemblage of marvelous cultivars that set profusions of fiery ruby, red, rose, pink, or white flowers along the branches. The double flowers, about ½ inch across, are set against needlelike, very dark green leaves, intensifying their color. Their rich hues are heartily appreciated in the overcast, cool, and wet days of February along the California coast.

Leptospermum scoparium 'Ruby Glow' is the most commonly seen of the early blooming tea trees, reaching about 8 feet tall with a many-branched habit. It's not particularly noticeable when not in bloom, but its tiny, dark leaves make a dim, hazy effect, a valuable backdrop for lower shrubs or perennials. The ideal situation would be near a deciduous tree that would throw a dense shade behind the tea tree in summer to set off masses of perennial flowers in the foreground, but reveal the shrub in winter.

While they make fine specimens, tea trees aren't usually used that way, more frequently being massed with other evergreen shrubby plants in borders and as screens and hedges. A cultivar with reddish leaves, called 'Red Damask', has an even denser habit than 'Ruby Glow', and develops its strontium-red flowers during winter, holding them into spring. A small, white cultivar called 'Snow White' begins to bloom as early as December, and continues for several months.

These are the February bloomers in mild-climate areas, beginning to smolder in the dead of winter and shocking us when they explode with bright flowers. They herald the many colors to come. Many other *Leptospermum scoparium*s bloom later in the spring in gorgeous shades of pink. One of the nicest is 'Nanum', a little 2-foot shrub with pink and red flowers. The Australian tea tree (*Leptospermum laevigatum*) grows to genuine tree size—about 30 feet. Its branching becomes progressively more graceful and its wood more muscular-looking with increasing age.

The tea trees don't seem to be bothered by pests, and require no pruning—an ideal, low-maintenance combination any gardener can appreciate.

A portrait of early spring bulbs: Iris reticulata, *top left, and* Scilla bifolia, *top right, associate with Johnny-jump-ups in the middle, crocus at the left, anemones and snowdrops at lower right. The wall helps them bloom earlier than unprotected bulbs.*

Daffodil, crocus, and other bulbs can be easily forced for February bloom. Cyclamens bloom now. Polyanthus primulas continue their cheery show of bright colors. And impatiens bloom nicely, provided you keep them free of whitefly and other greenhouse pests.

Annuals can brighten the February greenhouse or sunspace. Some people like to grow the calceolaria or pocketbook plant hybrids with their strange yellow blooms. *Calendula officinalis,* the pot marigold, is a reliable bloomer in the greenhouse or sunspace. The African daisies are used this way, too.

March (Early Spring)

Many plants bloom now in the South and West, but in the temperate climates, life is just beginning to return to the fields and backyards of mid-America.

Bulbs are among the first garden plants to bloom in March in Zones 5 and 6—the centrally located climate zones that run from coastal Maine through Long Island and the New York City area to southern Pennsylvania, Ohio, Indiana, and Illinois. These zones include all of Kentucky, southern West Virginia, and western Virginia.

"Bulbs" include, in our parlance, all the self-contained storage roots that reliably send up flowers each year. Also included are the true bulbs, as typified by an onion with its separate rings of tissue and distinct growing point. You'll notice that lilies also exhibit the properties of true bulbs.

The term also includes corms, which resemble bulbs except for their undifferentiated tissue. New plants start from the old corms, which wither away in favor of the new generations. In this way corms will naturalize. Crocus is a corm.

And "bulbs" include the tubers, swollen underground stems or roots with "eyes." Potatoes are familiar tubers. Among flowers, *Anemone blanda,* the windflower, is a tuber. New aerial parts emerge from the eyes, which are actually buds, and use the stored starch in the tuber as food for green herbaceous growth. The old tuber is used up and the plant forms new tubers and more tubers over the growing season. Thus tuberous plants may naturalize where they like the spot.

Bulbs are best planted in the fall, so that they have a chance to winter over, settle in, and acclimate themselves to their new surroundings. Plant your bulbs in good garden soil about three times as deep as the bulbs are wide. Make sure that drainage is quick so that the bulbs never sit in water.

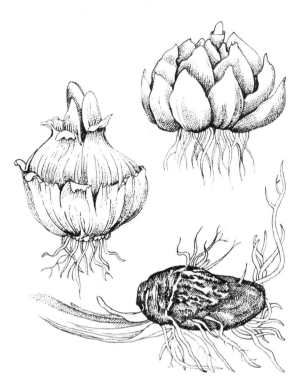

Three kinds of "bulbs" include true bulbs, like the lily bulb at top right; corms, such as the crocus corm (out of scale) in the center; and tubers, like the calla lily tuber at the bottom.

Bulbs that bloom in March in Zones 5 and 6 may begin blooming in January in Zone 9, February in Zones 7 and 8, and won't burst open in the coldest northerly zones until late April.

Creative Ways to Use Bulbs

Bulbs are loved for the intensity of their early effects—fields of daffodils and sheets of red tulips. How fitting and right that some of the first plants to bloom in our gardens reveal such delicate filigree and design, and splash the winter-weary world with such vivid colors. But bulbs can also produce some of the more subtle and delicate colors: chionodoxa's pale blue and gold, puschkinia's porcelainlike turquoise and cream.

Our favorite way to use bulbs is to plant some in every available nook. We like them to pop out in surprising places. The eranthis, or winter aconites, show the spring's first color, so tuck a few beside a well-used path. Create a golden pool of yellow daffodils under an old apple tree. A handful of chionodoxa tucked between stones consorts nicely with the emerging, tightly rolled spears of lily-of-the-valley.

Certain bulbs are wonderful for their jewellike appearance. It's fun to put some in an out-of-the-way part of the garden where they can be "discovered" by visitors, looking like charms on nature's spring bracelet. Two such finely tooled flowers are *Leucojum vernum,* the spring snowflake, which hangs out green- and gold-tipped bells, and *Fritillaria meleagris,* the checkered fritillary, with its surprising checkerboard markings.

Whether part of a color display, like daffodils, or set out for their charm, like snowflakes, or their perfume, like hyacinths, bulbs should be massed in clumps, not strung out in marching lines of single-file flowers, or trudging three abreast in endless circles around the edge of a flower bed. The clumps look best when they have oval, irregular shapes, reproducing the effect of dappled light, broken into its component prismatic colors, and arrayed in pools under trees, on banks, by shrubs, everywhere.

Some gardeners plant the seeds or transplants of their favorite annuals in the spring bulb gardens as soon as the soil thaws, so that the annuals eventually cover the fading bulb foliage. Others use perennials such as ferns and hostas to hide the yellowing leaves of their bulbs. Areas of naturalized bulbs can be over-planted with ground covers that will replace the spring show with one of their own. *Lamium* 'Beacon Silver' carries interesting silver-sheened leaves that will brighten a shady spot once the bulbs die down and the tree canopy closes overhead. Epimedium, liriope, vinca, and ajuga—all work to replace bulb foliage. Bulb foliage must be allowed to die away naturally. Cutting it off too soon prevents the bulb from manufacturing enough food to bloom properly the following year. Clipped too soon over several years, the bulbs will die out.

Start a spring bulb display in March with the earliest snowdrops (*Galanthus* spp.) and continue major bloom right through the tulip period in late May and early June. As the spring progresses, free-form drifts of bulbs mix beautifully with early spring perennials like blue mertensia and the forget-me-nots. Red tulips held above mats of white arabis are clean and pretty. By tulip time, your color palette ranges toward infinity.

Use bulbs for fun—pink and white tulips in association with pink and white dogwoods, or an all-blue, all-bulb, all-gorgeous garden with *Scilla siberica, Iris reticulata, Muscari botryoides, Bulbocodium vernum, Chionodoxa* spp., and *Anemone blanda*.

Most bulbs will slowly increase their numbers, although crowding may lessen their bloom. We've seen daffodils, grape hyacinths, blue squill (*Scilla siberica*), and puschkinias slowly add an extra stem or two each year and expand our meager plantings to respectable clumps. And most of us have seen the daffodils around long-abandoned properties, still coming up each year, but now expanded to room-size, even barn-size, patches. As we found out in Pennsylvania, after a dozen or so years, spring bulbs came up everywhere.

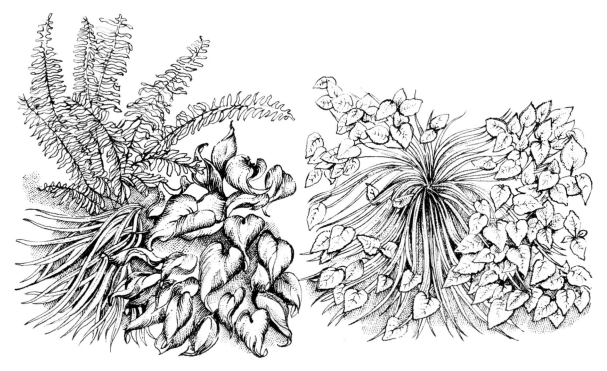

At left, ferns and hostas hide the spent foliage of daffodils. At right, the ground cover Lamium maculatum *'Beacon Silver' begins to cover fading bulb foliage.*

Shrubs, trees, and evergreens create little pockets where bulbs can be showcased for their finest effect.

Bulbs Indoors

Bulbs forced indoors brighten up late winter days. How wonderful the hyacinths smell when coaxed from their dormant bulbs in glass hyacinth vases on a bright windowsill. A miniature bulb garden can be planted in a long container. Small, perfect narcissus in individual pots lend a grace note to the table. Forcing bulbs indoors brings all their color and gaiety into the most tedious time of the year.

Bulbs for forcing need to undergo a cooling period (at root cellar temperatures of 35 to 45°F) for 100 days. Then they can be

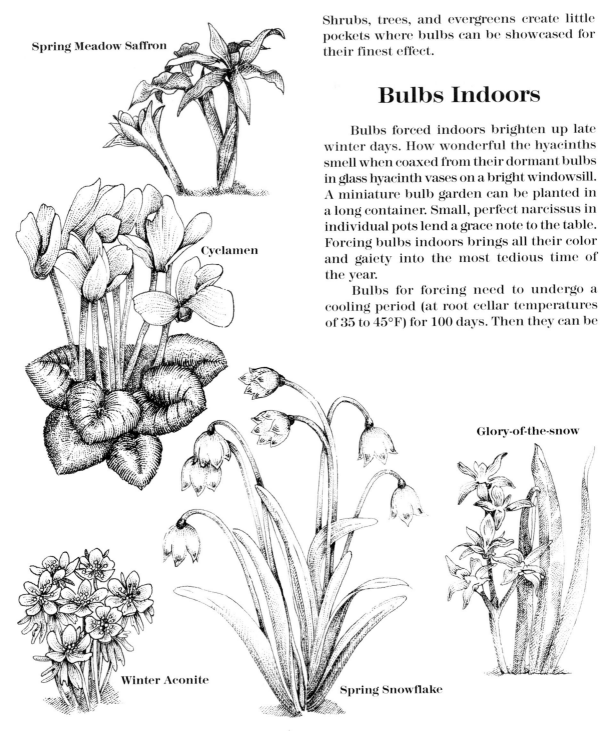

Spring Meadow Saffron

Cyclamen

Glory-of-the-snow

Winter Aconite

Spring Snowflake

Favorite Spring Bulbs

planted from early October (for January bloom) onward for a succession of indoor blooms. Bulbs for forcing include galanthus, *Iris reticulata,* all varieties of daffodil, narcissus, hyacinth, and crocus, plus eranthis, brodiaea, *Scilla tubergeniana,* and star of Bethlehem.

If you have a room or sunspace that receives at least a half day of sun, then you can grow bulbs indoors, allowing them to flower at their natural times, as opposed to forcing, which causes them to flower out of season. Grow frost-tender bulbs in pots for flowers you couldn't otherwise have. Plant a hanging basket full of *Achimenes ehrenbergii* and watch the lilac flowers with white throats, spotted with yellow, cascade out. Or pot up a kafir lily (*Clivia miniata*) for striking red

and yellow lilylike flowers. Grow freesias indoors in a cool room for their delicious scents and pretty jewellike colors in February and March.

Other tender bulbs you might like to try include *Cyclamen persicum;* eucharis (Amazon lily, which flowers two or three times a year with dainty, daffodil-like flowers); the rich purple and white gloxinias; the voluptuous, large-flowered hippeastrum (amaryllis); and gracefully curved vases of zantedeschia (calla lily).

In Zones 9 and 10, it's possible to grow a wide range of exotic bulbs outdoors, including the pink trumpets of crinums and picotee amaryllises, and the Luther Burbank cross between the latter two bulbs, the amarcrinum.

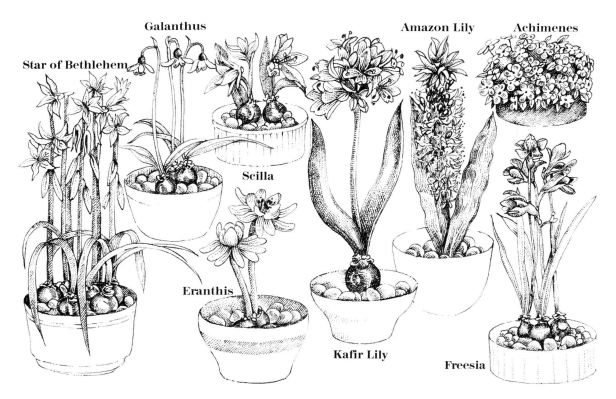

Some bulbs, such as the Kafir lily (clivia), Amazon lily, and Achimenes, are grown as houseplants all year, while others, including the freesias, star of Bethlehem, snowdrops, winter aconite, and squill, are grown in pots for forcing.

FEATURED FLOWER OF MARCH: CEANOTHUS

California is the native home of a shrub that resembles the eastern lilac, but is evergreen and thickly covers itself with profusions of intensely blue, tiny flowers, which on very close inspection are set off by little stamens resembling yellowish stars in the evening sky.

Although they look a bit like lilacs, these native ceanothus shrubs will grow in Zones 8 to 10 and are fully adapted to the summer drought, requiring summer water only in their first year, or until they become established. Most varieties have small to medium, glossy, dark green, evergreen leaves. I've seen them blooming wild on the rocky cliffs of Big Sur as early as January, although most of the cultivars in commerce begin their serious bloom in March.

Ceanothus produces flowers from light, pale blue to the deepest indigo. All give a real blue—not a magenta, or lilac. Along coastal California, it's widely used along roadsides and as foundation plantings in malls and industrial complexes. Such ordinary uses don't detract from the plant's rare beauty at all—in fact, the roads and malls look far better for the plantings.

Ceanothus's lovely blue mixes well with the western redbud (*Cercis occidentalis*), the New Zealand teas (*Leptospermum* spp.), and the soft yellow acacias. All three combinations have the advantage of being native, and do quite well without a lot of fussing, pruning, or watering.

Ceanothus, being native and having been selected and bred for many years, now takes many forms. Some of the most familiar include those in the following list.

Hybrid Ceanothus

'Blue Buttons': grows to 10 feet tall and nearly twice as wide. Carries light blue to light lilac blooms in big clusters.

'Dark Star': produces little 2-inch clusters of cobalt blue flowers. The bush grows only to 5 feet or so, maybe twice as wide.

'Frosty Blue': as the name implies, the blue flowers are frosted with white. Reaches 6 to 8 feet, spreads to 10 feet wide. An outstanding choice for the garden.

'Julia Phelps': covered with lots of 1-inch clusters of midnight-blue flowers. Reaches 5 to 6 feet tall, half again as wide.

'Ray Hartman': medium-blue flower clusters appear at tips of a big shrub, reaching 15 to 20 feet tall and nearly as wide. Has large leaves for a ceanothus, 2 to 3 inches long.

Ceanothus Species

C. gloriosus: hugs the ground in large mats that are covered with light blue flower clusters in spring. Likes the cool steady climate near the ocean.

C. griseus 'Horizontalis': another low-growing sort, commonly called the Carmel creeper. Has light blue clusters. More tender than *C. gloriosus*.

C. griseus 'Louis Edmunds': features medium royal-blue blooms. Reaches 5 to 6 feet and twice as wide. Leaves are bright green.

C. rigidus 'Snowball': a white-clustered ceanothus. Reaches 6 feet.

C. thyrsiflorus 'Snow Flurry': very profuse bloom covers the shrub, which reaches 8 to 10 feet.

Ceanothus 'Ray Hartman', at top, and 'Julia Phelps', at bottom, add splashes of blue to early spring in coastal California.

April (Mid-Spring)

Some of our first friends are trees. As toddlers venturing outside, we meet common yard trees like the flowering dogwood (*Cornus florida*) and the crabapple (*Malus floribunda*) in our front yards before we venture into the yards of others. April is when these trees start to bloom, and our early impressions of their gorgeous display make them special to us for a lifetime.

April's a dangerous month because of the ever-present possibility of frost—and April frosts are possible from New York to Santa Rosa. How many frost-blasted magnolia blossoms have graced—or rather, disgraced—our yards in April? How many tender young things, coaxed forth from dormancy by an early, abnormally warm spell (we experienced several days in the 90s in Pennsylvania one year), are subsequently frostbitten back to bare wood? Despite the setbacks, April—at last!—is full of flowers.

The old dogwoods of our early childhood may be gone—victims of the anthracnose disease that's decimating *Cornus florida* populations in the northeastern United States. A very disease- and insect-resistant dogwood you might substitute in a planting today is *Cornus mas,* the cornelian cherry. It flowers in early April in the Northeast, producing puffy yellow clusters that cover the bare branches. *Cornus officinalis* is a very similar plant, except that its slightly larger flowers appear a week earlier than *C. mas.* Both species are upright, with beautiful, rich brown, finely textured bark. Both branch extensively, and can be pruned to overcome their natural shrubbiness. A bonus is the cheery red berries that appear in late summer and early fall, a favorite of birds. Those of *C. mas* make a good jelly.

An exceptionally nice specimen tree for April bloom is *Magnolia stellata*, the star magnolia. It's hardy up through Zone 5 (but the flowers will often be nipped by hard frost in that zone, so it favors a slightly warmer climate). The star magnolia is a dense, shrubby tree, with lots of stems and branches thickly covered with green leaves. What could be more wonderful on a mild mid-April morning than to step into the early spring sunshine and find the star magnolia in full bloom, covered with fragrant white stars? Each 3-inch star is an aggregate of from 12 to 20 petals radiating out from the center. Some of the cultivars of this species are even more exciting: 'Centennial' has up to 32 petals blushed pink on their outer edges; 'Royal Star' is white with many petals, the innermost of which can be incurved; and 'Waterlily' is pink in bud, opening white, and highly fragrant.

There are hundreds of magnolia cultivars in commerce. Check the chart, Flowering Trees, on page 156 for several of the most important.

A weeping Higan cherry (*Prunus subhirtella* 'Pendula') is often chosen with good reason as the focal point of the April landscape. A well-displayed weeping Higan cherry can reach 30 feet tall or more, and nearly as wide, softly arching its delicate branches toward the ground, creating a waterfall of single, pale pink blossoms in foamy clusters. Because of its weeping habit, it remains interesting in leaf, especially in winter when its arching, curved branches are visible. Weeping cherries are breathtaking alone in a lawn, but they're also useful planted at the front of a group of trees that serve as a backdrop for a bulb and perennial garden. In April, the tree's pink fountains can pour into a bed of gaily colored bulbs. Later, its dark green leaves can provide contrast for elegant drifts of campanula and phlox. The tree serves again in fall when its foliage turns yellow.

Check the chart, Flowering Trees, on page 156 for other ornamental prunus (stone-fruit) varieties.

To the April show add the amelanchiers,

Flowers have textures too. Notice the differences between the flowers of cornelian cherry, at top; the star magnolia, below it; the weeping Higan cherry, third from top; the serviceberry, below it; and the ruby horse-chestnut at bottom.

or serviceberries. These multistemmed, shrubby trees grow to 25 feet tall and about 10 feet wide, creating an open, upright appearance. In April they cover themselves with pendulous clusters of pink buds that open into white flowers just as the leaves appear. These are followed by reddish-black berries in June. They taste good, but you'll have to hurry to beat the birds. *Amelanchier canadensis* is a shrubby form with slightly smaller flowers. Both *A. laevis* and *A. arborea* take to a tree form more easily, and *A. laevis* is fragrant.

A striking display of bright scarlet, conical, upright, 8 inch tall flower clusters that appear at branch tips in late April is provided by *Aesculus ×carnea* 'Briotii', the ruby horse-chestnut. Like other horse-chestnuts, the leaves are long and five to seven of them are grouped in a fan-shaped bunch, giving the tree a rather coarse appearance when not in bloom, and a messy habit in autumn when the leaves turn brown and fall. But the red panicles above the new green leaves are as festive a flower display as any tree's. Because of its rough look out of season and its dense, dark canopy, it's not a tree to feature by itself. But it adds exceptional interest to a group of background trees selected to coordinate flower colors as they bloom along with the ruby horse-chestnut.

Although relatively rare, the Carolina silverbell (*Halesia carolina*) produces a sweet profusion of white, bell-shaped flowers. Small clusters of the flowers hang beneath the new greenery in late April in Zones 5 to 8. Since the tops of these trees often die back due to midsummer droughts, it's often kept topped to form a low tree, although it will reach 30 feet high and just as wide in spots it favors. The gorgeous bells are hard to see when you're looking down on the limbs or from a distance, so Carolina silverbell should be given a spot atop a steep rise right next to a house

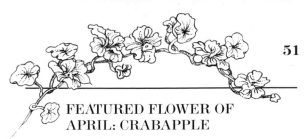

or well-used steps or pathway. The display of white bells only lasts a week, but it's a sight you'll remember the other 51 weeks of the year.

Another relatively rare tree is Persian parrotia (*Parrotia persica*), a witch-hazel family member that produces small flowers with showy clusters of red stamens on its bare branches in early April. It usually makes a brilliant autumn display of yellow and orange foliage. The bark of this tree is interesting because it peels off in various shades of gray, white, and buff.

April's bounty of wonderful trees is just the beginning of the flowering tree season. From now until frost, you can select trees that provide an overwhelming abundance of choice flowers to lure the bees and the birds, and to charm whatever appreciative souls wander through your landscape.

Before you head off to the nearest nursery with your head full of magnolias, dogwoods, crabapples, and a host of other ornamental trees, let us warn you again of a possible pitfall. When planting ornamental trees, plan for their full size. There's no use spending the money on stock that will have to be removed because of overcrowding within five or even ten years. These plants are usually in the garden for the duration, so plan accordingly. They should be the first plants you select, along with evergreen structural plantings, because they form the big masses in the landscape.

When siting trees, keep bloom times and flower colors in mind. White flowers look fine with any other color, especially with pink. Pink, on the other hand, may not look particularly nice abutting a yellow-flowered tree. For a thorough discussion of color harmonies and how to choose companions, see Chapter 2, Understanding Color Harmonies, in our previous book, *The Perennial Garden* (Rodale Press, 1985).

FEATURED FLOWER OF APRIL: CRABAPPLE

The question is not whether to plant flowering crabapples—they are so beautiful in so many ways that they must be among our first choices for early flowering trees—but how to choose wisely from the absolute welter of species and hybrid cultivars available.

For gardeners who like to rush the season, the earliest to flower is *Malus baccata* var. *mandshurica*, the Siberian crabapple, which blooms in mid-April with white, fragrant, 1½-inch flowers. Its fruits are ½-inch red ornaments.

A time-tested variety, one that's been a staple in American landscaping for over 100 years, is *Malus floribunda*, or Japanese flowering crabapple. This familiar crabapple is round and spreading, with a nice branching habit that responds well to pruning for artistic effect. In late April it takes on a reddish glow as the flower buds swell. These open rosy pink, which soon fades to white. In full bloom it carries the delicate fragrance of apple blossoms. It reaches full height as a tree of 20 to 25 feet, spreading even wider as it ages.

A more compact crabapple for small spaces is *Malus hupehensis,* the tea crabapple, which reaches only 20 feet when mature, and carries single white flowers in late April. Later in the season it produces very ornamental red crabapples about ½ inch across. Like many apples, it has a tendency to flower heavily only in alternate years. This species is very susceptible to fireblight.

For extremely small spaces or for a place in the landscape that requires a small tree, consider planting *Malus sargentii*, or sargent crabapple, which bears fruit every other year. It's even more compact than the tea crabapple, reaching only 10 feet when mature, but spreading to 15 feet or more. Sargent crabapples are hardy, reliable landscape plants with profuse flowering in their "on" years, when their fragrance is also apparent. The fruits are ½-inch, shiny red globes.

One reason for the crabapple's enduring popularity is the fruit that hangs late on the tree, sprinkling the landscape with red when everything else is tumbling down to killing frosts. The redbud crabapple, *Malus ×zumi* 'Calocarpa', produces the typical load of pinkish-white, fragrant

(continued)

flowers in alternate springs, but follows with deep red crabapples that hang into winter.

Many crabapples have such a crazy, mixed-up parentage that it's easiest to lump them together as, simply, hybrids. Here are some of the choicest, as selected by horticulturists at Longwood Gardens in Kennett Square, Pennsylvania.

Hybrid Crabapples

'Coralburst':   6- to 8-foot dwarf tree with coral pink buds and double, rosy pink flowers.

'Dolgo':   tall tree, rising to 30 feet, with large, fragrant white flowers and large red-purple fruits. Tends to bear in alternate years.

'Donald Wyman':   pink buds and large white flowers are followed by bright red fruit that hangs until winter.

'Jewelberry':   tiny crabapple, reaching only to 6 feet, with white flowers and bright red fruits.

'Red Jade':   popular crabapple variety with dark pink buds opening to white flowers along weeping, hanging branches. The name refers to the color of the fruit.

'Red Jewel':   single white flowers appear on a compact tree with pretty, spreading branches. The glossy red fruit hangs through December.

'Sentinel':   single, pale pink flowers are followed by small red fruit that hangs through fall.

A crabapple gives joy in bloom in the spring; shade in the summer; and, in some types, red or yellow fruit that hang into the winter.

May (Late Spring)

With the arrival of May, Nature begins her peak floral displays. Bulbs and early perennials carpet the garden floor, trees fill the sky overhead with bloom, and now the shrubs explode; the whole world returns to the full, vibrant life of summer.

When viewing a garden from a distance, shrubs provide the middle ground. Many are about as tall as we are and meet us at eye level, though some are taller. A good definition of a shrub is a woody plant with multiple stems that reaches not much higher than 15 feet. Much taller than that and we're talking about trees. There's a whole class of woody plants that grow 15 to 20 feet tall and are difficult to classify as either shrubs or trees. Shrubs form the walls of outdoor "rooms" and, in the months when they're not in flower, provide backdrops for other flowers placed in front of them. Most shrubs can be grown as hedges when planted in rows, but hedges can require a lot of work when kept formal or clipped. We prefer the easy informality of massed shrubs that suggests avenues to explore, rather than the formal lines that herd the garden's visitors along.

Colorful Shrubs

When choosing shrubs, you have a universe of plant material at your fingertips. There are something like 7,000 shrubs available in commerce, and many of them flower. Precisely because there is such a welter of material, we've limited our descriptions to those common varieties with a large number of benefits or exceptional beauty. We think the following shrubs are among the most useful and beautiful commonly available from nurseries or mail-order houses. Not all of these bloom in May, but each has a place in our list of top-notch shrubs.

The butterfly bush (buddleia) begins to bloom in high summer with long, densely packed racemes of lilac, blue, purple, deep burgundy, or white florets. *Buddleia davidii* 'Black Knight' throws rich, dark burgundy wands 10 to 12 feet into the air in graceful curves traced by the bending stems. A compact form is available, *B. davidii* 'Nanho Purple', that reaches only 5 feet.

Butterfly bush looks and smells exquisite. Better yet, it attracts butterflies, as its common name suggests. It has a loose, open habit and looks beautiful emerging from a puffy white cloud of gypsophila. The plant needs little care except to be cut back to a foot tall in late winter where the frosts haven't done the pruning for you. Buddleia flowers on new wood, so cutting it back promotes flowering.

For wonderful spring bloom, gardeners have a world of azaleas and rhododendrons in all imaginable colors. Many gardeners like to plan a spring spectacular around a crescendo of color from these shrubs, literally filling the garden with intense color. *Kalmia latifolia,* or mountain laurel, likes the same woodland conditions as the azaleas and rhododendrons. Its sweet, scalloped pink bells tinkle on short, open shrubs, which look particularly pretty teamed with a ground cover of deep blue ajuga. I grew up in Pennsylvania's Pocono Mountains, whose woods filled with mountain laurel in late spring, and this plant has retained a spot in my heart ever since.

Speaking of Pennsylvania, our driveway there was lined with wild chokecherries (*Prunus virginiana*), and I loved their spring blooms—white panicles tossing this way and that over the whole bush. I haven't seen chokecherries here in California, but we do have the bottlebrush buckeye (*Aesculus parviflora*), whose flowers give a similar effect. It grows as a wild tree here, but the *A. parviflora* cultivar of commerce forms a bush 10 feet high and 15 feet wide that covers itself with upright white racemes in July—a month when many shrubs are out of flower and the garden needs the kind of dramatic interest that bottlebrush can provide. It's hardy to Zone 5 and can be used as a specimen or massed with other shrubs. Just be sure to give it plenty of room to grow.

Common yellow scotch broom (*Cytisus scoparius*) has become a weed here in northern California, but that shows the plant's drought resistance and innate vigor. The cultivated varieties are not as rampant as the species, and are much prettier. We had scotch broom freeze out on us in Zone 6, but it will grow there in protected spots, and even in Zone 5, if given extra protection. One of the chief advantages of broom is its leggy, twiggy texture—small leaves on long stems, looking like an old-fashioned corn broom held upside down. Broom associates well with broad-leaved deciduous or evergreen shrubs. We like *C. scoparius* 'Lord Lambourne' for its red and creamy white flowers. Of the yellow sorts, *C. praecox* 'Moonlight' has sulfur-colored, pealike flowers in profusion in May.

One of the most useful garden shrubs of all is *Deutzia gracilis,* the slender deutzia. It reaches only 3 feet and explodes in a froth of pure white blossoms in May. This allows you to use it in massed plantings to light up a foreground, or plant it in the perennial garden to provide a splashy display while the perennials are still putting on vegetative growth. After flowering, it should blend back into a border or create a low backdrop with evergreens for small perennials or annuals placed in the front of the garden.

If you have a difficult spot—wet, rocky with poor soil, or shady—try *Clethra alnifolia* 'Pinkspire', a carefree shrub with fragrant, rose-pink spires of little florets from July to September. Clethra looks best after pruning out its excess stems, reducing them to several beautiful, graceful woody trunks. The shrub reaches just 6 feet or so. For added drama, underplant the stem-pruned specimens with *Liriope muscari,* so that the llriope's deep blue flower spikes and the clethra's sweet pinks harmonize.

The chaenomeles, or flowering quinces, are very early blooming low shrubs in colors from bright, rich red to the softest apricots. Most are hardy to Zone 5, and *Chaenomeles speciosa* 'Rubra Grandiflora' with large red flowers is hardy to Zone 4. Give these a featured spot where they'll be visible from the house in early spring.

A shady, humusy spot is perfect for the delightful *Fothergilla major* with its puffy, white, 2-inch flowers in spring and brilliant display of fall foliage color. Plant it with *Hydrangea quercifolia* with its large, odd leaves in summer, its brilliant red and purple fall foliage coloration, and the extra large, snowy flower clusters in midsummer.

Some flowers are lovely, others are fun. One in the latter category is *Kerria japonica* 'Pleniflora', which grows from 4 to 8 feet, and produces masses of ball-shaped, golden yellow, double flowers. The effect is playful and cheerful, especially when displayed against a dark evergreen or wall. It blooms in March in the warm zones and May in Zone 5, the limit of its hardiness.

Not well known is *Kolkwitzia amabilis,* also called the beauty bush. It's easy to grow and needs no care except removal of older stems from time to time to promote better flowering. The plant reaches from 6 to 10 feet and is covered in late spring with light pink bells. It's a good choice for the shrub border with white-flowered neighbors.

The potentillas are long-blooming little shrubs that reach 18 to 24 inches, then spread, forming busy mounds of roselike yellow flowers. Although most cultivars are shades of yellow, there are red, white, and salmon-coral shades, too. Use these in forward parts of the border, interrupting drifts of perennials, spilling out into the lawn.

Once you know the scent of a large, sprawling mock orange (*Philadelphus* spp.) blooming on a warm, early June morning, you'll find a place for one. The cultivar

Butterfly Bush

Mock Orange

Weigela

Spiraea

Slender Deutzia

Beauty Bush

'Virginal' has semidouble flowers with a strong, sweet scent that closely resembles the delicious odor of citrus blossoms. A very pretty type is the compact variety *Philadelphus* ×*lemoinei* 'Belle Etoile', which reaches only 5 to 6 feet and carries pure white, single flowers with cool red centers.

Spiraeas and syringas (lilacs) are both mainstays in the shrub border, or are often used alone as specimens. *Spiraea* ×*bumalda* 'Anthony Waterer' is a choice deep pink that will bloom most of the summer and even occasionally in fall. Another of our favorites is *Spiraea prunifolia* 'Plena', with its tiny, double white flowers that fill the slender branches with neat whorls of white bloom. As for the lilacs, choose them by the colors you like best. There are lavender, deep violet, pink, and white sorts. We love the deep violet kinds, and cut them freely to decorate the house with their bountiful look and fresh spring fragrance.

Weigela florida is a round shrub with spreading branches that arch over to touch the ground. It blooms in May with profusions of white, pink, or red flowers, depending on which cultivar you choose. It's a very effective choice to plant with a color-coordinated spiraea, as they will bloom together but contrast in foliage (the weigela has large leaves and the spiraea small ones).

Viburnums carry leathery, handsome leaves and pretty pink or white hemispherical clusters of blooms, and many have a wonderful spicy scent. One of our very favorites is *Viburnum* ×*burkwoodii*, hardy to Zone 5 and reaching to 10 feet. Its spring flowers are waxy domes with a sweet and spicy scent. If it's scent you're after, plant *V. carlesii*, considered by many (including us) to have the most beguiling fragrance of any shrub. Although its blooming period is only ten days, those who love it wouldn't be without it. One of its offspring, *V.* ×*carlcephalum*, blooms later and continues *V. carlesii*'s scent for another few weeks.

FEATURED FLOWER OF MAY: RHODODENDRON

When we think of rhododendrons, we usually think of evergreen, leathery-leaved shrubs with fancy hemispheres of brightly colored flowers in May and June.

Actually, there are over 900 species of rhododendrons, found wild from the mountains of the Himalayas to the hot coasts of Burma, from Olympia, Washington, to the hills of Virginia. Breeding work has produced over 10,000 named cultivars in horticultural commerce, so there's no end of choices as to blooming season, color, shape, and other qualities.

Culturally, rhododendrons include the azaleas. Azaleas are one of several series of related types of rhododendron, and thus are a subset of the genus. All rhododendrons like cool, woodsy conditions: an acidic, humusy soil that's always cool and moist, but not soggy, such as is found on the floor of pine forests; filtered shade; some protection from winter winds and summer's sun and blazing heat. When they like their spot, they require little care.

Because of the sheer volume of the plant material in this genus, it's important to know which species are superior on several counts. Here we'll discuss one of the all-around best rhododendrons, *Rhododendron yakusimanum*. For other noteworthy rhododendrons and azaleas, see the chart on page 236.

R. yakusimanum stays low and compact in habit, reaching only to about 3 feet, and produces masses of appleblossom-pink buds in May that open to 1- to 2-inch bells with the palest yellow stamens. Its leaves carry a gray-green fuzz when young, but lose this as they mature. The leaves form a dense, rounded canopy of substantial mass.

R. yakusimanum is hardy to -20°F, unusually hardy for such a pretty rhododendron. It grows well in a wide range of conditions, from the California coast and Pacific Northwest to the Rockies to the Atlantic seaboard. It finds the hot summers of the southeastern United States excessive.

Clumps of *R. yakusimanum*, which is native to the Japanese island of Yukushima, create a striking, delicate effect. Too often we see rhododendrons used for sheer color exuberance that tends to overwhelm the eye—masses of hard orange, for instance, or bright cherry red. We get tired of the overpowering colors pretty quickly, and much prefer the soft pink and white of this species.

Among hybrid rhododendrons, a similar effect to *R. yakusimanum* is given by 'Dora Amateis', bred earlier in this century by a sculptor with a fondness for rhododendrons. It's a diminutive form with small leaves, hardy to -15°F, and carries masses of light pinkish-white flowers with tinges of light green. It might be a good choice to plant in front of *R. yakusimanum* in order to continue the area of bloom to the ground.

The May garden is full of so much bloom that we should be careful not to let the color schemes shout, scream, or shriek—which they do when whole hillsides are given over to the harder colors of hybrid rhododendrons. Pastel masses, such as given by the Exbury azalea hybrids, also give large pools of color, but ones you can live with.

All azaleas are rhododendrons, but not all rhododendrons are azaleas. Azaleas usually have smaller, more rounded leaves, such as the Exbury azalea, at top. The Rhododendron yakusimanum, *at bottom, is smaller than the azalea, but its leaves are wider and longer.*

June (Early Summer)

June is the month when roses—the most beloved of all the flowering plants—everywhere burst into exuberant, often fragrant, bloom. Any fine garden must have roses, but how do we begin to select the right ones from the thousands of kinds that are available?

The answer is to focus on the functions you want your roses to perform. The rose that covers a pergola will be different from one for a shrub border. Roses have been classified into several categories that reflect such functions.

Miniature Roses   These are as diverse in shape as the other kinds of roses, but they never grow much past 8 to 10 inches tall. We have one planted among sedum by our mailbox, where we're sure it gives a visual hello to the mail carrier each day. Miniatures are great in containers and hanging baskets, as well as for in-ground uses where they are best displayed at the edges of walls and embankments.

Floribunda Roses   Reaching only from 1 foot to 3 or 4 feet tall, most floribundas make excellent hedges and masses for color in the landscape. Their profuse flowers appear in sprays at the branch tips, some remaining in bud while others are in various stages of opening. Most older forms have flowers somewhat smaller than the hybrid teas, but large-flowered forms, such as the pretty mauve blend 'Angel Face', have been developed. They can be pot grown for the patio or sunspace. Floribundas are excellent for landscaping because of the low maintenance they require. Their heritage makes them hardy and resistant to many of the diseases that attack other roses. Simply prune them back each dormant season to six or eight vigorous young canes, with an open center to prevent crowding in the middle.

Hybrid Tea Roses   The hybrid teas are large specimen roses, borne in sparse sprays, with finely turned buds and elegant petal structure. They are slightly larger than the floribundas, reaching 3 to 6 feet, and bloom from spring to frost. These are the roses with stems usually long enough for the flowers to be cut for vases. Hybrid teas require a bit of work: pruning back leaving three to six young, vigorous canes to shape the rose into an open-centered bush; using organic insect and fungus controls to ward off pests and diseases to which they are prone; and protecting them from bitter winter weather in the cold regions. But they're worth it, and their enormous popularity is a tribute to their enchanting beauty. They are sometimes pruned to a standard shape—that is, to resemble a small tree with a single trunk—with great effectiveness. 'Peace', probably the world's most beloved rose, is a hybrid tea.

Grandiflora Roses   Beautiful, big (10 to 12 feet) rose bushes, the grandifloras produce clusters of flowers nearly as big as those of the hybrid teas on long stems for cutting. As contrasted with floribundas, they tend to open their sprays of flowers all at once. If the eight or ten strongest canes are lightly pruned back, they will produce more but smaller flowers. If the bushes are pruned back to six canes, and these are clipped heavily, they will produce fewer but larger flowers. Grandifloras are best used in the background to shower the upper reaches of the garden composition with color.

Most grandifloras are fully double and many have a delightful fragrance. Regarding the doubleness of roses, the cooler the climate, the more time the buds take to develop, and the more petals those with the double capacity produce. During high summer's heat, buds come faster with fewer petals. Cool-climate rose growers should choose semidouble or single varieties to prevent buds with too many petals from opening improperly.

Polyanthas   These roses form clusters of small flowers at the end of flower stalks with many branches. One of the most popular roses of all time, 'Cecile Brunner', sometimes known as the sweetheart rose, is a polyantha. This type requires little care.

Shrub Roses   These are the survivors from an earlier time—the hardiest, most disease-resistant sorts with heavy flower production of lightly colored blooms. They grow to 8 to 10 feet in various forms, from upright to pendulous. These and the grandifloras are excellent for massing in the back of the sunny garden. Shrub roses are relatively carefree. Prune them to the shape you want when they're young, and check them periodically thereafter for old, graying canes, which should be removed. Among the shrub roses are counted the species and hybrids of *Rosa rugosa,* which produces dark, purple-red, single flowers, followed by very large, edible hips that are rich in vitamin C. (See the chart, Flowering Shrubs, on page 190 for more information on good shrub roses.)

Climbing Roses   Some climbers are extra vigorous sports of hybrid teas, floribundas, or other classes of rose. Others are ramblers—long-caned roses in their own right, usually extra hardy, and floriferous in an old-fashioned way. Many of your favorite rose varieties will be available as climbing sports, so that you can have 'Peace' or 'First Prize' draped over your doorway as well as along the walkway. Smaller, less vigorous kinds of climbing roses are sometimes called pillar roses, because they are just about the right size for twisting prettily up a post. Climbing sports produce long, permanent canes from which flowering laterals arise. To prune, cut these laterals back to just a few (two or three) buds each dormant season. Ramblers are handled differently. Prune off the 2-year-old canes each season after they flower. This will keep the ramblers in shape, without a lot of sparse and dead old canes cluttering up their effect. For a selection of climbing and rambling roses, see the chart on page 273.

Some Outstanding Roses

Besides the hybrids, there are some species roses with very good qualities. *Rosa hugonis,* for instance, is a pale yellow rose of exquisite form. *Rosa rubrifolia* is prized as much for the combination of its ruddy foliage and orange hips in the fall as it is for its flowers earlier in the year. *Rosa banksiae* is a thornless rose with long, green canes that grow to 20 feet or more and are covered over in May and June with very double, small, ball-like flowers of a most elegant pale yellow. (This rose is covered in more detail in the chart, Climbing and Rambling Roses, on page 273.)

The following rose selections, arranged by color, are based on rose growers' favorites summarized by the American Rose Society (ARS) of Shreveport, Louisiana.

Favorite Pink   Grandiflora 'Queen Elizabeth'. This rose, a cross between the hybrid tea 'Charlotte Armstrong' and floribunda 'Floradora', could be classified with neither parent, and so the classification of grandiflora was created. Some say that if a garden is to have just one rose, this would be it. 'Century Two' and 'Duet' are exceptional pink hybrid teas.

Favorite Bicolor   Hybrid tea 'Peace'. This rose thrilled the world when it survived the ravages of World War II as an unnamed sport and was released as 'Peace' on V-day, marking the end of the war in 1945. The center of the bloom seems to hide a golden light that fades to white and then achieves a pink blush on the petal tips. Both 'Peace' and 'Queen Elizabeth' claim to be the world's favorite rose. 'Chicago Peace', a pink blend rose, has gained great favor lately.

Favorite Red   Miniature 'Starina'. It is given a rating of 9.6 by the ARS, the highest of any rose of any color or type—and no wonder. 'Starina' produces perfect red roses

ROSE FORMS

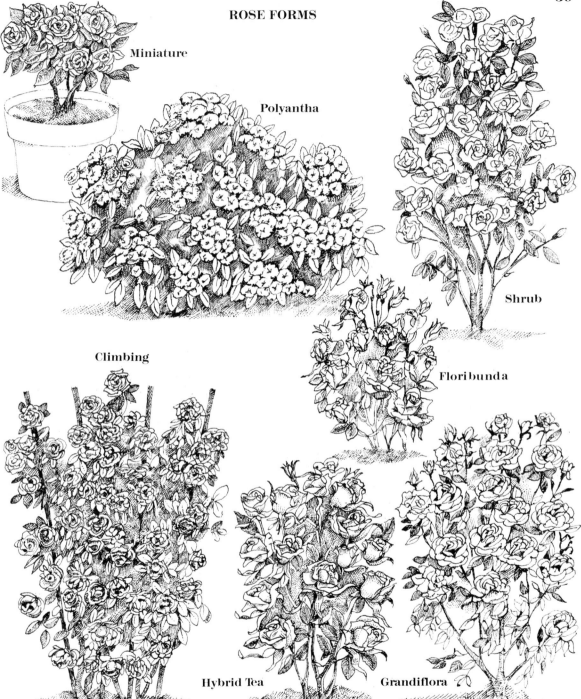

Miniature

Polyantha

Shrub

Climbing

Floribunda

Hybrid Tea

Grandiflora

with bits of yellow over a very long season. The leaves are shiny, dark green, and it stays under a foot tall.

Favorite White Floribunda 'French Lace'. This plant with a profuse blooming habit produces outstandingly beautiful creamy white roses with delicately ruffled edges. It recently won top awards from the ARS. Even more highly rated by the ARS are the white floribundas 'Evening Star', 'Iceberg', and 'Ivory Fashion'. Among hybrid teas, 'Garden Party' gets high marks.

Favorite Yellow Species rose *Rosa banksiae*. Who can resist the gay profusions of thornless yellow flowers spilling over walls and porches? 'Sunsprite' among floribundas is a disease-resistant form of rich color, and 'Lemon Spice' among hybrid teas combines a delicate yellow color, perfect form, and heady scent.

Favorite Lavender Floribunda 'Angel Face'. A fragrant rose that features ruffled petals edged with crimson. We also like the hybrid tea 'Lady X'. The lavender flowers carry pink highlights in the shadows and petal edges. An extravagantly sensuous rose with a name to match.

Favorite Apricot Floribunda 'Apricot Nectar'. The deep apricot-colored buds open into perfect buff-colored roses. It carries a sweet scent. Altogether charming when discovered in an out-of-the-way part of the garden.

The American Rose Society has also ranked favorite roses by category. So many hybrid cultivars and species roses are grown and sold that the ARS polls its 20,000 members every three years to establish ratings for almost all of the kinds available in commerce. A rating of less than 6.0 means that the rose is of questionable value. From 6.0 to 6.9, it's just fair. From 7.0 to 7.9, good; from 8.0 to 8.9, excellent; from 9.0 to 9.9, outstanding, and 10, we know, is perfect.

All the hybrid roses listed on page 61 are rated 8.0 or higher by the ARS membership. The rating system is based on form, color, length of bloom, fragrance, and disease and pest resistance—all of the quality points that make up the beautiful creature we call the rose. Thousands upon thousands of American rose growers think that the roses in this list are all-around champions.

Rose-Growing Tips

Organic rose growers will want to plant their roses in humus-rich, compost-improved soil with very good drainage. Include a shovelful of sand in each hole if your soil contains a lot of clay. Roses like lots of nutrients to show their best, so dust a handful of a mixture of wood ashes and bone meal into each hole. Side-dress the plant with some nitrogen-rich fertilizer like rotted poultry manure. In midsummer, water with fish emulsion regularly. Use a rich mulch in the fall when overwintering your roses, so that it will be actively decaying and releasing nutrients the following spring. Keep soil moist for roses, but not wet. Because many roses are susceptible to fungus diseases, drip irrigate or flood the soil with water, rather than watering overhead and wetting the leaves.

Hybrid Teas

Apricot Blend: 'Nantucket'

Mauve: 'Lady X'

Orange Blend: 'Folklore'

Pink Blends: 'Chicago Peace', 'Tiffany'

Deep Pink: 'Miss All-American Beauty'

Medium Pink: 'Century Two', 'Duet'

Red Blends: 'Double Delight', 'Lustige'

Dark Red: 'Chrysler Imperial', 'Mister Lincoln'

Medium Red: 'Olympiad', 'Red Jacket'

White: 'Garden Party', 'Lemon Sherbet', 'Pristine'

Yellow Blend: 'Peace'

Grandifloras

Pink Blend: 'Pink Parfait'

Medium Pink: 'Queen Elizabeth'

Floribundas

Mauve: 'Escapade'

Mauve Blend: 'Angel Face'

Orange Blend: 'Anabell', 'First Edition', 'Tony Jacklin'

Orange-Red: 'Orangeade', 'Sunfire', 'Trumpeter'

Medium Pink: 'Betty Prior', 'Cherish', 'Simplicity'

Dark Red: 'Europeana'

White: 'Evening Star', 'Iceberg', 'Ivory Fashion'

Yellow Blend: 'Little Darling'

Deep Yellow: 'Sunsprite'

Polyanthas

Medium Pink: 'China Doll'

Light Pink: 'The Fairy'

Shrub Roses

Apricot Blend: 'Alchymist'

Orange-Red: 'Summer Wind'

Pink Blend: 'Applejack', 'Cornelia', 'Dr. Eckener', 'Paulii Rosea'

Deep Pink: 'Cerise Bouquet', 'Flamingo', 'Vanity'

Medium Pink: 'Belinda', 'Frau Dagmar Hartopp', 'Pink Grootendorst'

Light Pink: 'Raubritter', 'Sparrieshoop', 'Wanderin' Wind'

Dark Red: 'Ruskin'

Medium Red: 'Dortmund', 'F. J. Grootendorst', 'Hansa', 'Will Scarlet'

White: 'Blanc Double de Coubert', 'Nevada', 'Prairie Star', 'Weisse aus Sparrieshoop'

Yellow: 'Golden Wings'

FEATURED FLOWER OF JUNE: FRAGRANT ROSE

When we think of rose fragrance, we usually mean the scent of the damask rose, *Rosa damascena*. Attar of roses, as the extract of rose scent is called, is usually made from this ancient species, which came originally from Damascus in Syria. But rose fragrances also run toward the citrusy, the spicy (cinnamon, cloves, and myrrh), and to a neutral sweet scent compared to orris root.

The American Rose Society has given a special award for fragrance to seven varieties of hybrid tea roses. They include the red 'Crimson Glory', 'Chrysler Imperial', 'Fragrant Cloud', and 'Papa Meilland'; the pink 'Tiffany'; 'Sutter's Gold', pale gold edged with pinkish-salmon; and the fancy red and gold 'Granada'. If you want extraordinary fragrance along with the beauty of color and form of a hybrid tea, these varieties head the list. But they by no means complete the list—there are thousands of delightfully scented hybrid teas. Red color usually indicates a relationship to the heavily scented species, especially *Rosa damascena*, but also *Rosa foetida*, *Rosa gallica*, and *Rosa moschata*.

Among climbing roses, 'Don Juan' is a superior deep red variety with an exceptional scent. There are climbing sports of 'Chrysler Imperial', 'Crimson Glory', and 'Sutter's Gold' as well. If you like the thornless *Rosa banksiae*, look for 'Lutescens', which carries single, fragrant, pale yellow flowers. Other Banksian roses have no fragrance. For fullest bloom, don't prune the 'Lady Banks', as she's known, for she flowers on shoots from older growth. This rose was introduced into England in 1796, and was named for the wife of Sir Joseph Banks, a famous English naturalist who sailed with Captain Cook on his first voyage to Australia.

Fragrant climbing roses combine a gorgeous scent with vigor and colorful bloom. They provide the gardener with good choices for partially covering a shed, running along a fence, covering archways, arbors, porches, and pergolas, and in other ways serving as architectural shrubbery.

Rose fragrance is usually strongest on warm, sunny mornings when the solar energy opens the rose blossom and evaporates its volatile scented oils into the air. If the day waxes hot, the fragrance will usually diminish. Exceptions include 'Chrysler Imperial' and 'Sutter's Gold', which retain a good fragrance throughout the day.

One rose that has it all is the coral-red 'Fragrant Cloud', which is easy to grow, vigorous, and disease resistant, and has a prize-winning scent. Trained to a small garden pillar or post in a sunny spot near a frequently used area, it will fill the air with its strong, genuine rose scent.

Fragrance intensifies the pleasure of beautiful roses. You can find fragrant varieties of every type of rose, including hybrid teas and climbers.

July (Midsummer)

Now it's high summer, and the common trumpet vine announces itself with a reddish-orange fanfare. The deep purple stars of *Clematis* 'Etoile Violette' open along the fence. The air is perfumed by the just-opened, sun-warmed florets of the honeysuckle. With summer's full-blazing sun, the vines—those seekers of the light—come into their own.

Vining is an evolutionary response to inadequate light levels. Plants in the dark understories of primordial forests either gave up the ghost or vined—that is, started elongating their stems and heading for the roof. Displaying their leaves above and among those of their hosts, vines get the benefit of sturdy trunks without the energy expenditure of making them. When sunlight is adequate, vines flower, often profusely.

Some plants in full sun are shrubs, but when covered over by an encroaching canopy of trees, begin to vine. Plants with this habit are called scandent, and many vines, such as the allamanda, show the tendency. The *Metrosideros robustus* of New Zealand climbs its host pine tree, then begins to thicken its stem into a full-size trunk. Eventually, it chokes and kills its host, standing upright by its now-massive trunk. Most vines, however, remain slender, although all use their vining habit to position themselves to receive optimum light levels.

When planning the use of vines in a garden or by a patio, it's important to keep this characteristic of vines in mind. Many will grow entirely too long, climbing out of visual reach and displaying their flowers to the birds. Choose your vines with a sense of how you want to view them, and train them to achieve that goal.

Vining Habits

It's worthwhile to focus on how vines grow and support themselves so you can select the best vine for the best location. Some vines, like *Tecomaria capensis*, have no structures to support themselves and rely on leaning to stay erect. The gardener will, of course, help these plants along by gently tying them to supports.

A more positive method of holding fast is exhibited by vines like bougainvillea and the rambling *Rosa wichuraiana*. These have thorns that dig into their supports and prevent the vines from sliding back or falling off.

A form of twining that creates a very effective support is weaving, where the vine's growing tip weaves back and forth through its supports. *Trachelospermum jasminoides*, star jasmine, exhibits this trait, and once it's woven itself into a chain link fence, it can't be pulled off.

A more common type of twining is shown by the morning-glories, whose growing tips twist round and round their upright supports. Others, like pea vines, have tendrils that encircle the stems of their hosts for support.

Then there are vines like *Bignonia capreolata*, the cross vine, which support themselves by means of tendrils that end in adhesive disks. Still others, among them *Solanum wendlandii*, the Costa Rican nightshade, have recurved hooks emerging from the leaf axils which hook into the host to provide support.

The trumpet vine, *Campsis radicans*, exhibits another form of supporting structure. It puts out rootlets from its nodes that will penetrate into crevices and cracks in bark, rock walls, or planking. Ivy, of course, has the same habit.

Using Vines in the Garden

Vines have some definite advantages for the gardener. They can make a vertical screen
(continued on page 66)

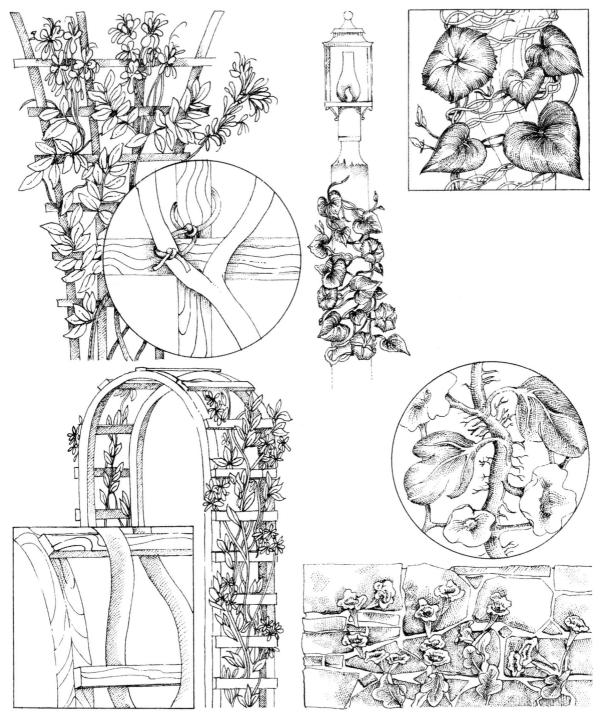

Four ways that vines climb, and supports they prefer. At top left, a leaning vine needs to be tied up to its support. At top right, a twining vine curls up a post. At lower left, a vine weaves through its supports, and at lower right, vines cling by small rootlets to a rock wall.

A glory bower grows over a doorway in a sunspace, transforming the cold entranceway into a living picture.

to provide privacy; they can be used to soften the hard lines of structures and tie them into the landscape plan; and they can be used on arbors, roofs, and overhead structures to throw a pleasant shade in outdoor living areas.

An effective use of vines is the floral cascade from a tall wall or roof. The vine is trained up the side away from the viewing area, or planted along a bermed top, and allowed to topple over in festoons of flowers. *Wisteria sinensis* and *Passiflora caerulea* make spectacular cascades.

A chief function of many delicate, pretty vines is to grace a wall that's frequently seen. *Ipomoea quamoclit*, with its feathery leaves and scarlet flowers, is a good choice for such an effect, as are many hybrid clematises. Larger vines with a coarser appearance, such as *Solanum jasminoides*, need to be placed in the background, away from the area where people will be spending a lot of outdoor time, so that the coarseness disappears with some distance.

Because vines trail, many of them make good ground covers when not given support. Those that produce rootlets at the leaf nodes are good at holding soil together, especially along a steep bank. In shady areas, *Vinca minor* and ivies will do a good job. In sunny areas, use *Rosa wichuraiana* or star jasmine. This latter vine doesn't have rooting nodes, but it does have tough roots that tenaciously hold the soil.

Many vines are beautiful enough in form and flower to be used as specimens. *Clerodendrum thomsoniae*, the glory bower, is such a plant. It makes a fine potted specimen that can be used outdoors in summer and indoors in winter. In addition, vines can be used to accent other plants, especially when they're in pots and can be moved as the season's color changes dictate.

Because they bloom so prolifically, vines can be breathtaking sights. Of all the flowering plants, vines are the romantics, as anyone who's leaned against a post of moonflowers on a soft summer night can attest. But be aware of the backgrounds they're seen against. When growing 'Heavenly Blue' morning-glory, for instance, it may be better placed against a background of tall, dark green foliage plants than on a pole where its blue flowers are seen against the blue sky and partially lost. Yellow flowers look exceptionally nice against a brick wall. Contrast is the key: the greater the contrast in color and in darkness to lightness, the more dramatic the flowers will appear. Some combinations are far too dramatic—the optical orange of *Thunbergia gregorii*, for instance, against a blue wall. Intense colors are much better used to accent softer harmonies of related colors.

Growing Tips for Vines

Vines offer a bounty of benefits for a minimal expenditure of planting space. And when they are flowering vines, especially fragrant ones, they perform double and triple duty.

In return, vines demand attention to pruning or they get woody and run out, producing dead waste and few flowers. Most of them also like their roots in the cool shade and their heads in the sun.

In the greenhouse or sunspace, vines become even more important than they are outside in the landscape, for they can fill the space from floor to ceiling with flowers while taking up very little growing room.

To prevent greenhouse vines from shading other plants, plant them against the interior wall, especially so they grow over a doorway leading into the sunspace. They can also be planted in the corners of the sunspace nearest the house wall. From these positions, they will open flowers toward the sun, which means toward people in the sunspace.

FEATURED FLOWER OF JULY: CLEMATIS

Clematis flowers are so gorgeous, it's sad to see how often they're strung up to a trellis against a wall and allowed to grow into spindly stems below and a tangled mass of foliage and flowers above. This unacceptable arrangement cuts down on the number of blooms and looks bad. It happens because the grower has given no thought to pruning, displaying the vines for best flower production, or to selecting plants that might be grown with clematis to hide the stems.

When you're working clematis into the garden design, think of plants to use with the vine. Roses are an excellent choice. Floribunda and grandiflora rose bushes will cover those spindly stems and shade the roots, allowing the vine to grow up through the inner structure of the bushes and display its flowers on the surface of the rose bush in color contrast or in harmony with the roses. Try the lavender 'Angel Face' grandiflora rose with pink clematis 'Nelly Moser' for a contrast or with lavender clematis 'Will Goodwin' for a harmony. The starburst shape of clematis blossoms also contrasts with roses' satiny swirls.

While shrub roses are frequently used in association with clematis, climbing roses can be used as hosts with great effect. Other shrubs, such as viburnums, spiraeas, syringas, and camellias, also make fine hosts.

When planting clematis with shrubs or climbers, plant them on the shady side, so that their roots get the cooling shade thrown by the shrub. Let the clematis find its own way to the sunlight, where it will disport itself to its own satisfaction.

If you intend to grow a clematis up into a small tree for support—say a fall-flowering *Clematis paniculata* into a rose-of-Sharon—plant the clematis toward the prevailing winds and give it a wire or cord attached to a tree branch to use for support until it reaches the tree limbs. This allows you to plant the clematis away from the tree trunk and its main feeder roots. Another way to get the clematis into the tree is to plant a shade-loving shrub that will act as the host most of the way to the tree's lower limbs. Clematis has elongated, arched leaf stems that hook over parts of its host.

When growing clematis in pots, you'll have success if you keep the pot out of direct sun—

clematis just hates to grow in hot, droughty soil. Make sure the drainage in the pots is excellent and keep the soil moist.

Keep after the pruning of clematis. They all need it, even the large, vigorous kinds, but some need far less pruning than others (see pruning recommendations for clematis groups in the chart, Clematis Large-Flowered Hybrids, on page 268). The chief purpose of the pruning is to remove dead and unsightly wood and get the remaining stems displayed so that the flowers that develop are seen to their best advantage. When planting several clematises together, keeping them in the same pruning group will make things simple.

Sweet autumn clematis climbs up a support hanging from the limb of an overarching rose-of-Sharon. Both bloom late in August.

August (Late Summer)

Most trees and shrubs are quietly in leaf now, their flowering period over. The pinks and blues of early summer are giving way to the deep greens, oranges, and reds of a year that's almost dead ripe.

Let the woody plants give background and structure now, for it's the perennials that step forward with the hot colors of August. These are the herbaceous plants that die back to the ground, insubstantial in the winter, but now they are the star performers in the waning garden.

Outstanding Perennials for Late Summer

Phlox paniculata, those sweetly scented balls that open in late July and August, give vibrant color to the beds of massed perennials. One of the strongest reds is given by *Phlox* 'Starfire', and orange by *Phlox* 'Orange Perfection'.

Quickly, the *Kniphofia uvaria,* or red-hot pokers, send up their flowering wands in bright orange-red and yellow. *Asclepias tuberosa,* the butterfly weed, blooms with a rich, pure orange.

Other reds in the August perennial garden include the rosy red *Physostegia virginiana* 'Summer Glow', called the obedient plant because of the florets' habit of staying put when pushed to one side or another. There are also red cultivars of *Aster novae-angliae,* or New England asters, and the deep crimson daisies of *Helenium autumnale* 'Crimson Beauty'. An intense red will be carried into early August by *Monarda didyma* 'Cambridge Scarlet', the crimson bee balm.

The August sun descends to earth with the yellows of the "heelies": *Helenium autumnale* 'Butterpat', *Helianthus* hybrid 'Loddon Gold', and *Heliopsis scabra* 'Incomparabilis'.

Because of all the yellow and red available, nature conveniently supplies a lot of cool lavenders and purples at this time of year, allowing gardeners to balance the hot colors. The New England asters feature many shades and hues in the purples. A pretty, light lavender resembling the annual ageratum appears in August atop *Eupatorium coelestinum.* The lavender of the fuzzy, flowering wands of *Liatris pycnostachya* is a purple variation of eupatorium's blue-lavender, while *Liatris scariosa* differs by the rich purple of its flowering spires.

The lavender bells that decorate the flower stalks of *Liriope muscari* and *Liriope spicata* make August a month we always look forward to. Something about liriope, with its grasslike foliage and neat appearance, makes it one of the most satisfying perennials in our garden. It takes a wide range of conditions, from full sun to partial shade, and makes an exceptionally fine ground cover.

Hostas bloom now, producing lavender or white trumpets held on a tall flower spike. Some gardeners remove these spikes, on the theory that the hostas are grown for their foliage and the flowers are not showy enough. But we like their cool lavender haze in the shady parts of the garden, and in the case of the August lily (*Hosta plantaginea* 'Grandiflora'), the white flowers give off an intense, sweet scent.

Among the August pinks, we love the soft color of *Physostegia virginiana* 'Bouquet Rose'. You will also get pink forms of *Aster novae-angliae.* A particularly luscious raspberry pink is given by the short, fuzzy spikes of *Astilbe chinensis* 'Pumila'. *Astilbe taquetii* 'Superba' has similar puffy pink spikes, but reaches 3 to 4 feet. The turtlehead, *Chelone lyonii,* has hooded mauve to pink florets on short spikes.

White forms of *Liatris scariosa, Physostegia virginiana,* and *Stokesia laevis* bloom now. Many flowers thought of as colored are

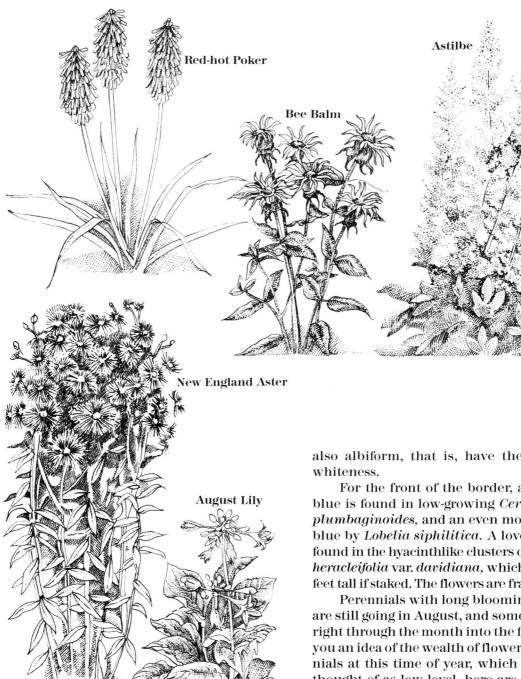

Red-hot Poker

Bee Balm

Astilbe

New England Aster

August Lily

Some favorite perennials: Red-hot poker and bee balm give red, hot colors; astilbe gives cooler pinks and whites, although there are red forms; New England asters bloom late for fall color; and August lily scents the air in high summer.

also albiform, that is, have the gene for whiteness.

For the front of the border, an intense blue is found in low-growing *Ceratostigma plumbaginoides,* and an even more intense blue by *Lobelia siphilitica.* A lovely blue is found in the hyacinthlike clusters of *Clematis heracleifolia* var. *davidiana,* which reaches 3 feet tall if staked. The flowers are fragrant, too.

Perennials with long blooming seasons are still going in August, and some continue right through the month into the fall. To give you an idea of the wealth of flowering perennials at this time of year, which is usually thought of as low level, here are some that we selected for our previous book, *The Perennial Garden.* They all begin blooming earlier in the year and finish blooming sometime in August or continue through the month. (If you're interested in a fuller treatment of this class of flowering plants, please see our book.)

Long-Blooming Perennials for Summer Color

Achillea filipendulina 'Coronation Gold':
 3 ft. tall, yellow.

Achillea millefolium 'Fire King':
 1½-2 ft. tall, red.

Aconitum napellus: 3-4 ft. tall, blue.

Anaphalis cinnamomea: 2 ft. tall, white.

Anchusa azurea 'Royal Blue': 3 ft. tall, blue.

Anemone vitifolia 'Robustissima':
 2½ in. tall, pink.

Anthemis tinctoria 'Moonlight':
 2 ft. tall, yellow.

Asclepias tuberosa: 2 ft. tall, orange.

Aster ×frikartii 'Wonder of Staffa':
 2½-3 ft. tall, lavender.

Campanula carpatica 'Blue Chips':
 8 in. tall, blue.

Campanula persicifolia 'Caerulea':
 2 ft. tall, blue.

Campanula rotundifolia 'Olympica':
 1-1½ ft. tall, blue.

Catananche caerulea: 1½-2 ft. tall, blue.

Centaurea dealbata: 2 ft. tall, red-violet.

Centranthus ruber: 3 ft. tall, red.

Chrysanthemum parthenium:
 1-3 ft. tall, white.

Cimicifuga racemosa: 6 ft. tall, white.

Coreopsis grandiflora 'Sunburst':
 20 in. tall, yellow.

Coreopsis lanceolata: 2 ft. tall, yellow.

Coreopsis verticillata 'Moonbeam':
 15 in. tall, yellow.

Corydalis lutea: 1 ft. tall, yellow.

Delphinium grandiflorum:
 1½ ft. tall, white, blue, purple.

Dicentra eximia: 1 ft. tall, pink.

Dicentra formosa: 1 ft. tall, pink.

Digitalis ×mertonensis: 3 ft. tall, pink.

Echinacea purpurea 'Bright Star':
 3 ft. tall, pink.

Echinops ritro 'Taplow Blue':
 4-5 ft. tall, blue.

Erigeron speciosus 'Prosperity':
 1½ ft. tall, blue.

Eryngium amethystinum:
 2 ft. tall, blue.

Gaillardia ×grandiflora 'Goblin':
 1 ft. tall, red and yellow.

Gentiana asclepiadea: 1½ ft. tall, blue.

Gentiana septemfida: 1½ ft. tall, blue.

Geranium cinereum 'Ballerina':
 8 in. tall, pink.

Geranium endressii 'Wargrave Pink':
 15 in. tall, pink.

Geranium sanguineum: 1 ft. tall, pink.

Gypsophila paniculata 'Bristol Fairy':
 3 ft. tall, white.

Gypsophila reptens 'Alba': 6 in. tall, white.

Hibiscus moscheutos 'Mallow Marvels':
 4-6 ft. tall, red, pink, white.

Inula ensifolia: 16 in. tall, yellow.

Lamium maculatum: 8-12 in. tall, pink.

Lathyrus latifolius: 9 ft. tall, pink.

Lavandula angustifolia 'Hidcote':
 1½ ft. tall, violet-blue.

Leucanthemum maximum 'Alaska':
 2 ft. tall, white.

Ligularia dentata 'Desdemona':
 3-4 ft. tall, orange.

Ligularia stenocephala 'The Rocket':
 5-6 ft. tall, yellow.

Lilium (Oriental hybrids):
2-7 ft. tall, red, pink, purple, white.

Lilium (Tiger lilies species):
3-5 ft. tall, salmon red.

Limonium latifolium:
1½ ft. tall, lavender-blue.

Linum flavum: 15 in. tall, yellow.

Linum perenne: 2 ft. tall, blue.

Lobelia cardinalis: 3-4 ft. tall, red.

Lysimachia nummularia:
1-2 in. tall, yellow.

Lysimachia salicaria 'Morden Pink':
3 ft. tall, pink.

Macleaya cordata: 6-8 ft. tall, white.

Myosotis scorpioides: 1 ft. tall, blue.

Nepeta ×*faassenii:*   1½ ft. tall, lavender.

Oenothera missourensis:
10 in. tall, yellow.

Oenothera tetragona 'Fireworks':
1½ ft. tall, yellow.

Penstemon barbatus 'Rose Elf':
1½ ft. tall, pink.

Penstemon gloxinioides 'Ruby King':
2 ft. tall, red.

Penstemon heterophyllus 'True Blue':
15 in. tall, blue.

Perovskia atriplicifolia:
3 ft. tall, blue.

Platycodon grandiflorus 'Blue':
2 ft. tall, blue.

Potentilla nepalensis 'Miss Willmott':
1 ft. tall, rose.

Potentilla ×*tonguei:*
3 in. tall, apricot.

Rudbeckia fulgida 'Goldsturm':
2 ft. tall, yellow.

Rudbeckia laciniata 'Goldquelle':
3 ft. tall, yellow.

Ruta graveolens 'Blue Beauty':
2 ft. tall, yellow.

Salvia jurisicii: 3 ft. tall, blue.

Salvia ×*superba:*   1½ ft. tall, blue.

Santolina chamaecyparissus:
1 ft. tall, yellow.

Santolina virens: 1 ft. tall, yellow.

Scabiosa caucasica 'Blue Perfection':
1 ft. tall, blue.

Sedum sieboldii 'Dragon's Blood':
10 in. tall, red.

Sedum spectabile 'Autumn Joy':
2 ft. tall, pink.

Sidalcea malviflora 'Elsie Heugh':
2-3 ft. tall, pink.

Solidago 'Goldenmosa':   3 ft. tall, yellow.

Stokesia laevis 'Blue Danube':
15 in. tall, blue.

Teucrium chamaedrys: 15 in. tall, rose.

Thalictrum delavayi: 3-5 ft. tall, lavender.

Tradescantia ×*andersoniana* 'Blue Stone':
2 ft. tall, blue.

Valeriana officinalis: 4 ft. tall, white.

Verbascum chaixii 'Album':   3 ft. tall, white.

Verbena rigida: 6 in. tall, purple.

Veronica incana: 1½ ft. tall, blue.

Veronica longifolia var. *subsessilis:*
2 ft. tall, blue.

Veronica spicata 'Blue Peter':
15 in. tall, blue.

Viola cornuta 'Chantreyland':
8 in. tall, apricot.

Yucca filimentosa: 4-6 ft. tall, white.

FEATURED FLOWER OF AUGUST: DAYLILY

Of all the flowering plants, the daylily (*Hemerocallis* species) is most extraordinarily lavish in its beneficence toward the gardener.

Consider that daylilies can be transplanted easily, hardly being aware of the move. They are also entirely edible (something most gardeners don't realize), from their crisp, juicy, white tuberous roots to the tissue of their flowers. They grow just about anywhere, even under trees, but prefer full sun for best bloom. Gardeners in the warmest zones will want to give daylilies some shade, or the searing sun will burn the color out of the flowers.

Most of all, however, daylilies are exquisitely beautiful. The great English horticulturist Graham Stuart Thomas found this quote from a poem of Ben Jonson's, penned in the seventeenth century:

It is not growing like a tree
In bulk, doth make Man better be;
Or standing long an oak, three hundred year,
To fall a log at last, dry, and sere:
A lily of a day
Is fairer far in May,
Although it fall and die that night—
It was the plant and flower of Light.
In small proportions we just beauties see;
And in short measures life may perfect be.

Take note of line 5: "A lily of a day." And note the translation of daylilies' botanical name into its original Greek: *hemera* means day, *kallos* means beauty, giving us beauty for a day. In fact, it was just about Jonson's time when the daylily was introduced into Europe from China, and it has remained a most beloved flower ever since.

Daylily breeders have been doing extensive work on colors and forms of the flower in recent years, with astounding results. Daylilies of the most exquisite pastel pinks, lavenders, yellows, peaches, salmons, apricots, and violets, plus vivid reds, burgundies, and golds, have been bred from two species: *Hemerocallis fulva,* the roadside, tawny daylily that naturalizes to the point of invasiveness, and *Hemerocallis flava,* the pretty lemon daylily.

Prices for the rarest and most cherished of the daylilies can reach up to three figures for a tuber. But don't feel left out. Many incredibly beautiful daylilies are available at very affordable prices. Start with local nurseries and check your favorite flower catalogs. The big mail-order firms, such as White Flower Farm, carry a nice selection, but there are a dozen or so large mail-order firms specializing in daylilies. Three of these include Houston Daylily Gardens, Busse Gardens, and Klehm Nursery (for addresses, see Mail-Order Sources for Ornamental Trees, Shrubs, and Vines on page 295).

*Beauty for a day—the daylily (*Hemerocallis *spp.).*

September (Early Fall)

Nature abhors a vacuum, and she can't stand bare soil either. Freshly turned soil quickly accumulates a wild collection of weeds and brambles, shrubs, and, eventually, trees. To cover bare soil, especially problem areas such as steep banks, gardeners turn to ground-hugging, low-growing plants known as ground covers.

Some ground covers are grown for tenacious roots that grasp the soil and prevent erosion; others are grown for their foliage and flowers. Here we'll look at the ground covers that can carpet your garden with flowers, including some that bloom in September, when most flowering plants are shutting down for the season.

Ground Covers of Note

You can have your ground cover and bushels of roses with *Rosa wichuraiana*. This trailing rose bears single white flowers early in the summer and red hips in September. A new variety of *Rosa wichuraiana* was recently discovered in Japan and has been named *Rosa wichuraiana* var. *poteriifolia*. It is lower and denser, makes a tighter mat, and is less rampant than the species. Few weeds can penetrate its mat, and it gives erosion control on steep banks. Other ground-covering roses include the miniature 'Red Cascade' (which grows to 3 feet high) and some of the ramblers (especially 'Evangeline'), which ramble over anything, even small trees, but also over worn-out, erosion-prone soil.

If soil-hugging roots aren't of primary importance, but you want to fill an area with a dense cover, plant *Hemerocallis* 'Stella d'Oro', a yellow daylily that begins to bloom in May on 2-foot masses of foliage and continues right through the summer to October. If you want an even smaller *Hemerocallis*, try 'Eenie Weenie', which reaches only 10 inches high.

Members of the dead nettle group make superb flowering ground covers. *Lamium maculatum* 'Beacon Silver' has silvery leaf variegations and lilac flowers, but you can also grow a white-flowered form known as 'White Nancy'.

The low-growing phloxes all make excellent ground covers. *Phlox stolonifera* and *Phlox divaricata* produce blue flowers, while *Phlox subulata*, often called mountain pink, makes mats of pink, scarlet, blue, or white—depending on the strain. *Phlox ovata* is a pink, low-growing species often used as a ground cover.

In the shade, hostas' wide leaves function beautifully as a ground cover. By using different species, it's possible to achieve leaf variations that include variegation, wavy edges, yellow and white margins, deep grooves, and silvery blue-green colors. They produce tall flower stalks in late summer, ranging in color from white to lilac or blue.

One of the cotoneasters, *Cotoneaster salicifolius* 'Autumn Fire', rapidly spreads into a 6 inch tall ground cover that blankets a circle 8 feet in diameter. While the flowers aren't showy, the red berries turn the plant to flame in the fall. *C. salicifolius* 'Scarlet Leader' is a similar ground-covering cotoneaster with deeper red berries.

Sarcococca hookerana var. *humilis* is a small, neat, tufted shrub with fragrant white flowers in spring. Its glossy evergreen leaves stay handsome all year. In warm zones, an equally effective ground cover is *Trachelospermum jasminoides*, the star jasmine.

Ajugas are common—but beautiful—flowering ground covers. 'Pink Beauty' is a particularly nice cultivar with light pink flowers mostly in early summer and scattered bloom in fall.

For erosion control on steep banks with very poor soil, it's hard to beat *Coronilla varia,* the crown vetch used along roadways in the East. The pretty cloverlike flowers are lavender-pink, and the plant makes dense mats only 2 feet high, flowering from June to frost.

A much more delicate ground cover is *Epimedium rubrum,* which bears little red and white spring flowers on reddish-green foliage. A white form, *E. youngianum* 'Niveum', is also available. Epimedium makes a very attractive display with its heart-shaped leaves, which are held in tiers.

Potentilla tonguei is a creeping form of the familiar woody shrub. Its dark green leaves are evergreen, and the flowers are single, yellow blooms with red centers. It's one of the more striking evergreen ground covers. *P. aurea* var. *verna* carries single yellow blossoms on 3-inch mats of strawberrylike foliage. Both bloom in either sun or shade.

Down by the sea, plant the bearberry, *Arctostaphylos uva-ursi,* which forms dense mats of little leaves and covers itself with pinkish-white flowers in spring and early summer. It's native to cold, maritime climates like New England's.

For scent and delicately beautiful flowers, plant lily-of-the-valley, your grandmother's old-fashioned favorite. It naturalizes to form a good ground cover, likes a shady spot, and its delicate little white or pink bells exude a sweet, perfumy scent.

Two shade-loving ground covers with grasslike foliage are *Liriope muscari,* known as blue lilyturf, and *Ophiopogon japonicus,* known as hardy lilyturf, although it's hard to understand how it acquired that common name, since ophiopogon won't grow much north of Washington, D.C., while liriope grows to Zone 5. Both produce lovely blue to purple flowers on short stalks.

One of our favorite ground covers is the tiny, rapidly spreading *Mazus reptans,* which grows scarcely taller than your thumbnail and produces little violet flowers in late spring. This one will withstand some trodding upon. There's also a white form of mazus that looks very pretty on the floor of a white garden.

If you want a vivid ground cover, try *Geum borisii,* which produces bright orange flowers in late spring and early summer, and will continue with light flowering until frost. It stays less than a foot tall and adds a hot accent to the front of a flower bed.

For showy mounds of bright yellow from June to August, plant *Lysimachia nummularia* 'Aurea'. Mix it with *Sedum spurium* 'Dragon's Blood', that blooms June through September.

Vinca minor or periwinkle, the familiar evergreen ground-covering vine with blue stars in spring, will naturalize in shady, woodsy spots. *Sagina subulata* is a mosslike evergreen that takes some foot traffic and covers itself with busy white flowers in high summer. It's good for edging walkways. *Daphne cneorum* and *Spiraea japonica* 'Alpina' are both low-growing, shrubby ground covers with delightful pink flowers, and both are useful for carpeting the ground around plantings of larger flowering shrubs.

Persian candytuft, *Aethionema* 'Warley Rose', is a choice ground cover for a dry, sunny spot in the garden. It reaches only 4 to 6 inches tall, and fills in when planted thickly to form a perennial mat of pink flowers in May. A look-alike plant is *Iberis sempervirens,* the white candytuft with a habit similar to aethionema's.

There are many, many more ground covers to discover, especially among the wildflowers native to America, such as *Cornus canadensis,* or bunchberry. In addition, there are wonderful types of ground-covering iris, such as *Iris cristata* with its small blue flags in late spring. And there are all the low-growing alpine versions of taller perennials that can be used as ground covers. It's easy to see that the floor of the garden can be strewn with myriads of flowers of all colors, at all times of the growing season.

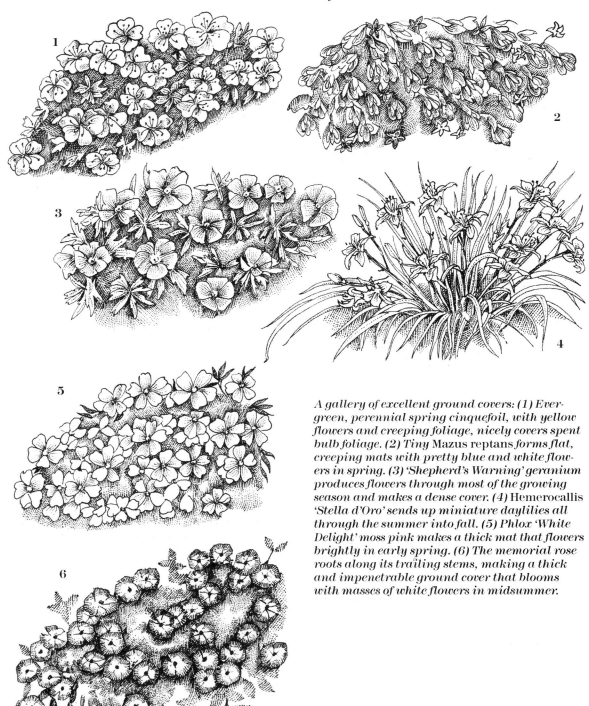

A gallery of excellent ground covers: (1) Evergreen, perennial spring cinquefoil, with yellow flowers and creeping foliage, nicely covers spent bulb foliage. (2) Tiny Mazus reptans forms flat, creeping mats with pretty blue and white flowers in spring. (3) 'Shepherd's Warning' geranium produces flowers through most of the growing season and makes a dense cover. (4) Hemerocallis 'Stella d'Oro' sends up miniature daylilies all through the summer into fall. (5) Phlox 'White Delight' moss pink makes a thick mat that flowers brightly in early spring. (6) The memorial rose roots along its trailing stems, making a thick and impenetrable ground cover that blooms with masses of white flowers in midsummer.

FEATURED FLOWER OF SEPTEMBER: HARDY GERANIUM

The hardy geraniums, or cranesbills, grow from 6 to 15 inches tall and make mounds of small leaves that persist nearly year-round, even in zones with January snow cover. Most species begin with a major bloom in May, and then continue to produce flowers right up to frost. Because of their long period of bloom, long period in leaf, toughness, and thick, weed-controlling, matting habit, the hardy geraniums are superb, useful ground covers, needing only a careful association with nearby flowers to be troublefree. They're a different genus altogether from the common bright red geraniums (*Pelargonium* spp.) so often seen potted.

Hardy geraniums like full sun and good garden soil. They grow well from upper New England to Georgia, and especially along the West Coast. Most species need moist soil, so irrigation of some kind in areas of summer drought is imperative. All are easily divided either in early April or early November. Most species have small, dark green or gray-green, deeply divided leaves, and wiry stems.

Probably the most well known of the hardy geraniums is *Geranium sanguineum,* called bloody cranesbill because of the species' tendency towards red flowers, and because its foliage turns reddish with the onset of cold weather in the fall.

The species produces flowers of a particularly vibrant magenta—not an easy color to use in a group. *Geranium sanguineum* 'Album' is a white cultivar much more easily assimilated into the border. *G. sanguineum* var. *prostratum* 'Shepherd's Warning' grows only 6 inches tall and produces salmon-pink flowers, making it one of the best for a low ground cover. It blooms from June through September, is a vigorous grower that covers large areas quickly, and is hardy to Zone 3. *G. sanguineum* var. *prostratum* also grows only 6 inches tall, and carries carmine red flowers.

Geranium endressii 'Wargrave Pink' is an easy-to-find cultivar and one of the prettiest. Its pink is charming and nice in combination with its sister, *G. endressii* 'Johnson's Blue', which makes mounds of lavender-blue flowers.

Although *Geranium himalayense* (also found as *G. grandiflorum*) blooms only in May and June, it's well worth considering as a ground cover in the front of the flower garden. Two-inch, cup-shaped flowers are an intense blue under the late spring sun, rivalling the displays of vibrant blue put on by the delphiniums.

Geranium cinereum 'Ballerina' is the lowest-growing of the cranesbills, reaching only 4 to 6 inches, but it produces loads of large, light pink flowers with purple-red centers and finely detailed red veining. It makes quite a show, even in Zone 10 (southernmost Florida and coastal southern California). Be careful with the related *G. cinereum* 'Splendens', which is also sometimes called *G. subcaulescens*. This plant's flowers are such an intense magenta that it swamps any nearby color. Use it, if at all, in an out-of-the-way place.

The bloody cranesbill is a hardy geranium with optically active magenta flowers.

October (Mid-Fall)

Finally, at the end of the growing season, when the trees, shrubs, and perennials have finished their bloom, it is the annuals that come to the forefront to lend color to the garden until the frosts mow them down. It is precisely because they are frost-tender that they are annuals.

Some annual flowers are perennials in warm climates where little or no frost occurs. Some are true annuals that set seed and disappear, wintering over to appear as seedlings the following year.

Annuals in Mixed Garden Design

In the mixed garden, with its many types of flowering plants—woody, herbaceous perennial, and annual—the annual flowers are useful in several ways.

First, they can be chosen for specific colors to work with the more permanent members of the garden community. For instance, it may be that you've planted a rosy red spiraea bush fairly close to a clump of yellow-orange daylilies, and the colors are clashing. One way to solve the problem is to move the daylilies. But an equally successful solution might be to separate the yellow-orange from the rosy red with a buffering color such as a splash of blue, which equally accents both the yellow-orange and the rosy red. For this purpose, you might choose the annual, *Brachycome iberidifolia,* the swan river daisy, with its shades of blue to violet with yellow-orange centers. Or, you might separate the offending colors with a buffer of neutral, buff, or white flowering plants— white carnations might be one choice.

An annual might also be chosen to harmonize with existing colors that are too close. In our yard we have an old, woody echium, which carries blue flower spires in spring but most of the year forms clumps of gray-green foliage on young, pink stems. A good choice for an associated annual might be a much darker blue, such as given by dark strains of bachelor's buttons or by lobelia. Another good choice might be an annual impatiens in a pink that harmonizes with the suggestion of soft pink in the echium.

Annuals are also excellent for filling in areas that need renovation, or for which you have future plans. And, of course, you may have favorite annuals—snapdragons, marigolds, nasturtiums—that you must have.

Interesting Annuals

Because their nature is to get up and out of the ground and reach sexual maturity to produce seed as rapidly as possible, annuals need full sun, lots of water, and a rich soil—usually. There are horticultural exceptions to every rule, but for most commonly found annuals, these requirements are essential. In this section, we'll look at some of the most common annuals for their habits and colors. You will find places for many of them in your flower gardens, for they are useful, quick splashes of color that augment your permanent plantings.

Many annuals are classified as Compositae, that is, members of the composite family, producing daisylike flowers. This group includes African daisy (*Arctotis* spp.), Swan River daisy (*Brachycome iberidifolia*), yellow ox-eye daisy (*Buphthalum salicifolium*), mountain daisy (*Celmisia*), Palm Springs daisy (*Caladanthus*), kingfisher daisy (*Felicia bergerana*), Transvaal daisy (*Gerbera jamesonii*), as well as calendula (*Calendula officinalis*), annual forms of chrysanthemum (*Chrysanthemum ×morifolium*), cineraria (*Senecio ×hybridus*), cosmos (*Cosmos bipinnatus; C. sulphureus*), sunflower (*Helianthus annuus*), and many more.

A very choice annual that is not daisylike is the flossflower, or ageratum. Fluffy mounds of these lavender-blue beauties provide a striking backdrop or understory to light pink flowers.

Among the annual amaranths, globe amaranth (*Gomphrena globosa*) flowers are pretty little balls in varying shades of pink, red, rose, and white. If picked just after blooming and dried, they hold their color perfectly through the winter in dried arrangements.

Alyssum (*Lobularia maritima*) is often used in planters and window boxes, and to edge old-fashioned gardens. It's a low-growing, small-leaved plant that spreads its white to purple flowers rapidly. The pungent pastel flowers range from white to pink and lilac to purple.

Annual asters, *Callistephus chinensis,* come in many sizes and colors and can be quite beautiful in a drift. Name your color and there's probably an aster to suit your preference.

One of the exceptions to the full-sun rule for annuals is browallia, which makes lovely mounds of low, blue to violet-blue flowers that like it best in a light shade. Browallia blooms all summer. Looking something like an allium (flowering onion), the blue lace flower (*Trachymene coeruleus*) makes lovely, soft-lilac flower balls 2 to 3 inches across, and deserves more recognition among annual growers.

Calendulas are hardy little pot marigolds that bloom in shades of cream, orange, or yellow all winter in Zones 9 and 10, and thrive in cool months elsewhere.

Canterbury bells, which can be either *Campanula medium* or *C. calycanthema,* cover their tall stems with the most wonderful mauve, rose, pink, or bluish bells in June and for some time thereafter. The candytuft, or iberis, is a low-growing flowering plant useful for low edging, and is available in white, rose, red, crimson, lavender, and purple.

For graceful intermixing with perennials, cosmos is a frequently chosen annual. Its colors are bright and cheerful, occurring in white, red, yellow, rose, and crimson. Blue bachelor's buttons are used the same way. We surrounded a deep carmine rose campion with these bright blue flowers one year with spectacular results.

Some perennial favorites also have an annual counterpart. There are annual geraniums (*Pelargonium* spp.), the bright red window-box favorites; annual gazanias, with red and yellow striping for a festive midsummer appearance; and an annual baby's breath (*Gypsophila elegans*) that should be sown every few weeks through the growing season for continuous bloom. Many cultivars are on the market, in many shades of carmine-red, rose pink, purple, and white.

Heliotropes combine good looks as a low edging plant with a pleasant fragrance of baby powder. The blooms are usually violet, but can sometimes be found in white.

Although most hollyhocks are perennials, there is an annual type, and one, 'Summer Carnival', won the All-America Award, with its very double, 4-inch flowers in shades of white, pink, rose, and red.

Impatiens are perfect for planting in moist, shady nooks, where they brighten up those little "in-between" places. You should have no trouble finding a color that suits your fancy, since breeders have given us hybrids in red, pink, orange, salmon, purple, white, and even variegated forms.

There's an annual delphinium, the larkspur, which may be found in shades of dark blue, pink, and white. For the darkest, most intense blues imaginable, choose the lobelia. It stays close to the ground and blooms continuously until frost.

Annual vines are nice to use to cover fences and to grow on trees. Purple, pink, blue, or white morning-glories will do the job in the morning, and moonflower (*Calonyction* spp.) will take over at night, opening its fragrant white flowers for the moths.

A fragrant daytime annual vine available in a rainbow of colors is sweet pea (*Lathyrus odorata*). Nasturtium serves double duty as a culinary plant and a pretty, flowering, viny grower, and blooms in bright yellows, oranges, and red-oranges.

The airy-looking, ferny-foliaged love-in-a-mist, nigella, is a thoroughly charming annual with lacy blue flowers. It associates well with denser but color-related perennials.

Pansies are usually grown as annuals, although they will come back in protected and warm climates. They're available in a profusion of colors. Almost as familiar—maybe more familiar—are petunias, with their dark violets and cheerful candy-stripe pink-and-white forms. Some of the very double blue petunias, such as the cultivar 'Blue Danube', could change your opinion if you're not usually a fan of petunias.

Polygonum capitatum is grown as an annual in the North, although it's perennial in warm zones. This is a graceful plant with bronzy green leaves that produces little flower balls of delightful pink hues. It works beautifully as a ground cover and as a plant to come tumbling out of a basket.

Two favorite annuals are California bluebell, *Phacelia campanularia*, with its intense deep blue, bell-shaped flowers, and portulaca, which could be the cheeriest flower in the garden as it opens single roselike flowers in many colors on its succulent stems from summer to frost. And, as an added bonus, it will reseed.

The annual Shirley poppy has double flowers in mixed colors, and is useful for filling in among perennials when sown successively for bloom from spring to summer. One of the many kinds of salvia is *Salvia splendens,* the annual sort, which usually is overused as an edging plant and comes in very bright red. The large, velvety trumpets of salpiglossis come in gold, rose, red, and blue. These flowers are similar to petunias, but finer, with interesting markings.

Another sweetly scented annual is sweet sultan (*Centaurea imperialis*). It has feathery puffs of subtly colored blooms in shades of pink, lavender, white and toned-down carmine.

Can any garden have enough snapdragons (*Antirrhinum majus*), with their symphonic color variations of crimson, white, yellow, rose, and cream? They can be found in tall varieties up to 30 inches, mediums to 18 inches, and dwarfs to 10 inches.

One of the prettiest hanging baskets is made with a planting of *Thunbergia alata,* the black-eyed Susan vine. Its flat flowers are a pale orange or cream, and the centers are dark purplish-brown, almost black. It twines its way up the basket's supports and then tumbles over in a gorgeous display of very subtle color.

Of all annuals, my very favorite is the tiny but spectacular torenia, or wishbone flower. *Torenia fournieri* 'Compacta' is a light lilac flower shaped something like a violet, with an intense robe of rich, dark purple and a bright yellow throat blotch.

If your garden is prone to drought, verbenas make a fine edging and ground cover, and withstand dry spells. So do venidiums, South African daisies of rich orange with purplish-black concentric rings. The foliage is gray, which makes this annual flower quite showy by contrast.

Zinnias find their way into many gardens, where they give bright colors in every shade but blue for cutting or for a sunny border. Their long bloom season, durability, and bold display make them favorites, especially in the late summer and fall gardens.

Another category of annuals for cutting includes the dahlias, whose roots can't stand frost and must be dug and stored in the cellar over winter. While the gardener handles them annually, they are really tender perennials. They come in single flowers to fully double pompons in every color except blue.

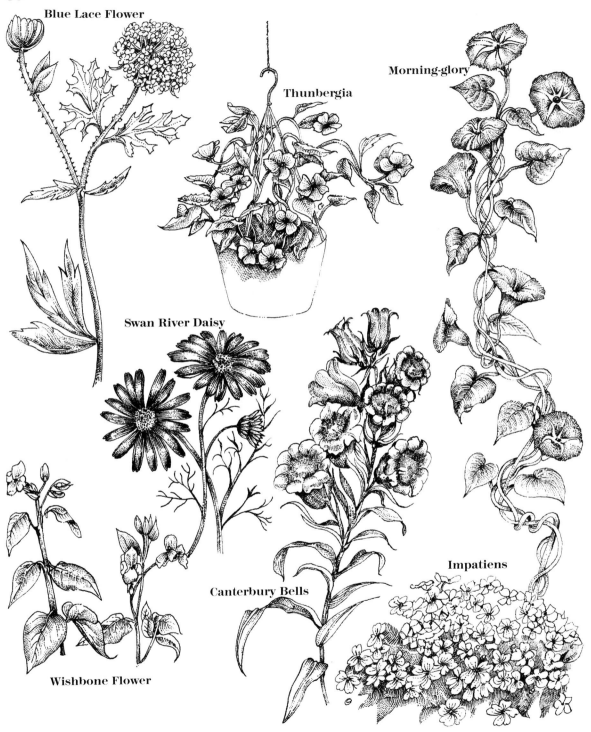

Blue Lace Flower

Thunbergia

Morning-glory

Swan River Daisy

Canterbury Bells

Impatiens

Wishbone Flower

Choice Annuals

FEATURED FLOWER OF OCTOBER: STOCK

The English have the climate for stock, the summer annual with the heavily scented towers of flowers. As a member of the mustard family, stock likes the same kind of cool weather that most cole crops (cabbage, kale, and broccoli) prefer. England's long, cool spring and summer give stock fanciers a long time to show off their prizes.

Botanically, stock is *Matthiola incana,* with felty, gray-green leaves on bushy plants between 1 and 2 feet tall, with either mounds or columnar spikes of scented flowers in an enormous color range, including white, yellow, pink, rose, lavender, blue, and purple. Excelsior stocks are the columnar-form variety, and one of the prettiest flowering annuals of all. Brompton stocks, of all the *M. incana* cultivars, probably have the heaviest scent. All stocks make great cut flower arrangements that perfume the air in the house. A separate species, *M. bicornis,* called night scented stock, opens its graceful lilac flowers' perfume chambers in the evening, producing a scent described by one seed catalog as "deliriously glorious and powerful."

In the United States, the Pacific Northwest comes remarkably close to England's climate, and similar conditions for growing stock prevail. But in most of the country, where very hot summers prevail, start seeds indoors to have seedlings ready for the mid-spring planting.

In Zone 6, the climate of New York City and Philadelphia, figure on setting out stock seedlings the first week of May. Count back eight weeks to arrive at the seed-starting date: the first week of March. On March 1 sow stock in flats in a mix of finished compost and vermiculite. If you don't have an adequate sunspace, supplement sunlight with artificial light. Grow seedlings at a temperature of from 55 to 60°F, no warmer.

When growing the 'Trysomic' strains, often found listed in seed catalogs as 'Trysomic Seven Weeks', you can select seedlings for the doubleness of the flowers they'll produce. When the first true leaves appear, lower the temperature in the sunspace or greenhouse to 50°F and thin out the seedlings with the darkest, greenest leaves. Leave those with the lightest, yellowest leaves. These seedlings are the ones that produce double flowers.

Grow the seedlings in the cool sunspace until the middle of April, repotting as necessary. Harden them off in a cold frame or on the back porch for a week. Then plant in the garden around the first of May. They like good, loamy garden soil with lots of organic matter and constant moisture. Grow in full sun from Zone 6 north, in partial shade in more southerly areas.

For continuous bloom, plant out areas of 'Trysomic Seven Weeks', 'Ten Week', and 'East Lothian'—they'll succeed each other in that order. Stocks will begin flowering in June and continue into July in the northern states. Move everything ahead a month in the warm zones. It's a good idea to plant stocks with a large perennial that will lend some shade by the end of June, helping to prolong stock's bloom in the hot weeks.

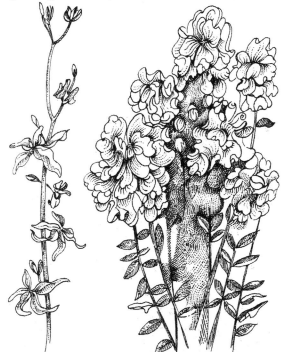

Matthiola incana, *more familiarly known as stock, pictured on the right, produces thick clusters of heavily fragrant flowers. On the left is* Matthiola bicornis, *called night-scented stock for its habit of perfuming the evening air.*

November (Late Fall)

A few chrysanthemums may be hanging on in the cold winds, but they are the last of the flowers as the world falls to winter's advancing ice. Fresh flowers for the house must come from the florist, or from the sunspace for those lucky enough to have one. The memory of summer's lush gardens can be kept fresh for most of us, however, by certain kinds of flowers that retain their color when dried.

These are the everlastings. They're best grown together in beds off to the side or out of the way of the main floral displays, as they will be harvested for drying just when they're looking good. Almost all like full sun and good garden soil, kept moist to make their best growth.

Dried flowers make excellent arrangements and centerpieces for the wintertime table. Dried flowers and herbs can be woven into wreaths—tapestries of soft pastels that the fresh colors attain when they dry. They always make wonderful gifts during the winter holidays, reminding their recipients of the summer's bright colors.

Some dried flowers, like strawflowers, need to have artificial stems, but most do not and will stand tall on their own dried stems. Proper drying means tying the cut flowers into small, loose bundles so that air can circulate freely around the stems. These are hung upside down in a very dry, dark, warm attic or room. When the stems are brittle, the flowers are dried.

Strawflowers should be harvested when their flower heads are just starting to open, not when the flower is full-blown. De-stem them just behind the flower head, and push green florist's wire stems into the back of the flower heads. The flowers will continue to open a little more as they finish drying on the artificial stems.

Remember, once you've created dried arrangements and wreaths from the flower garden's bounty, don't place them where direct sunlight will hit them, otherwise the sun will bleach out their colors.

Flowers for Everlasting Beauty

Along with dried flowers, you'll want to dry some of the foliage plants to add color and interest to your arrangements. What follows is a list of the main flowers and foliage plants for drying. These are by no means all the plants available for drying. If those covered here aren't enough, begin to experiment with shapes you find in nature and try to dry them for your arrangements.

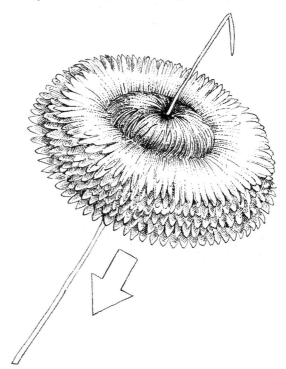

Strawflowers are given green wire stems for strength. The wire is inserted into the flower from the top, and the bent end is pulled tightly to the flower head to secure it.

Acroclinium   These double and semi-double daisies have strawlike petals and retain soft shades of rose, pink, and white.

Artemisia   'Silver King' and 'Silver Queen' dry to feathery gray foliage.

Bells of Ireland   The flower spire is covered with cuplike green bracts, in which inconspicuous flowers appear, then drop. When dried, the green cups turn a pale straw color and look nice in dried flower arrangements.

Celosia   Both the plumed varieties and the cock's-comb head varieties dry well and add interesting shapes to any arrangement.

Chinese Lanterns   These are the orange, papery husks often seen for sale in the fall, but much more economically grown in the garden.

Echinops   Everything about this plant is appealing; bluish-green, spiky balls offer superb contrast to feathery leaves and pendulous seed heads.

Globe Amaranth   A productive plant that offers masses of small, round flower heads in white, pink, orange, and reddish-purple from summer till frost. This is one of the best flowers to grow in the regular garden for drying because more flowers keep coming after cutting.

Golden Ageratum   This plant gives you little golden buttons when dried. They look delightful woven into decorative wreaths.

Goldenrod   A shapely and colorful plant growing wild in the fields, it's no less so after it's dried and placed in an arrangement.

Grasses   Foxtail looks nice, but it's such a weed in our gardens that we don't like to see it in an arrangement on our table. If you don't share our bias, Burpee sells a tall, mixed, annual grass seed packet that gives a wide range of upright and pendulous grass heads and stems.

Joe-pye Weed   An eastern weed of boggy meadows and low places, with beautiful, fragrant, pinkish-beige flower heads that dry perfectly.

Lamb's Ears   The soft, silvery gray flower rods, cut just when the first light purple flowers are opening along its length, retain all their best points when dried, and make very interesting additions to any arrangement.

Larkspur   The pink, blue, or white varieties of this annual delphinium retain good color when harvested young and dried.

Lavender   Harvest the flower heads on their long stems just before the florets pop open. These add a vivid lavender-blue to arrangements and are also good in potpourris.

Liatris   The raspberry pink spires dry well if picked when just opened.

Lunaria   Also known as honesty, or money plant. This plant produces silvery, round, flat seed pods that give extra interest to flower arrangements.

Pearly Everlasting   The plant is known as *Anaphalis cinnamomea,* sometimes listed in catalogs as *A. yedoensis.* It makes the most beautiful little pearly seed heads that hang gracefully from the tips of long stems. And it has a fragrant, haylike scent.

Pot Marjoram   A relative of culinary oregano, pot marjoram gives small purple heads that dry well, smell great, and look good.

Statice   Looks exactly the same dried and fresh. *Limonium sinuata* is the species commonly grown for drying, and cultivars and mixed shades come in packets that will grow to be yellow, rose, white, fawn, beige, lavender, blue, apricot, and shades in between. There are other species, less commonly seen, with wonderfully graceful flower stems, on which tiny florets appear. Look for perennial statice (*Dumosa* spp.), *Limonium latifolia,* and *Limonium caspia.*

Strawflowers   These are the helichrysums, with colors that are very bright when fresh in the garden, and hardly less bright after being dried. In fact, strawflowers feel dried, even when growing.

Tansy   This rampant weed makes pretty

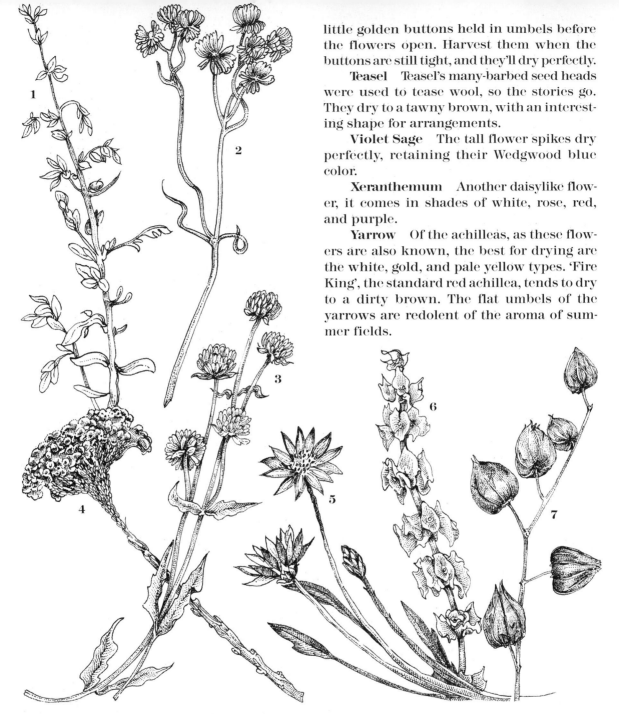

little golden buttons held in umbels before the flowers open. Harvest them when the buttons are still tight, and they'll dry perfectly.

Teasel Teasel's many-barbed seed heads were used to tease wool, so the stories go. They dry to a tawny brown, with an interesting shape for arrangements.

Violet Sage The tall flower spikes dry perfectly, retaining their Wedgwood blue color.

Xeranthemum Another daisylike flower, it comes in shades of white, rose, red, and purple.

Yarrow Of the achilleas, as these flowers are also known, the best for drying are the white, gold, and pale yellow types. 'Fire King', the standard red achillea, tends to dry to a dirty brown. The flat umbels of the yarrows are redolent of the aroma of summer fields.

Flowers for drying come in all sorts of shapes. Artemisia (1) lends its silvery gray dried foliage, while pearly everlasting (2) has a pleasant, haylike scent. Globe amaranth (3) contributes soft balls of pastel colors to the arrangement, and celosia (4), the cock's-comb, adds a splash of purple-crimson. Xeranthemum (5) has large, daisylike flowers in red and purple shades. Bells of Ireland (6) is green when alive, but dry to a papery beige. Another papery husked plant for the dried arrangement is Chinese lanterns (7) in bold reds and oranges.

FEATURED PLANT OF NOVEMBER: COTONEASTER

Cotoneaster only looks like it's flowering when it covers itself in fall and into winter with red berries. And so for those of us who endure winter's hard freezes, the genus offers a last hurrah of color, both outdoors and added to indoor arrangements.

Cotoneaster is a large genus, with family members ranging from tiny ground covers up to 20-foot shrubs. Some are evergreen, some deciduous, and some semi-evergreen. All like dry, poor soil, and produce more richly colored berries if given these conditions.

Although cotoneasters make lots of spring flowers, they are small and not particularly showy. Berries develop during the summer and turn bright red to orange-red in late summer or fall, persisting on the shrubs for months.

A choice low-growing cotoneaster is *Cotoneaster adpressus* 'Praecox', reaching only 1 foot high and spreading about 6 to 8 feet in diameter as it flows over low walls or rocks. Its berries are bright red, ½-inch spheres.

Another excellent ground-covering cotoneaster is *C. dammeri,* the bearberry cotoneaster. It throws branches of its woody structure out 10 feet, but never raises its leaves much more than 6 inches from the ground. It's evergreen and its berries are extra showy. Of this species, 'Coral Beauty' has coral berries and 'Royal Beauty' has darker red fruit.

Rock cotoneaster (*C. horizontalis*) also stays low, to about 2 feet, and carries its leaves in a twill pattern. The berries are a pretty bright red and very showy. Although this species is deciduous, it's only bare for a short time in the dead of winter.

The hybrid cotoneaster 'Lowfast' is aptly named, being low (reaching only a foot tall) and fast (quickly extending itself to 10 or more feet). It carries medium red fruit that is not as showy as many other kinds. 'Lowfast' is used because its vigor allows it to fill areas quickly, hold fresh cuts on banks, and heal over newly dug areas.

As its name implies, *Cotoneaster microphyllus* has tiny leaves, which help it show off its ¼-inch, light red berries to best effect. It seldom grows more than 3 feet tall, or reaches more than 6 feet across.

Clusters of small, bright red berries are borne on the prostrate branches of *Cotoneaster salicifolius* 'Autumn Fire' that grow only 6 inches high. *C. salicifolius* 'Repens' is similar, with a weeping form. Both of these cultivars reach spreads of 8 feet.

When growing cotoneaster, don't prune the branch tips because they die back and look bad. Remove old wood from the base where it arises. Watch for fireblight, which will blacken and kill cotoneaster quickly if it gets started. Prune off all affected branches, sterilizing your shears after every cut, and burn the blighted limbs.

Scarlet Leader Willowleaf Cotoneaster

December (Early Winter)

Even December's meager sun is enough to support a wide range of greenhouse plants, many of which flower just in time for the holidays.

New materials make greenhouse gardening more practical than ever. A lot of folks have the idea that they'll build a sunspace on the south wall of their house, and that it will become both a greenhouse for plants and a supplementary home heating unit. Experience has taught us, however, that you usually can count on only one use for a sunspace. If you plan to use it for flowering plants, the heat generated under the glass will have to stay in the sunspace and not be carried off to heat the home. Conditions in the sunspace will vary, depending on structure and supplemental heating ability, and these variations will determine what plants you can grow.

Warm and Humid Sunspaces

Sunspaces designed as greenhouses for tropical plants should be warm and humid. Daytime temperatures should go no higher than 85°F and nighttime temperatures no lower than about 60°F. It's best if you can wash down the place with a hose to provide good humidity.

These conditions allow for the widest range of plants, including some of our favorites. *Cattleya trianaei* is the Christmas orchid, with rose or white flowers decorated with purple edges and golden throats, guaranteed to brighten the December greenhouse. For fragrance, include a specimen or two of *Gardenia jasminoides,* which will reach 3 or 4 feet in greenhouse conditions and keep a supply of lovely white, fragrant flowers coming amid its glossy, dark green leaves.

Oncidium papilio, butterfly orchids, are gorgeous creatures with flower stalks that look like stems on which the most beautiful red and yellow butterflies have settled. Phalaenopsis orchids, or moth orchids, perform the same charade for the moths.

The warm and humid greenhouse is the place to grow gloxinias (*Sinningia* spp.) with their white, red, blue, violet, and lavender flowers in solid colors and in mixed shades and picotees. There are sweet little dwarf forms, too, that have the same gently sloping tubular flower shapes.

A wonderfully fragrant plant is the climbing *Stephanotis floribunda,* which grows to 10 feet or more. It and the hoyas have similar habits and will grow together.

Cooler and Less Humid Sunspaces

If it's impractical for you to keep the greenhouse at 60°F, there is still a range of plants to be chosen for a sunspace kept at no lower than about 50°F, with less humidity. This could be a sunny bay in the house, or an actual open sunspace subject to house temperatures and humidity. Here you can grow abutilons, the so-called flowering maples, with many new cultivars in shades of light pink, salmon, cream, reds, and oranges. Cacti and aloes will also do well in these conditions, and these produce spectacular flowers that appear to be from another world.

Gather your favorite pink begonias into pots for these conditions, and set clumps of billbergia among them. Our *Billbergia nutans* blooms in our living room in December, bathed in warm sunlight, and producing soft pink flower stems that elongate, then open to spill out jewellike, pendulous flowers of green, yellow, and dark purplish-blue.

To really splash your sunspace with color, grow *Bougainvillea buttiana* hybrids in lively, bright shades of red, pink, orange, yellow,

crimson, and magenta. They'll reach to 20 feet and more where they like the spot, so just two or three in large pots will keep a sunspace in bright color.

We like to grow a dwarf Seville-type orange, whose bonbon-sized fruit makes delectable marmalade, but you can also grow an 'Improved Meyer' lemon in a large tub for a good production of superior lemons, or a 'Washington' navel orange.

The less humid and cooler conditions of this sunspace are suited to cymbidium orchids that usually open a flush of blooms during the winter. And we always have a night-blooming jasmine around to freshen the winter air with its pungently sweet aroma. Freesias do well in the sunspace, and will produce lovely flowers with perhaps the most delicious scent of all. Pots can be brought to the table when in full bloom.

Fill a large pot with good loam and grow a specimen or two of *Hibiscus rosa-sinensis*, with their brilliant, showy, tropical flowers. They grow compactly in their tubs and bear crimson flowers. You can also find cultivars in apricots, oranges, reds, pinks, and yellows. Cover bare soil in the pots with impatiens to give contrasting or coordinating colors.

The passionflowers are space-saving climbers for the sunspace. Many bear edible fruit, but it's the fancy flowers that attract the grower. We love the intricate significance of *Passiflora ×alatocaerulea*'s unusual flower parts. These are likened to symbols of the passion of Christ, with the pistils seen as the nails, the five red stamens as the five wounds, and the filigreed halo as the crown of thorns. Lately we've grown fond of the red-flowered types of passiflora, *P. coccinea* and *P. jamesonii*.

You'll find that bird-of-paradise and the thunbergias do well in the conditions of the cooler greenhouse or sunspace. A pot full of calla lilies, with their gracefully unfurling white spathes, adds an elegant, even somber note to the sunspace.

Plants for a sunny, cool room in winter include cymbidium orchids at top, friendship plant placed so its spectacular flowers can be seen, a tub full of useful 'Improved Meyer' lemon, and the flaming tropical colors of bougainvillea at bottom.

Cold Sunspaces

If your sunspace loses its heat at night and temperatures fall to near freezing (but not below freezing) in the early hours, you can still grow a range of flowering plants. Agapanthus bulbs make handsome foliage and clear, light blue flowers that will begin to bloom in late January or February. *Jasminum polyanthum* carries pinkish buds and white, heavily fragrant flower clusters that will make the sunspace smell like a tropical garden. Camellias of various types, most of which take readily to pot culture, also will take these conditions.

The cup-and-saucer vine (*Cobaea scandens*) is interesting in this type of sunspace. Its flowers begin as a light green that turns creamy white, then darkens to purplish-violet. You might grow it out of a bed of the rose to purple flowers of *Bergenia crassifolia,* the winter-blooming bergenia.

Bulbs planted in the cold sunspace in fall will begin their growth in late January or February, giving you a spring bulb display much in advance of the outdoor season. Amaryllis with its huge trumpets comes in a wide range from pinks to reds to white, with variegations and markings in some types. The bright red variety is especially showy for the holidays.

Windowsills in Bloom

Even a sunny window qualifies as a sunspace. One of our friends has an old and beautiful *Schlumbergera bridgesii*, the Christmas cactus, in a sunny west window bay. The plant has reached a diameter of 3 feet, and at Christmas turns into a waterfall of hanging red flowers.

The merest pot of African violets on a windowsill makes this crucial statement: there are flowers here, in winter. They give hope for the lusher seasons to come.

FEATURED PLANTS OF DECEMBER: INDOOR ANNUALS

Gardeners can use their sunspaces to start seeds of annuals for indoor winter displays. Indoor growers have the same range of color possibilities as they have in the summer garden, but now miniaturized in pots and containers.

Lantana hybrids bring combinations of colors within the same flowers. They're usually grown in hanging pots to allow the pretty mosaiclike rosettes to spill out. 'Camara Mixed Hybrids' flower all winter in combinations of red and yellow, rose and yellow, lilacs, and white.

Annual ageratums, the puffy, raspberry lilac flossflowers, cover the bare soil of large pots or tubs with their unusual texture. Hybrid calceolaria, the pocketbook flower, has a pouchlike bloom that's fun to look at. Its popular cultivar, 'Anytime', blooms well all winter. Start seed for these in spring.

Calendulas, or pot marigolds, bloom for months in the cool greenhouse with typical marigold shades of orange and yellow, but also with softer apricots and peach colors. Start their seed in mid- to late summer for indoor plants that will start blooming when conditions turn harsh outside.

The beautiful blue bachelor's buttons (*Centaurea cyanus*) help liven up midwinter table displays. Sow their seed in fall and give them the most summery conditions you have—such as a south-facing window or sunspace—for best winter bloom. 'Jubilee Gem' is a compact form only 1 foot tall that's suited for pot culture.

Although carnations, *Dianthus caryophyllus,* and California poppies, *Eschscholzia californica,* both flower in the winter sunspace, put them at opposite ends of the sunspace, as the carnations' pink clashes with the poppies' orange-gold. The annual baby's breath, *Gypsophila elegans,* and rocket candytuft, *Iberis amara,* can be used to surround taller, stemmy plants, or at the base of climbers like the sweet pea, *Lathyrus odoratus,* growing up its trellis on the sunspace's interior wall.

The dancing little pink flowers of toadflax (*Linaria maroccana* 'Fairy Lights') make an elegant accent for more conspicuous greenhouse flowers. For an intense blue contrast, use *Lobelia erinus,* but use it sparingly, as its dominating blue is the color of fiery sapphire. A less intense blue than lobelia is provided by the forget-me-not, *Myosotis sylvatica*, which you may want to mix into beds or containers of primulas, either the *Primula ×kewensis* hybrids, or fairy primrose (*Primula malacoides*).

Sweet alyssum, *Lobularia maritima*, is an easy-to-grow, tidy little plant for the sunspace. It's available in colors from white to violet to purple, and has a light, delicate smell. For strong fragrance from a winter annual, grow stock (*Matthiola incana*).

Hybrid schizanthus 'Magnum' is known as poor man's orchid because of its orchidlike flowers on feathery foliage. The flowers are interestingly

marked with dark colors against rose and lilac backgrounds. Start the seed for these in September. Senecio hybrid 'Hansa' is a pretty cineraria for the cool sunspace, taking the same conditions as the primulas and schizanthus. Sow the seeds of blue lace flowers (*Trachymene coerulea*) in October for late winter and early spring bloom. Myriads of tiny blue florets form lacy flower balls 2 to 3 inches across on fine-leaved, 2-foot plants. Give them plenty of sunlight in a cool greenhouse for best bloom.

Nasturtiums (*Tropaeolum majus*) and Johnny-jump-ups (*Viola tricolor*) serve double duty, as their flowers can brighten up both the sunspace and winter salads.

Indoor annuals like plenty of light, moisture, and warmth. If you can give them these conditions, they'll produce gorgeous blooms. Lantana hybrids are shown spilling from a hanging basket. At left, Linaria maroccana 'Fairy Lights' dangles its flowers from a small pot, in the center is hybrid schizanthus 'Magnum', and the foot-tall dwarf bachelor's buttons open blue flowers at right.

Chapter 3
A Color Tour of Flowers through the Seasons

Time lapse cinematography of flowers captivates people because it concentrates reality and reveals secret patterns in the movements of plants.

The 79 photos in this section similarly concentrate what flower lovers might see if they had traveled widely over a full cycle of the seasons.

We begin with indoor bloomers that provide intense doses of color in sunny rooms, preserving a bit of summer's sumptuous flower extravaganza in miniature.

The phalaenopsis orchids **(Photo 1)** produce their waxy blooms anytime through the winter, with a spring peak. Their common name is moth orchid because the flower form is said to resemble a group of moths resting on a branch. But few moths have the delicious colors of these easy-to-grow epiphytes, which require only to be potted in chunks of moist fir bark, and a daily watering, to brighten winter days in the frozen heart of North America. When the sun returns to the zenith, phalaenopsis requires partial shade and jungle conditions, as its foliage will burn in direct summer sun.

Our winter photography continues outdoors in the warm zones—the coasts of Florida, the Gulf, and the southern Pacific—where flowers are always blooming, even in January. Those of you who live in these areas will find familiar garden plants in our photos, but most readers will know them only as houseplants, if at all. Some are only seen on visits to these favored climates.

As we pass into spring and summer, the photos reflect the variety and color of plants that bloom in all regions of the country. Summer ends, fall's languid days arrive, and the photos thereafter reflect once again those sun-warmed areas where the blooms continue outdoors through the winter.

When we looked through the final selection of photos, we were struck by the brilliance of the flower colors in the coldest months. Look at the reds of December's photo selection, or the phalaenopsis orchids opposite, for examples.

A photograph, by its nature, isolates a bit of reality and calls our attention to it. When the photographer has an artistic eye, the photograph reveals harmonies in its colors and shapes that seem almost too perfect. We think **Photo 1** has that quality, with its candy-colored flowers, rich turquoises, and lush, light pinks. The truth is that there is so much beauty in the world, we hardly see any of it.

Photo 1

Photo 2

January

The pretty pattern of the petals of a rich pink *Camellia japonica* (**Photo 2**) make this woody shrub especially welcome in winter in Zones 9 and 10. The flower's mathematical regularity gave rise to the name of its style, formal double. Camellias grow into dense, 6- to 8-foot shrubs with glossy, evergreen leaves.

Florist's cyclamen, *Cyclamen persicum* (**Photo 3**) blooms all winter where freezes are few, but hardier types like *C. coum* and *C. cilicium* will also bloom in January in Zone 9. Types hardy enough for cold-winter areas bloom from July to September.

Photo 3

Photo 4

If you could close your eyes and smell the spicy flowers of *Jasminum polyanthum* in **Photo 4**, you might open them in a Mediterranean garden where the romance of antiquity hangs like the jasmine's perfume in the air. As January closes, the jasmines open in the warmest regions of the country.

The jasmine's light pink is echoed in the delightful shell pink of a formal double *Camellia japonica* **(Photo 5)**. Notice the deep green of the camellia's leathery leaves, which makes the shrub as useful when out of flower as it is beautiful in bloom.

Photo 5

February

February sunshine along the California coast coaxes *Leptospermum scoparium* 'Helen Strybing' **(Photo 6)** to open its exquisite pink flowers. Commonly called the New Zealand tea tree, the brushy shrub's tough little leaves enable it to withstand months of drought. This variety derives its color harmonies from the red-brown/salmon pink side of the spectrum, while other varieties play on deep rose red and white.

Photo 6

Photo 7

Hummingbirds love to press their ruby throats against the bright red bristles of *Callistemon citrinus,* the bottlebrush **(Photo 7)**, as they sip its nectar. This showy plant forms a dense bush if unpruned, or a 20-foot tree if pruned to a single trunk. The brushy flowers form in cycles throughout the year, and there always seems to be a splotch of red somewhere on the branches. Where frosts don't nip it back, the common calla lily, *Zantedeschia aethiopica* **(Photo 8)**, will unfurl its mystical shrouds to reveal golden spikes of tiny true flowers in the center of the blossoms.

Photo 8

Photo 9

One of the first butterflies of spring, a young swallowtail, chases its dreams among the watery blue flowers of *Agapanthus orientalis,* the February-blooming lily-of-the-Nile **(Photo 9).** About mid-month, the acacia trees explode into masses of yellow flowers. Here, *Acacia dealbata* **(Photo 10)** throws a long truss of puffy flowers into the California sunshine. In **Photo 11,** creative pruning gives us a pleasing assemblage of dense, rounded mounds. The gold of new leaves covering the California golden privet, *Ligustrum ovalifolium* 'Aureum', in the foreground, and the red of the *Leptospermum scoparium* 'Ruby Glow' behind it artfully meld colors as well.

Photo 10

Photo 11

Photo 12

The brilliant royal purple of *Tibouchina urvilleana,* the princess flower **(Photo 12)**, brightens a balmy day along California's coast. In cold winter regions, this small Brazilian tree can be kept pruned to make a great potted plant for a sunny room. In **Photo 13**, the latches on the tibouchina's flowers have opened and the petals have fluttered to the ground. At the same time, February's chill causes it to shed some leaves onto the carpet of baby's tears. Here, nature suggests all the seasons in one subtle scene.

Photo 13

March

With spring's arrival, Nature begins to show her penchant for profuse variety. A hybrid ceanothus (**Photo 14**) shows why it's called wild lilac in its native California.

Photo 14

Photo 15

A warming sun illuminates a *Kerria japonica* 'Pleniflora' **(Photo 15)** tossing its cheerful orange-yellow flower balls into the air. Kerrias bloom in March in the mildest zones, but not until May in the cold regions. The gracefully arching branches stay green all winter, and are used in oriental plant arrangements for their beauty of form. In **Photo 16**, the tulip-shaped flowers of *Magnolia* ×*soulangiana* dance above familiar yellow daffodils, one of spring's common, but always thrilling sights. In **Photo 17**, the reborn world is swaddled in the pinks of flowering crabapples and the rich, warm yellows of the shrub beneath, *Forsythia* ×*intermedia* 'Spectabilis'.

Photo 16

Photo 17

Photo 18

The pink and yellow theme of spring is restated **(Photo 18)** in the pink blossoms of a hybrid chaenomeles (flowering quince) and *Forsythia ×intermedia*'s yellow bells. Where the twigs and branches of shrubs cross, as they do here, unplanned but beautiful color combinations may appear. **Photo 19** shows what an ordinary housefront can become when thoughtfully planted with flowering shrubs and trees. The red icing of bloom over the surface of a rhododendron and the glowing pink cloud of ornamental cherry flowers frame a window, wherein appears an abstract image of the world in the street. The choice of light pink above and deep red below is an artful use of one small portion of the color spectrum.

Photo 19

Photo 20

The rosy pink flower bracts of *Cornus florida* 'Rubra', the eastern dogwood **(Photo 20),** decorate the garden's wooded spots in warm climates. Filling the air with pink, established ornamental crabapples **(Photo 21)** and a sward of green grass make a simple but powerful early spring landscape.

Photo 21

April

A heavenly April light falls through purple-leafed plums and crabapple to touch on a hybrid rhododendron, 'P. J. Mezitt' or 'P.J.M.' **(Photo 22).** Dandelions dot the nicely naturalized blue carpet of spring star flower, *Ipheion uniflorum*.

Photo 22

Photo 23

Sometimes the simplest plants and arrangements are the most dramatically beautiful. **Photo 23** shows *Wisteria sinensis* gracing a smooth, white wall. The window frame's blue coordinates with the light violet-blue of the wisteria. A single, early red rose and a deep pink azalea add the right color accents at the base of the wall. It's not the color scheme as much as the pattern that amazes those who find the checkered fritillary, *Fritillaria meleagris* **(Photo 24),** which arises from bulbs each spring in quiet meadow settings.

Photo 24

Photo 25

The light pink, double flowers of a
Prunus serrulata 'Kwanzan', or Japanese
flowering cherry, tumble over the top of
Nandina domestica **(Photo 25).** In the hot,
dry regions, the colors of summer return in
April **(Photo 26).** Here, *Aloe striata* lifts
heavy umbrellas of salmony flowers in
front of the intense red blossoms of *Cal-
liandra tweedii,* the Trinidad flame bush.

Photo 26

Photo 27

Little leaves, long green stems, a brushy habit, and rich strawberries-and-cream flowers make *Cytisus scoparius* 'Lord Lambourne' one of the showiest of the Scotch brooms **(Photo 27).**

May

Pinks, lavenders, reds, oranges, and whites are represented in this magnificent stand of large hybrid rhododendrons **(Photo 28)** that have overgrown the cold, stony facade of a church. The pure colors of the rhododendrons are pulled together, concentrated, and fired into glass in the stained glass rosette above the bushes, reminding parishioners of May's colors all year round.

Photo 28

Photo 29

An exquisite harmonization of colors is found in these hybrid waterlilies **(Photo 29)** growing in a pool of dark water. Set out in May, waterlilies will bloom all summer. *Laburnum ×watereri* 'Vossii' **(Photo 30)** spills its yellow, wisteria-like flower clusters before a red barn wall. This tree would not be nearly as effective against a white wall or the sky. In **Photo 31,** a front yard on the West Coast turns to a mass of colors: pinkish-blue hydrangeas, red and white pelargoniums, and bright yellow echeveria in a swirl of shapes.

Photo 30

Photo 31

The sight of a bed full of 'Lucky Strike' hybrid tulips **(Photo 32)** announces May, the most floriferous period of the year. Now the air's warmth and the moisture mingle with the earth's sweet breath to bring the scents of summer back to us. The sun, only a month from its peak intensity, burns above a hillside of red azaleas **(Photo 33)**. The deep bronzy-red leaves of *Acer palmatum,* Japanese maple, and the chartreuse layers of evergreen chamaecyparis shade a stone bench, keeping a spot cool for visitors coming down the garden path.

Photo 32

Photo 33

Photo 34 shows a wooded garden crackling with the electricity of life reborn, brooding under the sudden heat and humidity of late May, almost liquid in the delicate new flesh of its leaves and flowers. In the face of such raw earth energy, we can only stare, until the trees become living lightning and the colorful shrubs become their echoing thunder.

Photo 34

June

A white arc of *Deutzia gracilis* blossoms cascades
into a pool of white roses **(Photo 35)**, presenting pure
colors just right for a June wedding.

Photo 35

Photo 36

Every shade of green seems to find a place along the wooded path to a garden shed **(Photo 36).** The spiky white wands of foamflower, *Tiarella cordifolia,* edge the path, while hybrid clematis hangs its white stars on a background fence. In **Photo 37,** the regular white flowers of *Acanthus mollis* demurely cover an Art Deco figure carved in low relief on fine marble, while the small, fragrant stars of *Trachelospermum jasminoides,* or star jasmine, twinkle overhead.

Photo 37

The strong light of June first coaxes the rhododendrons and azaleas into bloom, then transfixes them with
sly sunbeams that penetrate the surrounding leaves
(Photo 38). The sun-shot petals reveal patterns of pink
within their delicate tissues.

Photo 38

The long, graceful branches of *Buddleia alternifolia* carry clusters of lightly fragrant lilac flowers. **Photo 39** shows it trained to a single trunk, giving it the look of a weeping cherry. It can also be grown as a shrub with many trunks. *B. alternifolia* heralds June's wild display of flowers with a rare and special beauty all its own.

Photo 39

Photo 40

Color becomes summer-rich as June progresses. The intense rosy red flower balls of a large rhododendron frame a garden path edged with lavender spikes of *Polygonum bistorta* var. *superbum* and shimmering white *Viburnum plicatum* var. *tomentosum* 'Mariesii' **(Photo 40)**. The deep coppery background color is given by *Acer palmatum*. **Photo 41** shows an old-fashioned climbing 'Blaze' rose covering a rustic arbor above a hot pool of orange 'Gingersnap' hybrid tea roses. These colors match the heat of new summer.

Photo 41

124

Photo 42

Photo 43

The crinkly petals of *Cistus hybridus,* the white rock rose **(Photo 42)**, resemble the finest linen, or cloth painted by Vermeer. This plant's leaves are pleasantly fragrant when crushed. Spring's golden yellow makes its June reprise in the massed blossoms of *Cassia surattensis,* the senna bush **(Photo 43)**.

July

The lavender-blue flowers of hybrid clematis 'Ramona' perfectly decorate this door and trellis **(Photo 44)**. Notice that the clematis is not underplanted to hide its bare stems, but rather left bare to reveal the trellis work.

Photo 44

Photo 45

Ipomoea purpurea, the morning-glory **(Photo 45),** smothers its
supports under a wild embrace.
Roses, such as the 'Katherine Loker'
in **Photo 46,** are blooming in every
corner of the United States as high
summer begins. July gives gardeners everywhere nature's maximum
potential for color.

Photo 46

Dahlias, like the "formal decorative" type shown in **Photo 47,** are frost-tender natives of Mexico and Central America that have been bred into hundreds of hybrid types. The yellow center buried beneath the pink petals seems Mexican in design. Northern gardeners must dig and store the tuberous roots over winter.

Photo 47

Glowing, flossy pink flowers decorate the ferny, blue-green foliage of *Albizia julibrissin*, the mimosa **(Photo 48).** One of the most heat-tolerant of ornamental trees, the mimosa responds to torrid weather with blooms like lights on a summer version of a Christmas tree.

Photo 48

Photo 49

Photo 50

Big, showy flower clusters of *Hydrangea macrophylla* (**Photo 49**) respond to soil conditions with pink or blue coloration. The more acid the soil, the more blue or purple the flowers; neutral or alkaline soils give pink or red flowers. The color red spills its variations everywhere this month. **Photo 50** shows the bright red-pink bracts of bougainvillea hybrid 'Rosea'. These are the papery outer leaves that surround the inconspicuous flowers.

Photo 51

Bougainvillea spectabilis pours baskets of magenta-red flowers down a set of steps, setting off the color of the blue tiles **(Photo 51)**. Permanent color features of the landscape form the basis for choosing the changing colors of associated flowering plants.

August

A cottage garden inundates its visitors with flowers in early July **(Photo 52)**. Red and pink hollyhocks appear on this side of the fence, tawny daylilies peek over from the other side, while *Lythrum salicaria* 'Morden's Pink' sends its tall, magenta sprays overhead in the background.

Photo 52

The dead ripe and optically active orange flowers of *Thunbergia gregorii*, orange clock vine **(Photo 53)**, tell the time of summer's fulfillment. The August air is hot and tropical, like the colors of the 'Fleurzauber' rose in **Photo 54**. But no matter how warm the days, *Felicia amelloides*, blue marguerites **(Photo 55)**, add their notes of cool color.

Photo 53

Photo 54

Photo 55

What bee could resist the mixture of the glowing,
buttery cups of *Rosa bracteata* 'Mermaid' mingled with
the beelike flowers of *Senecio angulatus* **(Photo 56)**? An
August river of gold given by perennial *Rudbeckia
fulgida* 'Goldsturm' flows past banks made of ornamental grasses, overhung by the white flower balls of a
peegee hydrangea, *Hydrangea paniculata* 'Grandiflora',
trained as a tree **(Photo 57).**

Photo 56

Photo 57

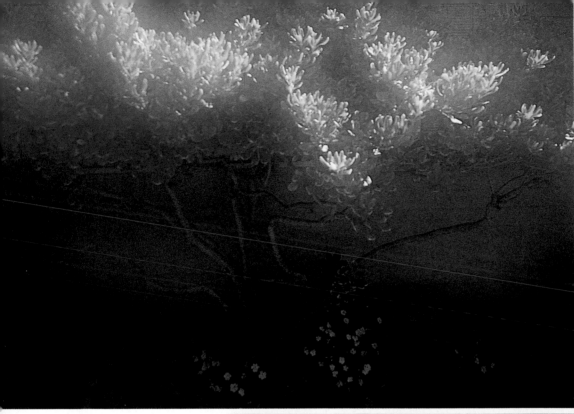

Photo 58

Photo 59

The undulating stems of *Pittosporum tobira* arise from a glowing bed of impatiens in this romantic, evocative photograph **(Photo 58)**, revealing the power of artful pruning in even a simple arrangement. In **Photo 59,** *Lonicera sempervirens* 'Dropmore Scarlet', trumpet honeysuckle, opens showy blossoms in the cooling days of late August, as it has been doing since June.

September

Summer's displays subside in September, but not without some final fanfares. The pink blooms of *Geranium endressii* are surrounded by the last spires of *Veronica spicata* **(Photo 60),** as they flank a series of descending garden pools.

Photo 60

Photo 61

Soft plumes of fountain grass, *Pennisetum setaceum* (**Photo 61**), are framed in an arch of vines and set against drifts of billowing white flowers. It's in September that ornamental grasses begin their quiet symphony of color. **Photo 62** shows a close-up of *P. setaceum*'s seed heads hanging among the elegant, purplish flower spikes of *Salvia leucantha*, Mexican bush sage.

Photo 62

The dusty, bluish greens seem more prominent at this time of the year, as the days cool off and nights can turn chilly. The succulent gray-green rosettes of *Sempervivum tectorum,* hen-and-chickens, in **Photo 63** are strewn with fallen rose petals and bordered by the cheery little flowers of wax begonias. Proving the adage that a garden's greatest beauty is never immediately apparent, *Rosa polyantha* 'The Fairy' peeks out of a soft blue haze created by *Artemisia* 'Silver King' **(Photo 64).**

Photo 63

Photo 64

Two elements turn an ordinary window into a charming scene right out of an Italian back street **(Photo 65):** the wrought iron grating and a thriving pot of *Pelargonium ×hortorum,* the common potted geranium. As cold weather returns, many gardeners pot up flowering plants to take indoors.

October

The lush clustered flowers of stock are grown for their heady fragrance as well as their rich colors **(Photo 66).** Stock is an outstanding cut flower. Its color spectrum includes blue and purple as well as the red, pink, white, and creamy yellow shown here. The plants prefer cool weather, and will bloom beautifully in October and, where winters are mild, in winter and spring.

Photo 65

Photo 66

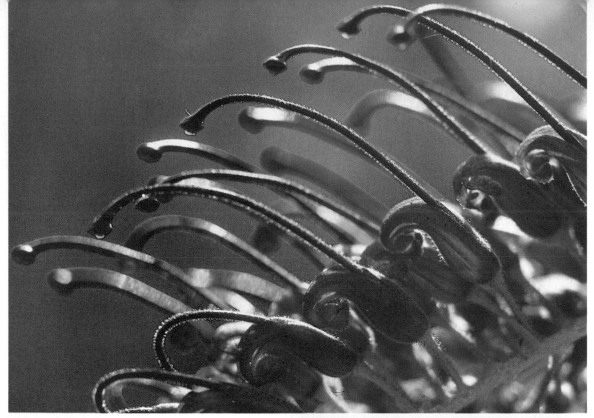

Photo 67

A rare, smoky light calls forth the coral pinks of *Grevillea* 'Robin Gordon' (**Photo 67**) and *Passiflora jamesonii* (**Photo 68**). The grevillea forms a shrub about 5-6 feet tall, while the passion vine is a vigorous grower that will cover a bank or corner of a building. In **Photo 69**, the slender red and white bells of a hybrid fuchsia decorate the cool green columns of a classic portico. A wisteria twines along the top of the portico. It will create a lilac and green color scheme in spring, for then the fuchsia will be out of bloom.

Photo 68

Photo 69

Photo 70

The rich red leaves of *Liquidambar styraciflua*, American sweet gum **(Photo 70)**, have tumbled into a bed of rose-lilac flowers of *Lantana montevidensis*—an annual ground cover in the North, but an evergreen perennial in the warm zones.

November

When flowers fail in the hardening frosts, rich red clusters of cotoneaster berries brighten the November landscape **(Photo 71)**. Cotoneasters aren't known for their flowers, but do produce masses of white clusters in late spring. Some deciduous varieties have good fall leaf color and an interesting twig structure.

Photo 71

Photo 72

Frost has cut down the flowers, but what's this? The whole world is ablaze with the colors usually reserved for flowers **(Photo 72)**. The fiery display advances down the eastern seaboard, leaving behind it the bare trees of winter. **Photo 73** discovers a mad but colorful partnership between the prickly pear cactus, *Opuntia occidentalis,* with its yellow flowers and red fruits, and the busy, self-absorbed little California fuchsia, *Zauschneria californica,* in the center.

Photo 73

December

The advent of winter doesn't spell the end of the flowering season. The sunroom is still bright with the vibrant colors of flowering annuals and tender perennials. *Lantana camara's* showy flower clusters **(Photo 74)** open yellow, then turn orange, red, lavender, or all three. Other striking plants for the sunroom include calceolaria (pocketbook plant), bachelor's buttons, California poppies, candytuft, Johnny-jump-ups, lobelia, nasturtiums, and carnations.

Photo 74

The December sun fails and the continent grows cold, but along its warm Pacific edge, plant visitors from other realms may open their exotic flowers. One of the most spectacular is the red and yellow *Camellia sasanqua* 'Yuletide' **(Photo 75).** The first camellia to bloom, it announces the holidays.

Photo 75

Glad that it's winter and that it can bloom, *Eucalyptus erythrocorys*, or red-cap gum, displays exuberant yellow blooms and fleshy red caps against a freshly washed sky **(Photo 76)**. As the red of the dying ember is often the reddest of colors, so the red bracts of *Euphorbia pulcherrima*, poinsettia **(Photo 77)**, mark the final days of the year indoors throughout the country, and outdoors in the warm climates.

Photo 76

Photo 77

Photo 78

Photo 78 shows the Nepalese native, *Rhododendron arboreum,* or tree rhododendron, beginning to bloom. It's hard to decide whether the soft green foliage or the red shades of the flowers are more beautiful.

At the end, it's just a shadow that passes in favor of a growing light, a quick step and shuffle into a new year and new life, like the graceful dance here performed by *Rosmarinus officinalis,* or the blue-flowered rosemary, and *Leptospermum scoparium* 'Ruby Glow', the New Zealand tea tree **(Photo 79).**

Photo 79

Chapter 4
Guide to Flowering Trees, Shrubs, and Vines

The three charts in this chapter are designed to simplify the task of selecting plants for your property. We've selected trees, shrubs, and vines that can be found in nurseries and mail-order catalogs, emphasizing varieties of surpassing beauty or utility.

We've arranged them so that a quick glance down the categories of plant characteristics will give you the plant you need, for the conditions you have, in the shortest amount of time. We believe you'll find these charts especially handy when working with your favorite nursery catalog or plant lists.

Terms regarding light and soil conditions are the same through the three charts. They bear a bit of explanation:

Full sun means just that; the plants receive sunshine all day. Partial shade means that the plants are in the sun for less than six hours a day, but for at least a couple of hours. Light shade means a bright shade, such as that found beside a stand of trees but not under them, or in a site that receives light reflected from a wall. Shade means a constant but medium shade, and full shade means the kind of conditions found under the closed canopy of a forest.

Many of the descriptions in the chart read, "Partial shade to full sun," which means that the plant prefers partial shade, but tolerates full sun. "Full sun to partial shade" means that the plant prefers full sun, but tolerates partial shade.

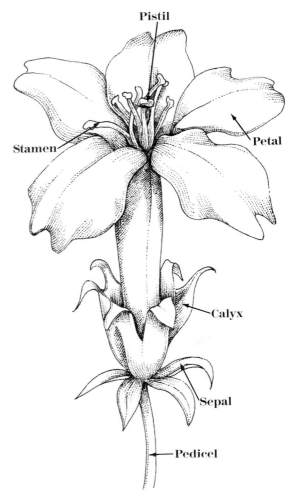

An idealized flower showing the major anatomical parts.

154

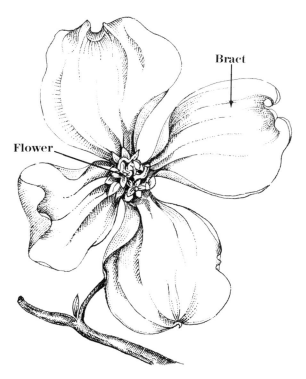

In some flowers, the bracts are large and showy, the actual flowers inconspicuous, as with this dogwood blossom.

As for soil descriptions, average soil means one not too rich in nutrients, with some organic matter but not humusy. Good garden loam means a soil with a good supply of nutrients, humus, and some actively decaying organic matter to give a crumblike structure. A deep soil is one that has been deeply worked and is open to drainage, and in which the nutrients are mixed deeply under the surface. A woodsy soil is full of decayed organic matter, usually acidic, without much nitrogen. A humusy soil implies the organic matter content of woodland soil with a full range of fertilizing nutrients. Compost is humusy soil.

The Zone category refers to the USDA Hardiness Zone Map on page 297, and lists the coolest zone in which the plant can grow outside.

The sizes given for plants in the charts are mature sizes. It will take a decade or more for your new plantings to reach these sizes, but eventually they will, and you'll be glad you planted them at mature-size spacings. For trees and shrubs, mature sizes are given height first, followed by width: "25 by 20 ft." means 25 feet tall and 20 feet in diameter at maturity. For vines, mature sizes are given as the length of the longest shoots. Tree shapes given in the chart are shown in the illustration on page 15, in Chapter 1, Creating Combinations of Flowering Plants.

With these clarifications, we feel the charts are self-explanatory.

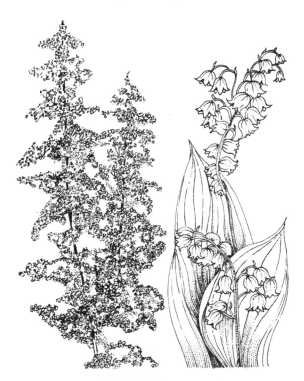

Flower cluster shapes: An astilbe (left) is characteristic of flowers that bloom in panicles, pyramidal, loosely branched flower clusters. The lily-of-the-valley (right) bears its flowers in racemes, in which flowers are borne on short stalks and are spaced evenly along a tall stem.

FLOWERING TREES

Place of Origin	Zone	Plant Type	Mature Size	Shape

Acacia baileyana   (ah-KAY-shah bay-lee-AN-ah)   BAILEY'S ACACIA

Australia	9	Evergreen	20 by 30 ft.	Rounded, spreading.

Culture: Full sun. Good garden loam.
Comments: Although acacias are short-lived, with weak wood, they reach mature size in just a few years. At home along California coast.
Cultivar: 'Purpurea', new foliage is gray-blue tinged with lavender-purple. Very striking tree.
Other Species: *A. dealbata*, silver acacia, like *A. baileyana*, only longer-lived; *A. farnesiana*, sweet acacia, fragrant, orange-yellow flowers.

Aesculus ×carnea   (es-KOO-lus KAR-nee-ah)   RUBY HORSE-CHESTNUT

Hybrid origin	5	Deciduous	40 by 40 ft.	Pyramidal, becoming rounded.

Culture: Full sun to partial shade. Deep soil.
Comments: Excellent specimen plant. Long-lasting, tough, compact compared to other horse-chestnuts.
Cultivars: 'Baumanii', white, double flowers; 'Rosea', pink blossoms; 'Briotii', deep red, 10-in. panicles, grows 20 by 20 ft.

Albizia julibrissin   (al-BIZ-ee-ah ju-lee-BRY-sin)   MIMOSA, SILK TREE

Central Asia	6-10	Deciduous	15 by 30 ft.	Flat-topped, spreading.

Culture: Sun to partial shade. Average soil. Tolerates poor soil and drought.
Comments: Pretty when viewed from above. Throws a light shade, so other plants may be grown underneath.
Cultivars: 'Alba', white; 'Rosea', rich pink; 'Ernest Wilson', bright pink.

Amelanchier grandiflora   (am-eh-LANK-ee-er grand-ih-FLOR-ah)   APPLE SERVICEBERRY

Eastern United States	4	Deciduous	25 by 10 ft.	Upright, irregular.

Culture: Full sun to partial shade. Tolerates wide range of soils.
Comments: Blooms early. Produces delightful, edible, berrylike fruit, and the bark is handsome, too.
Other Species: *A. canadensis*, serviceberry, many-stemmed tree bears white flowers; *A. laevis*, Allegheny serviceberry, drooping white flowers and treelike form; *A. arborea*, downy serviceberry, large white flowers produced on treelike form.

Plant Description	Season of Bloom	Flower Color	Flower and Fruit Description
Fernlike fronds of blue-green to gray-green leaves densely cover the tree's many twiggy branches. Fast-growing.	Jan.-Feb.	Yellow	Profuse, puffy clusters of yellow flowers appear at the branch tips, completely covering foliage.
Stocky, solid tree with dull brown bark. Leaves are long, lustrous, dark green, throwing dense shade.	Apr.-May	Rosy red	8-in. rosy red panicles adorn tree's branch tips. Seedpods are prickly balls.
Feathery, fernlike leaves and spreading habit make good canopy over outdoor areas. Has a lacy appearance.	June-July	Pink	1-2-in. pink-and-white puffs are held above light green foliage on sinuous, spreading branches. Volunteer seedlings can be pesky.
Multistemmed, with an open appearance. Young leaves are bronze to purple.	Apr.	White	Large flowers are pink in bud, opening white in drooping clusters just as leaves emerge. Edible, dark red berries follow in June. Leaves turn yellow-red in fall.

(continued)

Place of Origin	Zone	Plant Type	Mature Size	Shape

Bauhinia blakeana (baw-HIN-ee-ah blake-ee-ANN-ah)   **HONG KONG ORCHID TREE**

China	9	Deciduous	20 by 25 ft.	Flat-topped, spreading, and irregular.

Culture: Full sun to light shade. Moist, humusy soil. Doesn't transplant well once established.
Comments: All *B. blakeana* have been propagated from cuttings from a single specimen in Canton, China.
Other Species: *B. fortificata*, Brazilian orchid tree, creamy white, 3-in. flowers; *B. variegata*, orchid tree, flowers vary from pink to white to lavender.

Brachychiton acerifolius 'Majestic Beauty' (brahk-ee-KYE-ton ay-seer-ih-FOAL-ee-us) **AUSTRALIAN FLAME TREE**

Australia	9	Semi-evergreen	40 by 60 ft.	Upright, pyramidal.

Culture: Full sun. Prefers deep, moist soil.
Comments: Brachychiton is a messy tree that drops leaves and pods.
Other Species: *B. discolor*, scrub, Queensland lacebark, or hat tree, popular in southern Florida, 2-in. pink flowers appear in June–July.

Callistemon viminalis (kal-ih-STEM-on vy-min-AL-iss)   **WEEPING BOTTLEBRUSH**

Australia	8	Evergreen	20 by 30 ft.	Upright, with weeping branches.

Culture: Full sun. Adaptable to most soils.
Comments: Tolerates long periods of drought once established.

Calodendrum capense (kal-oh-DEN-drum kap-EN-say)   **CAPE CHESTNUT**

South Africa	10	Semi-evergreen	25–30 ft. by 25–30 ft.	Rounded, spreading.

Culture: Full sun. Well-drained, average soil.
Comments: Takes several years to bloom. Plant in sheltered spot.

Cassia leptophylla (KASS-ee-ah lep-toe-FY-lah)   **GOLD MEDALLION TREE**

Brazil	9	Semi-evergreen	20 by 25 ft.	Low, spreading, umbrella-shaped.

Culture: Full sun. Average, well-drained soil. Tolerates dry spells.
Comments: With its rich color and graceful shape, a superior specimen tree for the lawn.
Other Species: *C. excelsa* (also called *C. carnaval*), known as crown-of-gold tree, 12-16-in. flower clusters appear on branch tops in Aug.-Sept.; *C. fistula*, golden-shower tree, fragrant, hanging yellow clusters measures to 1½ ft. long, best suited to Zone 10.

Plant Description	Season of Bloom	Flower Color	Flower and Fruit Description
The gray-green, kidney-shaped leaves fall during the tree's blooming season; it stays bare just a short time between leaf drop and blossoming.	Dec.–Apr.	Pink to purple	6-in., orchidlike flowers decorate the tree in winter and early spring.
The leaves are wide, light green, with 5-7 lobes. Leaves drop just before bloom. The sturdy trunk is smooth and green.	May–June	Red-orange	¾-in. tubular blossoms are borne in masses of flower spikes over parts or all of the top of the tree. Blooms sporadically to fall. Fruits are woody pods with black seeds.
Pendulous branches sweep to the ground in a soft haze of narrow, light green leaves.	May–July	Red	Branches are covered with brushy rows of red bristles resembling a bottlebrush; blooms sporadically in fall.
Oval, medium green leaves arrayed on the tree's sturdy structure give a dense shade beneath. Slow-growing.	May–July	White, rose, or lilac.	1 ft. long spikes of white to rosy lilac florets are held erect above foliage, much like a horse-chestnut (*Aesculus* spp.).
Fast-growing, small tree of pleasing shape; pendulous compound leaves comprise many narrow leaflets.	July–Aug.	Yellow	Rich yellow, 3-in. flowers are borne in clusters; scattered bloom spring to summer.

(continued)

Place of Origin	Zone	Plant Type	Mature Size	Shape

Catalpa bignonioides　(ka-TAL-pa big-nohn-ee-oh-EYE-deez)　**COMMON or SOUTHERN CATALPA, INDIAN BEAN TREE**

Place of Origin	Zone	Plant Type	Mature Size	Shape
Southeastern United States	5	Deciduous	30-40 ft. by 20-35 ft.	Upright, irregular, rounded.

Culture: Prefers full sun and moist, fertile soil, but does well in most climates.
Comments: Catalpas litter the yard with fallen leaves and fruit, so plant in out-of-the-way areas. Often used to fill in until other trees reach mature size.
Cultivar: 'Aurea', yellow foliage instead of the usual green.
Other Species: *C. speciosa*, western catalpa, a larger tree, less showy bloom than southern catalpa.

Cercis canadensis　(SIR-sis can-a-DENSE-iss)　**EASTERN REDBUD**

Place of Origin	Zone	Plant Type	Mature Size	Shape
Eastern United States	4	Deciduous	30 by 25 ft.	Rounded, shrubby.

Culture: Sun or shade in eastern or northern exposure. Fertile, moist, sandy loam.
Comments: Nice with dogwoods in a woodland planting.
Cultivars: 'Alba', white; 'Oklahoma', reddish-purple; 'Pinkbud', bright true pink; 'Wither's Pink Charm', soft pink.
Other Species: *C. occidentalis*, native western redbud, hardy to Zone 8; *C. chinensis*, Chinese redbud, has a shrubby, compact shape, suited to Zone 7; *C. siliquastrum*, judas tree, a compact grower in Zone 7.

Chionanthus virginicus　(kye-o-NAN-thus ver-JIN-ih-kus)　**FRINGE TREE**

Place of Origin	Zone	Plant Type	Mature Size	Shape
Southeastern United States	5	Deciduous	20-30 ft. by 25-35 ft.	Rounded, spreading.

Culture: Full sun. Deep, moist, fertile loam.
Comments: Good specimen tree for the small garden when artfully trained and shaped.

Chorisia speciosa　(kor-EEZ-ee-ah spee-see-OH-sah)　**FLOSS SILK TREE**

Place of Origin	Zone	Plant Type	Mature Size	Shape
Brazil	9	Semi-evergreen	30 by 60 ft.	Tall, stately tree with cylindrical crown.

Culture: Full sun. Well-drained soil. Water monthly during drought.
Comments: When the world is entering autumn, the floss silk tree breaks into cheerful bloom. Its studded trunk is highly unusual looking.
Cultivars: 'Majestic Beauty', deep pink flowers on a thornless tree; 'Los Angeles Beautiful', burgundy flowers.
Other Species: *C. insignis*, white floss silk tree, flowers range from white to pale yellow, good for Zone 10.

Plant Description	Season of Bloom	Flower Color	Flower and Fruit Description
Fast-growing, softwood tree with large, heart-shaped leaves.	June	White	2-in., bell-shaped, white florets with yellow and brown throat markings held in pyramidal clusters above the yellow-green leaves; followed in fall by long beans.
Horizontal tiers of zigzag branches covered with reddish-brown bark. Leaves are an attractive heart shape.	Apr.	Magenta	The pealike flowers form right on the slender branches before the leaves appear, brushing the tree with color.
Oval, dark green leaves appear late in spring. Pretty gray bark.	June	White	6-8-in. fleecy panicles of feathery, slightly fragrant flowers followed by clusters of small, dark blue fruit. Leaves turn golden in fall. Dioecious, meaning some plants have male flowers, others have female flowers.
Thorny trunk. 5-in., light green leaflets form fan shape.	Sept.–Dec.	Pink, rose, or purple	6-in., showy, starlike flowers borne singly until frost. Fruit bursts into cottony masses of fluff.

(continued)

Place of Origin	Zone	Plant Type	Mature Size	Shape

Cladrastis lutea   (klah-DRASS-tiss LOO-tee-ah)   YELLOWWOOD

Place of Origin	Zone	Plant Type	Mature Size	Shape
Southeastern United States	3	Deciduous	30-35 ft. by 20-25 ft.	Vase-shaped to cylindrical, with rounded top.

Culture: Full sun. Average, well-drained soil.
Comments: Worth the wait for its spectacular floral show. Good specimen for a featured, but out-of-the-way, spot.
Cultivar: 'Rosea', pale pink flowers.

Cornus alternifolia   (KORE-nuss all-turn-ih-FOAL-ee-ah)   PAGODA DOGWOOD

Place of Origin	Zone	Plant Type	Mature Size	Shape
Eastern United States	3	Deciduous	15-25 ft. by 30-40 ft.	Spreading, irregular.

Culture: Sun to partial shade. Moist, well-drained, humusy soil.
Comments: Needs a spot where its "layered look" can be displayed well.
Cultivar: 'Variegata', variegated leaves, prefers shade.

Cornus florida   (KORE-nuss FLOR-ih-dah)   FLOWERING DOGWOOD

Place of Origin	Zone	Plant Type	Mature Size	Shape
Eastern United States	5	Deciduous	25 by 25 ft.	Spreading, flat-topped.

Culture: Partial shade. Moist, woodsy soil.
Comments: A most elegant tree for the understory. Threatened in the East by anthracnose disease. Good by the terrace, or below a deck.
Cultivars: 'Cherokee Chief', ruby red flowers, new growth is red; 'Cloud 9', blooms early and profusely in white; 'New Hampshire', hardy for northern gardens, white flowers; 'Pendula', has a weeping habit, white flowers; 'Plena', double white flowers; 'Rubra', soft pink flowers; 'Weaver's White', large and white, suited for southern gardens; 'Welchii', variegated foliage adds a nice touch, flowers inconspicuous pink to white; 'Williams Red', covered with rosy red flowers, suited for southern gardens; 'Xanthocarpa', has white flowers, yellow fruits.
Other Species: *C. mas*, cornelian cherry, round, yellow flower clusters in late winter followed by scarlet berries.

Cornus kousa   (KORE-nuss KOO-sah)   JAPANESE FLOWERING DOGWOOD

Place of Origin	Zone	Plant Type	Mature Size	Shape
Japan, Korea	5	Deciduous	20 by 25 ft.	Upright, spreading.

Culture: Full sun. Deep, rich, humusy soil.
Comments: Use as a specimen in front of dark, evergreen background. Resistant to anthracnose.
Cultivars: 'Gold Star', smaller, growing to 10 by 12 ft., features variegated foliage and white and green flowers in June; 'Summer Stars', blooms white in June-Aug.; 'Rosabella', pink flowers.

Plant Description	Season of Bloom	Flower Color	Flower and Fruit Description
Bright, yellow-green compound leaves turn clear yellow in fall. Bark is smooth, light gray.	June	White	Irregular bloomer. Flowers every 2 or 3 years when mature with intensely fragrant, hanging clusters of white, pealike flowers. Quite showy.
Branches held horizontally give a tiered look, hence the common name.	May–June	White	Flat, 2-3-in. clusters of creamy white flowers followed by blue-black fruit later in summer.
Long branches held horizontally give a very open effect. Has scaly, gray-brown bark. Dark green leaves turn scarlet in fall.	Mid-Apr.–May	White	Clusters of small, stamenlike florets are cupped by 4 wide petals (actually bracts) notched at their tips. Red berries follow in Sept.
Branches spread with age. Older bark flakes to reveal gray-brown patches. Dark green leaves are shiny on top.	May–June	White	Flower petals (bracts) are pointed, turn creamy pink as they persist for a month. Fruits are raspberrylike spheres, appearing from Aug.–Oct.

(continued)

Place of Origin	Zone	Plant Type	Mature Size	Shape

Cornus nuttallii   (KORE-nuss nut-AL-ee-eye)   PACIFIC DOGWOOD

| Northwest United States | 7 | Deciduous | 50 by 20 ft. | Conical, becoming pyramidal with age. |

Culture: Partial shade. Woodsy, well-drained soil. Likes to naturalize in favored habitats.
Comments: Plant as understory tree, as in nature. Dislikes summer waterings. Showy flowers make it a good specimen.

Cotinus coggygria   (ko-TYN-us ko-JIG-ree-ah)   SMOKE TREE

| Europe | 5 | Deciduous | 15 by 20 ft. | Upright, spreading, irregular. |

Culture: Full sun. Average soil.
Comments: Dramatic plant with very unusual appearance and color. Good in shrub and small tree borders.
Cultivar: 'Royal Purple', foliage appears wine red in spring changing to purple in summer.

Crataegus laevigata   (kra-TEEG-uss lee-vih-GATE-ah)   ENGLISH HAWTHORN

| Europe, North Africa | 4 | Deciduous | 15 by 20 ft. | Round, globelike. |

Culture: Full sun. Average to slightly alkaline soil.
Comments: Slow-growing, compact, pretty landscape tree in spring, summer, and fall.
Cultivars: 'Toba', hardy to Zone 3, flowers open white, turn rose; 'Crimson Cloud', red petals with white centers; 'Paula's Scarlet', rose red, sterile flowers.
Other Species: *C. nitida*, glossy hawthorn, ¾-in. white blossoms appear in clusters; *C. phaenopyrum*, Washington hawthorn, best for fall foliage color, red berries remain all winter; *C. viridis*, winter king hawthorn, features extra-persistent red berries.

Davidia involucrata   (da-VID-ee-ah in-vahl-you-KRAH-tah)   DOVE TREE, HANDKERCHIEF PLANT

| China | 6 | Deciduous | 30 by 40 ft. | Broad pyramid with rounded crown. |

Culture: Sun to light shade. Average soil.
Comments: Best displayed as a specimen against a grove of dark evergreens.

Plant Description	Season of Bloom	Flower Color	Flower and Fruit Description
The gray-barked branches are held horizontally. Single tree may form several trunks. Rich green leaves turn red and yellow in fall.	Apr.–May	White	Flowers with 4-8 creamy white petals (bracts) open early on bare branches, fade to pinkish blush. Clusters of shiny red-orange fruit follow.
Forms multiple stems with small, rounded, bluish-green leaves that turn yellow, red, and purplish in fall. Can be trained to single trunk.	July–Aug.	Pinkish or lavender-brown.	Flowers are not showy, but pedicels elongate and are covered with purplish-pink hairs that produce cloudlike puffs of color.
Glossy, dark green leaves borne on dense, spreading branches. Young plants carry thorns.	May	White	Small, ½-in. flowers appear profusely in clusters at branch tips. Crimson "haws," ½-in. scarlet berries, appear Sept.–Oct.
Neat tree with good-looking branches and heart-shaped leaves.	May	White	Small, reddish flowers appear with 2 large, but unequal, creamy white bracts; the top one is 3-4 in. across and the bottom one 6-7 in. The appearance is of white hankies (or doves) in the tree. 1½-in. brown fruit hangs on tree into winter.

(continued)

Place of Origin	Zone	Plant Type	Mature Size	Shape

Delonix regia (dih-LON-iks REE-jee-ah) POINCIANA

Place of Origin	Zone	Plant Type	Mature Size	Shape
Madagascar	10	Deciduous	20-30 ft. by 50-60 ft.	Rounded, spreading, umbrella-shaped.

Culture: Full sun. Average, sandy soil.
Comments: Southern Florida's showiest tree. A rapid grower that turns messy when pods fall.

Erythrina caffra (er-ih-THREE-nah KAF-rah) KAFFIRBOOM CORAL TREE

Place of Origin	Zone	Plant Type	Mature Size	Shape
South Africa	10	Deciduous	25 by 40 ft.	Broad, spreading.

Culture: Full sun. Moist, well-drained, average soil.
Comments: Flowers drip a watery sap. One of the largest erythrinas, with showiest bloom.
Other Species: *E. coralloides*, naked coral tree of Mexico, grows to 30 ft., fire-red candles bloom Mar.-May at ends of leafless, thorny branches; *E. crista-galli*, cockspur or coral bean tree of Brazil, grows to 20 ft., semi-evergreen, produces loose clusters of pink to burgundy flowers; *E. humeana*, natal coral tree, grows to 20 ft., clusters of orange-red flowers bloom Aug.-Nov., above heart-shaped leaves.

Eucalyptus ficifolia (you-kah-LIP-tus fiss-ih-FOAL-ee-ah) FLAME EUCALYPTUS

Place of Origin	Zone	Plant Type	Mature Size	Shape
Australia	9	Evergreen	30 by 30 ft.	Round, upright.

Culture: Full sun. Light, rich, well-drained soil. Outside of native habitat, likes San Francisco and California coast best.
Comments: Tolerates city stresses, but not frost. Showiest eucalyptus.
Other Species: *E. caesia*, smaller, growing to 20 ft., needs staking and pruning to maintain its graceful, weeping habit, offers dusty pink to deep rose flower clusters in Feb.-Apr.; *E. erythrocorys*, red-cap gum, reaches 25 ft., red calyxes tip up and drop to show gold flowers in winter; *E. leucoxylon* 'Rosea', small, very ornamental tree with crimson flowers; *E. pyriformis*, pear-fruited mallee, grows to 20 ft., 2-3-in. red, pink, orange, yellow, and cream flowers bloom sporadically from late winter to early summer; *E. sideroxylon*, red illyarie, the largest at 60 ft., pendulous clusters of pale to dark pink flowers bloom sporadically from fall to spring, specimens with darkest leaves have darkest flower colors; *E. torquata*, coral gum, reaches only 20 ft., coral buds open to red flowers all year.

Evodia danielii (eh-VOH-dee-ah dan-YELL-ee-eye) KOREAN EVODIA, BEE TREE, BB TREE

Place of Origin	Zone	Plant Type	Mature Size	Shape
Northern China, Korea	5	Deciduous	25 by 25 ft.	Upright, rounded.

Culture: Full sun. Average soil.
Comments: Blooms when few other trees are flowering. Bees love blossoms.

Plant Description	Season of Bloom	Flower Color	Flower and Fruit Description
Graceful, fine-textured, compound fronds 2 ft. long make dense foliage mass on wide-spreading branches.	June–July	Red	Huge clusters of 3-4-in. scarlet flowers engulf the tree for 6 weeks. Bloom followed by 2 ft. long, brown seed pods that hang for months.
Light green, compound leaves have 3 leaflets. Trunk and branches are sturdy, with gray-brown bark. Thorns of youth disappear with age.	Jan.–Feb.	Orange-red	Fiery, 2-in., tubular florets in clusters turn tree to flame just after leaves fall around year's end. 4-in. pods contain poisonous red seeds.
6-in., dark reddish-green leaves make tree resemble ficus, the common houseplant. Dense, thickly branched, with brown-gray, coarse, furrowed bark. Slow-growing.	July–Aug.	Red	Showy clusters of 6 or 7 red to pink flowers sporadically engulf areas of tree in summer. Fruits are thick, woody cups that persist on tree.
Open, airy arrangements of dark green compound leaves. Quick-growing, shrubby wood.	Late July–Aug.	White	Clusters of small flowers soon followed by shiny red and black berries.

(continued)

Place of Origin	Zone	Plant Type	Mature Size	Shape

Franklinia alatamaha   (frank-LIN-ee-ah ah-lat-ah-MAH-hah)   **FRANKLIN TREE**

Place of Origin	Zone	Plant Type	Mature Size	Shape
Southeastern United States	5	Deciduous	20 by 15 ft.	Upright, spreading.

    Culture: Full sun to partial shade. Protect from strong winds. Moist, well-drained, humusy soil. Likes a mulch within dripline.
    Comments: Found in the wild in Georgia by John Bartram and named after Benjamin Franklin. Disappeared from the wild in 1790.

Grevillea robusta   (greh-VIL-ee-ah ro-BUS-tah)   **SILK OAK**

Place of Origin	Zone	Plant Type	Mature Size	Shape
Australia	9	Evergreen	50 by 25 ft.	Pyramidal when young, becoming rounded and irregular.

    Culture: Full sun. Tolerates wide variety of soils, but must be well-drained.
    Comments: Flowers best inland in southern California and Florida. Good for quick screen while more substantial trees grow to size.

Halesia carolina   (HALE-zee-ah care-oh-LINE-ah)   **CAROLINA SILVERBELL**

Place of Origin	Zone	Plant Type	Mature Size	Shape
Southeastern United States	5	Deciduous	30 by 30 ft.	Pyramidal when young, turning round with age; has an upright profile.

    Culture: Full sun to partial shade. Rich, humusy, well-drained soil.
    Comments: An understory tree of southern mountain slopes. Looks good in natural, woodsy setting. Flower display lasts only a week, but worth it.
    Other Species: *H. monticola* 'Rosea', grows to 40 ft. with large, pale pink flowers.

Jacaranda mimosifolia   (also called ***J. acutifolia***) (jack-ar-AN-dah mih-mohs-ih-FOAL-ee-ah)
    JACARANDA

Place of Origin	Zone	Plant Type	Mature Size	Shape
Brazil	10	Semi-evergreen	30 by 20 ft.	Open, irregular, rounded.

    Culture: Full sun to light shade. Average, sandy soil. Withstands drought.
    Comments: Good for hot climates. Give it a sheltered spot out of the wind.

Plant Description	Season of Bloom	Flower Color	Flower and Fruit Description
6-in., glossy green leaves, loose and open, turn a leathery red to red-orange in fall. Slender branches have gray-brown bark.	Aug.-Sept.	White	White flower buds look like big marbles, open a few at a time to 5-petalled white cups holding center spray of yellow stamens. Strikingly beautiful when last blooms displayed against red leaves.
Dark green, fernlike leaves are silvery beneath. Wood very fast growing, but soft and weak.	Apr.	Orange-yellow	6-in. sprays of soft golden yellow flower spikes bloom in early spring.
Leaves dull yellow-green, turn soft gold in fall. Several stems form clumps with upright branches. Gray bark.	Late Apr.-Early May	White	Strings of 1-in. bells hang prettily beneath new leaves. Light brown, winged seedpods sought by squirrels.
Finely divided, mimosalike foliage drops for short period in Feb. Brittle, often multi-trunked wood needs protection, and staking when young.	May-July	Lavender-blue	Fragrant clusters of 2-in. tubular flowers make spectacular display. Flat seed capsules used in dried arrangements.

(continued)

Place of Origin	Zone	Plant Type	Mature Size	Shape

Koelreuteria paniculata   (koal-roy-TEER-ee-ah pan-ik-you-LAH-tah)   **GOLDEN-RAIN TREE**

Place of Origin	Zone	Plant Type	Mature Size	Shape
China, Korea	5	Deciduous	30 by 30 ft.	Rounded, open, flat-topped with age.

Culture: Full sun to partial shade. Tolerates widely varying soils, city conditions.
Comments: Prune to shape when half-grown. Gorgeous specimen for landscape transition.
Cultivar: 'September', small lawn tree produces masses of yellow flowers in Sept.

Laburnum ×watereri   'Vossii'   (la-BER-num WAH-ter-er-eye VAWS-ee-eye)   **GOLDEN-CHAIN TREE**

Place of Origin	Zone	Plant Type	Mature Size	Shape
Europe	5	Deciduous	20 by 15 ft.	Upright, vase-shaped.

Culture: Full sun to light shade. Average soil. Give sheltered position away from winds.
Comments: Flower clusters resemble golden wisteria. Effective lining walkway, trained to arch overhead.

Lagerstroemia indica   (lah-ger-STREEM-ee-ah IN-dih-kah)   **CRAPE MYRTLE**

Place of Origin	Zone	Plant Type	Mature Size	Shape
China, Korea	7	Deciduous	20 by 15 ft.	Upright, open, rounded.

Culture: Full sun. Dry, sandy soils. Moist coastal conditions cause mildews.
Comments: Can be grown in tubs. Prune regularly when dormant to increase flowering.
Cultivars: Many cultivars available in wide range of colors and sizes.

Leptospermum laevigatum   (lep-toe-SPER-mum lee-vih-GATE-um)   **AUSTRALIAN TEA TREE**

Place of Origin	Zone	Plant Type	Mature Size	Shape
Australia	9	Evergreen	30 by 25 ft.	Upright, twisted, sprawling.

Culture: Full sun. Well-drained, sandy, acid soil.
Comments: The artistic sculpture of the trunks and masses of early flowers make this a favorite of the California coast. Good as hedge or specimen tree.

Magnolia ×'Betty'   (mag-NOLE-ee-ah)   **LITTLE GIRL HYBRID MAGNOLIA**

Place of Origin	Zone	Plant Type	Mature Size	Shape
Hybrid origin	4	Deciduous	10 by 15 ft.	Rounded, multi-stemmed.

Culture: Full sun to partial shade. Deep, humusy, well-drained soil.
Comments: This is one of the Kosar-Devos hybrids called "The Eight Little Girls," developed at the National Arboretum. Ideal for small gardens.
Other Cultivars: The rest of the Little Girl Hybrid magnolia series includes: 'Ann', earliest of the Little Girls to bloom; 'Jane', slow-growing and the last to flower; 'Judy', reddish-purple, 3-in. flowers; 'Pinkie', light pink flowers; 'Randi', slow-growing with rose-purple flowers; 'Ricki', extra-large rose, lavender, and white flowers; 'Susan', 6-in., red-purple flowers with slightly twisted petals.

Plant Description	Season of Bloom	Flower Color	Flower and Fruit Description
Large, compound leaves with up to 15 toothed, oval leaflets on an open-branched structure.	July	Yellow	Soft yellow flowers in very showy, upright, fragrant, 1-ft. clusters that appear over the foliage masses. Papery husks contain hard black seeds.
2-in. leaves form dense foliage on compact, upright structure. Young bark is smooth and green; older bark is brown.	May	Yellow	Beautifully hung with 1½-ft., slender panicles of rich golden yellow, pea-shaped flowers. Dull brown, 2-in., flat seedpods are poisonous.
Small, oval, glossy, dark green leaves make dense upper foliage. May be multi-trunked or pruned to single trunk. Multitrunked specimens' bark, mottled red and gray, provides winter interest.	July–Sept.	Red, pink, lavender, or white	Electric, varied colors of red and pink on crepe-paper petals held in round clusters above foliage. More profuse on multitrunked trees.
Tiny, stiff, dull, dark green leaves appear along twisty, sinuously curved, gray-brown trunks with shaggy bark.	Feb.–Apr.	White	Masses of ½-in. white blossoms cover the tree in late winter and early spring.
A shrubby habit with smooth, 4-in. leaves and silver-gray bark.	Mid-Apr., sporadic throughout summer.	White	Upright, red-purple buds open into white, lightly fragrant, 8-in. flowers.

(continued)

Place of Origin	Zone	Plant Type	Mature Size	Shape

Magnolia grandiflora   (mag-NOLE-ee-ah grand-ih-FLOR-ah)   SOUTHERN MAGNOLIA

Place of Origin	Zone	Plant Type	Mature Size	Shape
Southeastern United States	7	Evergreen	40-80 ft. by 25-40 ft.	Pyramidal.

Culture: Full sun to partial shade. Deep, humusy, well-drained soil.
Comments: From May–Sept., fallen leaves and seeds need tidying up.
Cultivars: 'Baby Doll', a miniature form; 'Cairo', extra-shiny leaves; 'Delilah', 12-in. flowers; 'Harold Poole', choice compact version with narrow leaves; 'St. Mary', compact and blooms while young; 'Victoria', hardiness allows use in Pacific Northwest.

Magnolia heptapeta   (mag-NOLE-ee-ah hep-ta-PET-ah)   YULAN MAGNOLIA

Place of Origin	Zone	Plant Type	Mature Size	Shape
China	5	Deciduous	35 by 30 ft.	Rounded.

Culture: Full sun to partial shade. Deep, humusy, well-drained soil.
Comments: The oldest cultivated magnolia, it graced the temple gardens of ancient China.
Cultivars: 'Moon Garden', pure white, fragrant flowers; 'Purpurescens', rose red on outside, pink on inside; 'Lacey', large white flowers measure 8 in. across.

Magnolia ×loebneri   'Merrill'   (mag-NOLE-ee-ah LOBE-ner-eye)   MERRILL'S MAGNOLIA

Place of Origin	Zone	Plant Type	Mature Size	Shape
Hybrid origin	4	Deciduous	20-30 ft. by 20-35 ft.	Spreading, round-topped to pyramidal.

Culture: Full sun to partial shade. Deep, humusy, well-drained soil.
Comments: Reliably hardy, free-flowering (at 5 years old) and pretty, this magnolia should be more widely planted in Zones 5 and 6.

Magnolia ×soulangiana   (mag-NOLE-ee-ah sue-lan-jee-AN-ah)   SAUCER MAGNOLIA

Place of Origin	Zone	Plant Type	Mature Size	Shape
Hybrid origin	5	Deciduous	20-30 ft. by 15-25 ft.	Rounded, spreading.

Culture: Full sun to partial shade. Deep, humusy, well-drained soil.
Comments: The most popular, widely planted magnolia in the North; flowers often ruined by late frosts; keep roots shaded.
Cultivars: 'Alba Superba', fragrant white flowers are tinged with purple; 'Alexandrina', large, early-flowering type; 'Burgundy', early red-purple flowers; 'Lennei', Large, wine red flowers; 'San Jose', rosy purple flowers; 'Samuel Sommer', creamy white flowers measure up to 14 in.

Plant Description	Season of Bloom	Flower Color	Flower and Fruit Description
Large, leathery leaves, shiny above and russet beneath, give a rather coarse texture and tropical look to the tree, which otherwise is grand and dignified. The bark is brownish-gray.	Apr.-Aug.	White	Large, showy, 10-in. flowers with waxy white petals have a sweet, citrusy scent.
Tree becomes ever rounder and more floriferous with age. 4-8-in. leaves are pointed, dark green above, lighter green and slightly downy beneath.	Apr.	White	Large, shaggy flower buds open to extremely fragrant, white, 3-in., chalice-shaped flowers.
Glossy, 4-in. foliage decorates the dark brown, spreading limbs and twigs.	Mid-Apr.	White	Similar in color to *M. stellata*, one of its parents, with its pinkish tinge to the base of the petals.
Spreading limbs hold buds covered with brown fuzz during the winter. Leaves are long, glossy, exotic-looking in northern gardens.	Apr.	White	Large, saucer-shaped, and slightly fragrant flowers open white with pink to mauve tinge around petal base.

(continued)

Place of Origin	Zone	Plant Type	Mature Size	Shape

Magnolia stellata (mag-NOLE-ee-ah stell-AH-tah) STAR MAGNOLIA

Japan	4	Deciduous	20 by 15 ft.	Rounded, spreading.

Culture: Full sun to partial shade. Deep, humusy, well-drained soil.
Comments: In areas of heavy frost, plant out of full sun to help delay bud burst.
Cultivars: 'Centennial', 5-in., pink-tinged blossoms; 'Rosea', pink flowers fade to white; 'Royal Star', white blossoms, blooms 2 weeks later than the species; 'Water Lily', very fragrant, pink buds open to large white flowers.

Magnolia virginiana (mag-NOLE-ee-ah ver-jin-ee-AHN-ah) SWEET BAY MAGNOLIA

Eastern United States	5	Deciduous in North; semi-evergreen in South.	25 by 15 ft. in North; to 60 ft. tall in South.	Irregular, spreading.

Culture: Full sun to partial shade. Likes wet soil.
Comments: Flowers sparse when young. Silver-bellied leaves shimmer in the wind. Good for swampy area.

Malus baccata var. *mandshurica* (MAL-us ba-KAH-tah mand-SURE-ick-ah) SIBERIAN CRABAPPLE

East Asia	3	Deciduous	35 by 30 ft.	Upright, spreading.

Culture: Full sun. Well-drained, slightly acid soil.
Comments: Earliest of the crabapples and one of the hardiest.

Malus floribunda (MAL-us flor-ih-BUN-dah) JAPANESE FLOWERING CRABAPPLE

Japan	4	Deciduous	25 by 30 ft.	Rounded.

Culture: Full sun. Average, well-drained soil.
Comments: Vigorous grower, blooms at an early age. One of the first crabapples in cultivation.

Plant Description	Season of Bloom	Flower Color	Flower and Fruit Description
Multibranched, compact, shrublike tree with a spreading habit. Dark green leaves give a medium texture. Slow-growing.	Apr.	White	3-in., fragrant, multipetalled starbursts appear singly but profusely over the bare branches in early spring.
Multistemmed tree with gray bark. Has shrubby habit in the North. Handsome foliage wherever it grows.	June–Sept.	White	2-3-in., citrus-scented flowers, borne singly and never in profusion along green twigs over several months. Leaves and flowers appear together.
Dense, bright green foliage with no autumn color. Upright habit in youth, becoming rounded with age. Fast-growing.	Mid-Apr.	White	Masses of fragrant, white, 1 in. wide blossoms fill the tree. Fruit is dull red, ½ in. in diameter.
Fine-textured, bright green leaves are massed in a spreading mound. No autumn color. Grayish, scaly bark.	Apr.–May.	White	Red-pink buds open as large, 1½-in., fragrant, white blossoms to smother the tree in spring bloom. Fruit measures ½ in. or slightly less, comes in yellow and red.

(continued)

Place of Origin	Zone	Plant Type	Mature Size	Shape

Malus hupehensis (MAL-us hoo-pah-HEN-sis)   **TEA CRABAPPLE**

China	4	Deciduous	20 by 20 ft.	Upright, vase-shaped, irregular.

Culture: Full sun. Average, well-drained soil.
Comments: Flower-covered branches thrust up and out from trunk. Flowers in alternate years.

Malus ×'Red Jade' (MAL-us)   **RED JADE CRABAPPLE**

Hybrid origin	4	Deciduous	20 by 25 ft.	Pendulous.

Culture: Full sun. Average, well-drained soil.
Comments: Sinuous branching habit and late-hanging, cherry red fruit make this variety worth growing. Blooms in alternate years.

Malus sargentii (MAL-us sar-JENT-ee-eye)   **SARGENT CRABAPPLE**

Japan	4	Deciduous	8 by 15 ft.	Spreading, shrubby tree.

Culture: Full sun. Average, well-drained soil.
Comments: As much a shrub as a tree. Bears annually, but makes a big display every other year.

Malus ×zumi 'Calocarpa' (MAL-us ZOO-mee cal-oh-CAR-pah)   **REDBUD CRABAPPLE**

Hybrid origin	4	Deciduous	20 by 20 ft.	Rounded, spreading.

Culture: Full sun. Average, well-drained soil.
Comments: Bears alternate years. Very ornamental late in the year.

Melaleuca linariifolia (Mel-ah-LEW-kah lin-AR-ee-eye-FOAL-ee-ah)   **SNOW-IN-SUMMER, FLAXLEAF PAPERBARK**

Australia	9	Evergreen	25 by 20 ft.	Upright, open, columnar when young; rounded and dense in maturity.

Culture: Full sun. Average soil. Tolerates moist to dry conditions.
Comments: A slow-growing tree with a unique texture and a dazzling display of summer flowers.

Plant Description	Season of Bloom	Flower Color	Flower and Fruit Description
Young foliage is purplish, changes to dark green when mature. Autumn color is coppery yellow. Scaly, gray-brown bark.	May	White	Soft pink buds open to fragrant white or pale pink blossoms, 1½ in. wide along length of branches. Fruit is ½ in., greenish-yellow to red, inconspicuous, not ornamental.
Bright green leaves hang from weeping, sinuous twigs and branches. Bark is brownish-gray.	May	White	Named for its dramatic ½-in., bright red fruit. Flowers open white from pink buds. A particularly showy crabapple.
Densely branched and twiggy multistemmed form. Dark green leaves turn orange in fall. Bark dark gray-brown.	May	White	Light pink buds open to small, fragrant white flowers that cover the tree. Dark red, shiny, ½-in. fruit hangs well into autumn.
Medium green leaves give fine effect. Grayish-tan bark.	May	White	Pink buds open to 1 in., fragrant, single flowers. Bright red, ½-in. fruit hangs well into winter.
Blue-green, needlelike leaves on pale tan twigs. Young bark is whitish and spongy, turning amber brown and peeling with age.	July–Sept.	White	Creamy white spikes of fuzzy florets cover the entire tree in midsummer. Flowers mature into cup-shaped fruits that stay on branches for years.

(continued)

Place of Origin	Zone	Plant Type	Mature Size	Shape

Oxydendrum arboreum   (ox-ee-DEN-drum ar-BOAR-ee-um)   SOURWOOD

Place of Origin	Zone	Plant Type	Mature Size	Shape
Eastern United States	7	Deciduous	30 by 15 ft.	Slender, pyramidal, upright.

Culture: Full sun to partial shade. Rich, acidic, peaty soil. Prefers cool summer conditions.
Comments: Showy in all seasons, and gives an oriental effect when planted in groups.

Parrotia persica   (par-OAT-ee-ah PER-sik-ah)   PERSIAN PARROTIA

Place of Origin	Zone	Plant Type	Mature Size	Shape
Iran	5	Deciduous	35 by 25 ft.	Upright, rounded.

Culture: Full sun in North; light shade in hot regions. Average, well-drained soil.
Comments: Easy to grow, pest-free, and interesting in all seasons.

Paulownia tomentosa   (paw-LOW-nee-ah toe-men-TOE-sah)   EMPRESS TREE

Place of Origin	Zone	Plant Type	Mature Size	Shape
China	6	Deciduous	30-40 ft. by 30-40 ft.	Rounded.

Culture: Full sun. Average, well-drained soil.
Comments: A trashy tree, always sending down detritus. Dense shade and surface roots preclude gardening beneath it.

Prunus cerasifera   'Thundercloud'   (PROO-nuss sara-SIFF-er-ah)   PURPLE PLUM, MYROBALAN PLUM

Place of Origin	Zone	Plant Type	Mature Size	Shape
Asia	4	Deciduous	25 by 20 ft.	Rounded, upright.

Culture: Full sun. Average, well-drained soil.
Comments: Excellent for bloom, and for purplish foliage in summer.

Prunus × 'Hally Jolivette'   (PROO-nuss HAL-ee jo-liv-ET)   HALLY JOLIVETTE CHERRY

Place of Origin	Zone	Plant Type	Mature Size	Shape
Hybrid origin	5	Deciduous	15 by 20 ft.	Rounded.

Culture: Full sun. Average, well-drained soil.
Comments: Hot weather shortens (and cool weather lengthens) its long blooming time.

Plant Description	Season of Bloom	Flower Color	Flower and Fruit Description
Shiny, leathery, dark green, narrow leaves on drooping branches turn rich red to rich plum purple in fall.	June	White	Fragrant clusters of bell-shaped florets arranged in graceful 7-10-in. panicles, followed by hanging racemes of greenish capsules persisting into winter.
Leaves are reddish when they first appear, then turn shiny green. Leaves measure 3-4 in. long. Scaly, flaking bark shows attractive patches of green, gray, white, and brown on multistemmed trunks.	Mar.-Apr.	Red	Showy red stamens held in fuzzy brown bracts cluster in dense heads before leaves appear. Brilliant yellow, orange, and scarlet leaf color in fall.
Large catalpalike leaves on fast-growing brittle wood throw a dense shade.	Mid-May	Violet	8-10-in. pyramidal clusters of 2-in., violet-blue trumpets appear before the leaves.
Garnet-purple leaves retain color all summer. Reddish-brown bark has big horizontal lenticels.	Apr.	White	¾-in. white flowers are massed on branches before the leaves appear. Few plums are produced.
Narrow, fine-textured, medium-green leaves are held on densely branched structure. Dull gray-brown bark. Yellow foliage in fall.	May	White	Pinkish buds open consecutively over 2 to 3 weeks, producing 1¼-in. double flowers.

(continued)

Place of Origin	Zone	Plant Type	Mature Size	Shape

Prunus × *'Okame'*   (PROO-nuss oh-KAHM-ee)   **OKAME CHERRY**

Place of Origin	Zone	Plant Type	Mature Size	Shape
Hybrid origin	5	Deciduous	20-25 ft. by 10-15 ft.	Upright, compact.

Culture: Full sun. Average, well-drained soil.
Comments: Because of short spread and good height, useful in small spaces.

Prunus sargentii   (PROO-nuss sar-JENT-ee-eye)   **SARGENT CHERRY**

Place of Origin	Zone	Plant Type	Mature Size	Shape
Japan	4	Deciduous	40 by 40 ft.	Upright, rounded, symmetrical.

Culture: Full sun. Average, well-drained soil.
Comments: Gets to be a big tree, so give it room.

Prunus serrulata   'Shogetsu'   (PROO-nuss sair-oo-LAHT-ah show-GET-soo)   **JAPANESE FLOWERING CHERRY**

Place of Origin	Zone	Plant Type	Mature Size	Shape
Japan	6	Deciduous	15 by 20 ft.	Flat-topped, spreading.

Culture: Full sun. Average, well-drained soil.
Comments: Especially showy and lovely cultivar of oriental cherry. Among those varieties planted along Washington D.C.'s Tidal Basin drive. Late-season bloomer.
Other Cultivars: 'Amanogawa', ¾-in., shell pink, semidouble flowers, mid-season; 'Kwanzan', 2-in., deep pink, very double flowers, mid-season; 'Shirofugen', pink buds open to white blooms, late season; 'Shirotae', fragrant, white, semidouble, nodding blooms, mid-season.

Prunus subhirtella   'Pendula'   (PROO-nuss sub-her-TELL-ah PEN-dew-lah)   **WEEPING HIGAN CHERRY**

Place of Origin	Zone	Plant Type	Mature Size	Shape
Japan	6	Deciduous	25 by 25 ft.	Spreading, weeping.

Culture: Full sun. Average, well-drained soil.
Comments: The most popular of all the weeping Japanese cherries.
Other Cultivars: 'Autumnalis', pink and white, semidouble flowers spring and fall; 'Yae-shidare-higa', double-flowered form of 'Pendula'.

Plant Description	Season of Bloom	Flower Color	Flower and Fruit Description
Narrow, graceful leaves arranged on vertical branch structure. Choice satiny, chestnut brown bark with large horizontal lenticels.	Apr.	Pink	Maroon buds open to light pink flowers, which last a week. Red calyxes that cup flowers persist for several weeks after petals fall.
Young foliage is bronze, then turns deep green, before turning orange to red in fall. Tree throws dense shade in full leaf. Young bark a satiny, mahogany brown.	Apr.-May	Pink	1½-in., deep pink, single flowers are held in small clusters on slender stems.
Stays low, with deep green leaves, dense shade. Bark is dark gray-brown. Fast-growing.	May	Pink	2-in. flowers, very double and pink on margins with white centers. Blossoms cover the tree before leaves appear.
The weeping branches are usually grafted to the top of a 6-ft. trunk, growing upward, outward, and downward over time.	Apr.	Pink	Single, pale pink flowers mass along the slender branches, giving a fountain effect.

(continued)

Place of Origin	Zone	Plant Type	Mature Size	Shape

Prunus yedoensis   (PROO-nuss yed-oh-EN-sis)   YOSHINO CHERRY

| Japan | 5 | Deciduous | 35 by 30 ft. | Upright, rounded, spreading. |

Culture: Full sun. Average, well-drained soil.
Comments: A variety planted along Washington D.C.'s Tidal Basin. Very floriferous and early.

Pterostyrax hispidus   (tehr-oh-STY-raks HISS-pid-us)   EPAULETTE TREE

| Japan | 5 | Deciduous | 25-35 ft. by 25-35 ft. | Rounded, low-branching. |

Culture: Full sun. Moist, sandy, slightly acid soil.
Comments: An attention-getting plant for landscape transitions.

Pyrus calleryana   (PY-russ kal-er-ee-AN-ah)   CALLERY PEAR

| China | 6 | Deciduous | 30 by 20 ft. | Rounded, upright. |

Culture: Full sun. Tolerates dry, city conditions and a wide range of soils.
Comments: A trouble-free early bloomer often used in commercial settings.
Cultivars: 'Aristocrat', leaves are shinier, darker green than the species; 'Bradford', Bradford pear, thornless form of familiar street tree; 'Capital', narrow, upright, to 15 ft.; 'Chanticleer', thornless and very formal, with an upright form; 'Fauriei', more compact (to 25 ft.) Bradford type; 'Redspire', narrow, oval shape with flowers larger than usual ⅓ in.; 'Select', choice for its pretty form.

Pyrus kawakamii   (PY-russ ka-wa-KAHM-ee-EYE)   EVERGREEN PEAR

| Taiwan | 9 | Evergreen | 25 by 20 ft. | Upright, open, irregular. |

Culture: Full sun. Average, well-drained soil.
Comments: Widely used in California. Good container plant. Needs yearly pruning.

Pyrus salicifolia   'Pendula'   (PY-russ sal-iss-ih-FOAL-ee-ah PEN-dew-lah)   SILVER FROST WEEPING PEAR

| Southeast Europe | 5 | Deciduous | 20 by 15 ft. | Upright, pyramidal, weeping. |

Culture: Full sun. Average, well-drained soil.
Comments: As beautiful out of flower as in. Use in the shrub border or as specimen.

Plant Description	Season of Bloom	Flower Color	Flower and Fruit Description
Fast growth and dense foliage give a quick, deep shade. Trunk and branches show pleasing shape.	Apr.	White	Pale pink buds open to lightly almond-scented, 1-in., single white flowers appearing before the leaves. Birds eat small, black fruit.
Leaves 3-7 in. long, light green above, silvery beneath. Open branching habit.	June	White	Fragrant, creamy white tufted flowers in drooping 9-in. panicles that are said to resemble braided epaulettes on military uniforms.
Glossy leaves emerge with flowers in spring, turn scarlet to purple in fall. Gray bark and sturdy, neat limbs spread with maturity.	Apr.	White	Dainty, white, 1/3-in. flowers are held in 3-in. bouquets over entire tree. No fruit.
Glossy, light green, wavy-edged leaves. Branch ends droop. Forms a thicket if unpruned. Most often pruned to one or a few trunks.	Feb.-Apr.	White	Flowers appear from Nov. on, but mass over tree in late winter to early spring. 1/2-in. red fruit appear in fall.
Graceful, silver-gray, willowlike leaves arrayed on pendulous, curving branches.	Apr.	White	3/4-in., pure white flowers open lightly along the drooping branches as the leaves emerge. 1-in. yellowish fruit of no culinary value.

(continued)

Place of Origin	Zone	Plant Type	Mature Size	Shape

Pyrus ussuriensis   (PY-russ you-SUR-ee-en-sis)   USSURIAN PEAR

Northern China	4	Deciduous	30-40 ft. by 30-40 ft.	Upright, rounded, spreading.

Culture: Full sun. Tolerates wide range of soils, but does best in average loam.
Comments: Vigorous, resistant to pests and fireblight, maintenance-free.

Robinia pseudoacacia   (ro-BIN-ee-ah su-doe-ah-KAY-shah)   BLACK LOCUST

Eastern United States	3	Deciduous	40 by 25 ft.	Upright, sparsely branched, open.

Culture: Full sun. Tolerates most conditions, soils.
Comments: Not for most home landscapes because of invasive, suckering roots, pests, and litter. Good for difficult, inaccessible, or semiarid conditions.

Sophora japonica   (SOF-or-ah ja-PON-ih-kah)   JAPANESE PAGODA TREE

China, Korea	5	Deciduous	50 by 50 ft.	Rounded, spreading.

Culture: Full sun to partial shade. Average soil.
Comments: Tolerant of city life, withstands heat and drought. Floppy growth. One of the last of the big landscape trees to flower.
Cultivar: 'Pendula', an attractive, pendulous form, but with sparse, infrequent flowering.

Sorbus alnifolia   (SOAR-bis all-nih-FOAL-ee-ah)   KOREAN MOUNTAIN ASH

China, Korea, Japan	3	Deciduous	40 by 35 ft.	Pyramidal.

Culture: Full sun. Average, well-drained soil.
Comments: Resistant to the borers that afflict European mountain ash.

Sorbus aucuparia   (SOAR-bis awk-you-PAIR-ee-ah)   EUROPEAN MOUNTAIN ASH, ROWAN TREE

Europe	3	Deciduous	30 by 30 ft.	Upright, round, spreading.

Culture: Full sun. Moist, acid, well-drained soil.
Comments: A pretty tree for fall with fruit that birds love. Susceptible to borers and scale. One of the mystical trees of ancient Celtic Druids.
Cultivars: 'Apricot Queen', apricot berries; 'Brilliant Pink', pink berries; 'Carpet of Gold', yellow-orange berries; 'Scarlet King', scarlet berries; 'Xanthocarpa', amber-yellow berries.

Plant Description	Season of Bloom	Flower Color	Flower and Fruit Description
Glossy, dark green leaves turn red to reddish-purple in fall. Becomes large, sturdy tree with wide branches.	May	White	Light pink buds open to showy white flowers. 1½ in. long fruit inedible.
Feathery, gray-green foliage turns dark green over the season. Often multitrunked. Bark is thorny, thick, rough, and deeply channelled.	May-June	Magenta	Long, hanging clusters of magenta to rose, pealike flowers carry light vanilla scent. Flat brown pods hang on tree during winter.
Dark green foliage on wide-spreading, dense branches that grow near ground.	July-Aug.	Creamy white	After 8-10 years, many upright, pyramidal clusters of yellowish-white, pea-shaped flowers appear and open all at once. 3 in. long fruit pods turn from green to yellow to brown.
Shiny, bright green leaves turn orange-red in autumn, and resemble beech leaves. Bark is smooth, gray.	May	White	Flowers ½-¾ in., held in bouquets of 6-10, are not showy. Eye-catching clusters of scarlet berries appear in late summer, fall.
Dull green leaves, gray underneath, turn red-orange to deep red in autumn. Sturdy frame, dense crown.	May	White	Creamy white florets in 3-5-in. clusters are not an outstanding feature. Grown more for the showy clusters of orange-red berries in Sept.

(continued)

Place of Origin	Zone	Plant Type	Mature Size	Shape

Stenocarpus sinuatus   (sten-oh-KAR-pus sin-you-AH-tus)   FIREWHEEL TREE

Place of Origin	Zone	Plant Type	Mature Size	Shape
Australia	10	Evergreen	30 by 15 ft.	Narrow, upright.

Culture: Full sun to partial shade. Deep, rich, moist, well-drained, acid soil.
Comments: Striking flowers make it a good specimen tree in the lawn.

Stewartia pseudocamellia   (stu-ART-ee-ah sue-doe-ka-MEEL-ee-ah)   JAPANESE STEWARTIA

Place of Origin	Zone	Plant Type	Mature Size	Shape
Japan	6	Deciduous	40 by 30 ft.	Upright, pyramidal.

Culture: Semishade with morning sun in South; full sun in North. Moist, acid, humusy, woodland-type soil.
Comments: Good appearance in all seasons due to choice bark, flowers, fall foliage.
Other Species: *S. koreana*, Korean stewartia, compact grower, reaching to 20 ft., less colorful bark, but more colorful fall foliage color than *S. pseudocamellia*; *S. monadelpha*, to 60 ft., white flowers have violet stamens; *S. ovata* 'Grandiflora', small stewartia, growing to 15 ft., shrubby and lacks mottled bark, 4-in. white flowers have lavender stamens.

Styrax japonicus   (STY-raks ja-PON-ih-kus)   JAPANESE SNOWBELL

Place of Origin	Zone	Plant Type	Mature Size	Shape
China, Japan	5	Deciduous	20-30 ft. by 20-40 ft.	Broad, spreading.

Culture: Full sun to light shade. Rich, moist, humusy, well-drained soil.
Comments: One of the most graceful and prettiest of small trees, especially when viewed from below. Plant along steep steps.
Cultivars: 'Pendula', weeping form; 'Rosea', pink blooms.

Styrax obassia   (STY-raks oh-BASS-ee-ah)   FRAGRANT SNOWBELL

Place of Origin	Zone	Plant Type	Mature Size	Shape
China, Japan	6	Deciduous	25 by 20 ft.	Upright, rounded.

Culture: Full sun to light shade. Rich, moist, humusy, well-drained soil.
Comments: Fragrant white racemes and large foliage make this a showy tree.

Plant Description	Season of Bloom	Flower Color	Flower and Fruit Description
Dense, shiny, rich green leaves 8-10 in. long and lobed when tree is young, smaller and unlobed when mature. Slow-growing.	Sporadically throughout autumn.	Red and yellow	Clusters of 12 or more striking, tubular, 2-3-in., fiery-colored flowers arrayed in clusters like radiating spokes of a wheel.
Leaves 3 in. long with elliptical shape. Dark green foliage turns to red, yellow, or purple in fall. Bark of major interest, mottled like sycamore in patches of gray, beige, and silver, and red and yellow ochres.	June-July	White	2½-in., camellialike, single white blossoms cup a puff of golden yellow stamens.
Rich green leaves, turn yellow in fall. Narrow trunk with wide, spreading branches.	June	White	Profusion of ¾-in., lightly fragrant, white bells hang beneath horizontal branches.
Large, handsome, light green leaves turn yellow in autumn. Bark reddish-gray-brown.	May-June	White	¾-in. fragrant flowers in 4-in. racemes droop from beneath large leaves.

(continued)

Place of Origin	Zone	Plant Type	Mature Size	Shape

Syringa reticulata   (sir-RING-gah reh-tick-you-LAH-tah)   **JAPANESE TREE LILAC**

Place of Origin	Zone	Plant Type	Mature Size	Shape
China	4	Deciduous	25 by 20 ft.	Upright, pyramidal, rounded with age.

Culture: Full sun. Well-drained, acid soil.
Comments: A hardy tree that withstands drought. A Victorian favorite. Makes good specimen.
Cultivar: 'Mandshurica', rises to 12 ft., leaves and flowers are smaller than on species.

Tabebuia chrysotricha   (ta-beh-BEW-ee-ah kry-so-TRY-kah)   **GOLDEN TRUMPET TREE**

Place of Origin	Zone	Plant Type	Mature Size	Shape
Brazil	9	Semi-evergreen	20 by 20 ft.	Rounded, spreading.

Culture: Full sun. Rich, well-drained soil.
Comments: Spectacular flowers. Blooms while still young. Protect from wind.
Other Species: *T. impetiginosa*, rose-purple flowers.

Xanthoceras sorbifolium   (zan-tho-SEAR-us sorb-ih-FOAL-ee-um)   **YELLOWHORN**

Place of Origin	Zone	Plant Type	Mature Size	Shape
Northern China	5	Deciduous	20 by 20 ft.	Upright, shrubby.

Culture: Full sun to light shade. Rich, well-drained soil.
Comments: An interesting tree for landscape transition, conversation piece.

Plant Description	Season of Bloom	Flower Color	Flower and Fruit Description
Leaves dark green with gray-green undersides. Slender trunk, or multitrunks, have lustrous bark.	June	White	Loose, creamy white pyramids of florets, from 6-12 in. tall and nearly as wide. Intense privetlike odor; best kept at a distance.
Compound leaves have 5 leaflets, 2-4 in., smooth above, fuzzy tan beneath. Spreading branches. Quick grower.	Apr.-May	Yellow	Tree blossoms with 3-4-in. golden yellow trumpets, often with burgundy stripes in the throat.
Glossy, rich green, compound leaves and stiff, upstanding branches.	Apr.	White	8-10-in. panicles of white flowers with a colorful spot at the base that changes from yellow to red as flowers age.

Place of Origin	Zone	Plant Type	Mature Size

Abelia ×grandiflora   (ah-BEE-lee-ah grand-ih-FLOR-ah)   BUSH ARBUTUS

Place of Origin	Zone	Plant Type	Mature Size
Garden origin	6	Evergreen in South; deciduous in North.	5 by 5 ft.

Culture: Sun to partial shade. Humusy, well-drained soil.
Comments: Frosts nip it to the ground in Zone 6, but regrows each year from roots, flowering on new growth. Makes a hedge plant in warm zones.
Cultivars: 'Edward Goucher', showy, deep pink flowers, Zone 7; 'Prostrata', grows to 2 ft., spreading.

Abeliophyllum distichum   (ah-BEE-lee-oh-FY-lum diss-TY-kum)   WHITE FORSYTHIA, KOREAN ABELIALEAF

Place of Origin	Zone	Plant Type	Mature Size
Korea	5	Deciduous	3-5 ft. by 3-5 ft.

Culture: Full sun to partial shade. Average, well-drained soil. Blooms on previous year's wood, so prune immediately after flowering.
Comments: Hardier and far less rank than forsythia. Makes a good, very early display.

Abutilon hybridum   (ah-BEW-till-on HY-brid-um)   FLOWERING MAPLE

Place of Origin	Zone	Plant Type	Mature Size
Hybrid origin	9	Evergreen	8 ft. by 8-10 ft.

Culture: Partial shade. Rich, moist, humusy, well-drained soil.
Comments: A good container plant; blooms all year in greenhouse.

Aesculus parviflora   (ESS-kew-lus par-vih-FLOR-ah)   BOTTLEBRUSH BUCKEYE

Place of Origin	Zone	Plant Type	Mature Size
Southeastern United States	5	Deciduous	8 by 15 ft.

Culture: Full sun to shade. Flowers best in sun, but will grow under trees. Humusy, moist, well-drained soil.
Comments: Spreads into large mound with age. Give it room to grow.
Cultivar: 'Rogers', 15-30-in. flower spikes bloom 2 weeks later than species.
Other Species: *A. pavia*, red buckeye, red blossoms in May, Zone 6; 'Atrosanguinea', dark red flowers; 'Humilis', prostrate form.

Alyogyne huegelii   (AL-ee-oh-jine hoo-GELL-ee-eye)   BLUE HIBISCUS

Place of Origin	Zone	Plant Type	Mature Size
Australia	9	Evergreen	6-8 ft. by 4 ft.

Culture: Full sun. Average, well-drained soil. Prune to prevent legginess.
Comments: The lovely, light violet-blue flowers are welcome through the seasons.

Shrub Description	Season of Bloom	Flower Color	Flower Description
½-in., glossy, oval leaves give medium-fine texture on dense, compact bush. Leaves reddish when new, bronze in winter.	July-frost	White to pink	Small clusters of ¾-in., tubular, lightly fragrant blossoms appear abundantly in leaf axils over long season.
Small, oval, blue-green leaves on a compact shrub with gently arching stems.	Apr.	White	½-in., forsythialike flowers open palest pink, soon fade to white with orange centers; clusters borne along length of leafless branches.
Medium green, large leaves resembling maple held delicately on upright, arching, open structure.	Apr.-June	White, pink, purple, yellow, red, or orange	Pretty, 2-3-in., bell-like flowers appear singly in axils, often hang below leaves.
5-7 dark green, 4-in. leaflets form fan-shaped leaves that turn yellow in fall. Spreads by advancing roots that send up suckers.	July	White	8-12-in., erect spikes are studded with slender white flowers, like bristles on a brush.
Deeply divided, coarse-textured leaves borne on upright stems; soft wood.	Intermittently throughout the year	Lilac-blue	Whorled petals form a flower 4-5 in. across. Flowers appear freely through the year, stay open several days on the bush.

(continued)

Place of Origin	Zone	Plant Type	Mature Size

Aralia elata   (ah-RAIL-ee-ah eh-LAH-tah)   **JAPANESE ANGELICA**

Northern China, Korea, Japan	4	Deciduous	20-40 ft. by 10-20 ft.

Culture: Full sun to partial shade. Average, well-drained soil.
Comments: Gives a tropical look in summer, and a stiff, spiny appearance in winter. Don't plant where bare feet will walk.
Other Species: *A. spinosa,* American angelica, native to eastern United States, compound leaves can reach 6 ft., flower clusters 3 ft., very spiny, clublike stems and branches.

Arbutus unedo 'Compacta'   (ar-BEW-tus you-NEED-oh)   **STRAWBERRY TREE**

Southern Europe	7	Evergreen	12-20 ft. by 12-20 ft.

Culture: Full sun to partial shade. Average, well-drained soil.
Comments: Flowers carry a sweet honey scent. Fruit not very appealing to taste.

AZALEA (See the chart, Rhododendrons and Azaleas, on page 236.)

Berberis darwinii   (BER-ber-iss dar-WIN-ee-eye)   **DARWIN BARBERRY**

Chile	8	Evergreen	5-7 ft. by 5-10 ft.

Culture: Full sun to shade. Moist, humusy, well-drained soil. Spreads by creeping stolons.
Comments: Showiest flowers among the barberries. Quickly reaches 3 ft., slower growing to 5 ft. Keep in check by root pruning.
Other Species: *B. koreana,* Korean barberry, Zone 5, 4-6 ft. tall. Showy yellow flowers appear in 3-4-in. racemes in May. Makes excellent thorny barrier hedge.

Brunfelsia pauciflora   'Floribunda'   (brun-FEL-zee-ah paw-sih-FLOR-ah flor-ih-BUN-dah)   **YESTERDAY-TODAY-AND-TOMORROW**

Brazil	8	Evergreen	3-6 ft. by 3-6 ft.

Culture: Partial shade to full sun. Moist, humusy, rich, well-drained, fertile soil. Prune to keep compact, as it grows tall in sheltered spots.
Comments: Excellent container plant; prune to shape when young.

Shrub Description	Season of Bloom	Flower Color	Flower Description
3-ft., dark green, glossy, compound leaves turn reddish-orange in fall. Slender, spiny stems arise from suckers.	July	White	Small white flowers occur in 1½-ft., showy, many-branched clusters.
Large bushy shrub or small tree when trained to a single trunk. Foliage gives fine-textured effect.	Oct.-Dec.	White	Urn-shaped, ¼-in. white flowers in pendulous clusters and round, prickly, ¾-in. strawberry red fruit hang on tree at same time.
¾-in., stiff, spiny leaves are darker green above, yellow-green beneath. Reddish stems are thorny, many-branched.	May	Yellow	4-in. pendant clusters of yellow blossoms tinged with red. ¼-in. berries are dark blue to plum red, favored by birds.
3-4-in., glossy, oval leaves make a medium-textured shrub; upright but compact.	May-June	Purple to white	Small clusters of tubular, 2-in. flowers open deep purple, turn light lavender their second day, and white their third day (hence the common name). Borne freely over the shrub.

(continued)

Place of Origin	Zone	Plant Type	Mature Size

Buddleia davidii 'Charming' (BUD-lee-ah dah-VID-ee-eye) BUTTERFLY BUSH

Place of Origin	Zone	Plant Type	Mature Size
China	6	Deciduous	6-10 ft. by 6 ft.

Culture: Full sun. Humusy, well-drained soil.
Comments: Dies to ground in winter in Zones 6 and 7, but blooms on new growth. Protect crown in cold zones. Not long-lived. Flowers attract butterflies.
Other Cultivars: 'Burgundy', wine-colored flowers; 'Black Knight', deep, dark blue-black to purple flowers; 'Dubonnet', dark reddish-purple flowers; 'Empire Blue', violet-blue flowers; 'Fascinating', lilac-pink flowers; 'Fortune', soft lilac; 'Nanho Purple', purple flowers, dwarf habit; 'Royal Red', red flowers; 'Snowbank', white flowers; 'White Profusion', white flowers, dwarf habit.
Other Species: *B. alternifolia*, hardy (no dieback) to Zone 6. A fountain of fragrant, lilac, flower-flocked stems with willowlike leaves in June. Beautiful companion to yellow roses; *B. globosa*, round, orange flower balls in June.

Calliandra haematocephala (kal-ee-AN-drah hee-mat-oh-SEFF-ah-lah) PINK POWDERPUFF

Place of Origin	Zone	Plant Type	Mature Size
Bolivia	10	Evergreen	6 by 10 ft.

Culture: Full sun to partial shade. Moist, average, well-drained soil.
Comments: Will grow in Zone 9 in well-protected spots.
Other Species: *C. tweedii*, Trinidad flame bush, Zone 9. Finer, lacier leaves than *C. haematocephala*. Crimson puff-balls form at ends of branches from Feb.-Nov.

Callistemon citrinus (kal-ih-STEE-mun sih-TRY-nuss) BOTTLEBRUSH

Place of Origin	Zone	Plant Type	Mature Size
Australia	9	Evergreen	10-20 ft. by 15 ft.

Culture: Full sun. Tolerates drought, wide range of soils.
Comments: Best used as an informal screen or hedge. Low-maintenance plant.
Other Species: *C. viminalis*, weeping bottlebrush, grows to 30 ft., flowers May–July on pendulous branches.

Calluna vulgaris 'J. H. Hamilton' (kah-LOON-ah vul-GAIR-iss) SCOTCH HEATHER

Place of Origin	Zone	Plant Type	Mature Size
Scotland	5	Evergreen	1 ft.

Culture: Full sun. Sandy, humusy soils. Low-nitrogen soils beneficially force roots deep for water and nutrients.
Comments: Especially suited to Pacific Northwest and northeastern coastal areas.
Other Cultivars: 'Alba Plena', double white flowers; 'Aurea', foliage gold in summer, copper in winter, purple flowers; 'H. E. Beale', to 2 ft., silvery pink flowers; 'Miss Pat', pink foliage in spring, 8 in. tall, light purple flowers; 'Mrs. Ronald Gray', 4 in. tall, reddish flowers.

Shrub Description	Season of Bloom	Flower Color	Flower Description
Large, coarse, deep green leaves with silvery undersides on long, gracefully arching, open, and rangy stems.	July	Lavender-pink	12-22 in. long, pyramidal nodding panicles of densely packed florets at ends of stems make superb displays, carry honeylike scent.
Velvety, dark green, compound leaves give tropical look to spreading shrub.	Oct.-Mar.	Pink	3-in., clear pink stamens form puffy ball-like flowers in profusion during peak bloom. 5-in. fruit pods follow.
3-in., narrow, bright green, lemon-scented leaves held stiffly on open, rangy structure. Suckers from base of stems.	Throughout year, with best display in spring.	Red	4-6-in. bristly cylinders of pure red florets appear at branch ends.
Four ½-in., slender leaves emerge from closely spaced nodes on stiff, upright, interlaced stems.	Aug.-Oct.	Pink	Little double pink flowers crowd the stems in late summer.

(continued)

Place of Origin	Zone	Plant Type	Mature Size

Calycanthus floridus   (kal-ih-KAN-thus FLOR-ih-duss)   CAROLINA ALLSPICE

Place of Origin	Zone	Plant Type	Mature Size
Southeastern United States	6	Deciduous	8 by 10 ft.

Culture: Full sun to partial shade. Moist, well-drained soils. Trouble-free.

Comments: Make sure your specimen has the sweet scent, as many plants offered for sale either lack scent or carry an off odor.

Camellia japonica   (kah-MEEL-ee-ah ja-PON-ih-kah)   JAPANESE CAMELLIA

Place of Origin	Zone	Plant Type	Mature Size
China, Japan	8	Evergreen	8–12 ft. by 6–10 ft.

Culture: Partial shade. Well-drained, humusy, deep soil. Mulch to keep roots cool.

Comments: A major winter bloomer from coastal Carolinas, along Gulf Coast, and on Pacific coast. Adds oriental effect to garden. Thousands of named cultivars.

Cultivars: 'Alba Plena', formal double white, mid-season; 'Carter's Sunburst', semidouble pink, mid-season; 'Chandler's Elegans', rose-pink anemone form, mid-season; 'Colonel Firey', large dark red formal double, late; 'Debutante', large pink peony form, early; 'Finlandia Red', red semidouble, mid-season; 'Glen 40', rose red, compact formal double, late; 'Jordan's Pride', light pink with deep pink marginal markings, semidouble peony form, mid-season; 'Kramer's Supreme', crimson peony form, mid-season; 'Nuccio's Gem', white formal double, mid-season; 'Pink Perfection', light pink formal double, mid-season; 'Reg Ragland', red semidouble, mid-season; 'Tiffany', very large pink, rose form, late.

Other Species: *C. hiemalis* 'Shishi Gashira', rose red semidouble, early through mid-season; *C. reticulata* 'Butterfly Wings', 9 in. rose-pink semidouble, mid-season; 'Captain Rawes', large rose-pink semidouble, mid-season; 'Nuccio's Ruby', large dark red semidouble, mid-season; 'Purple Crown', purplish-red peony form, mid-season; 'Shot Silk', bright pink semidouble, early; 'Valentine's Day', large dark pink to reddish-orange formal double, mid-season; *C. sasanqua* 'Apple Blossom', light pink single, early; 'Bonanza', red semidouble, early; 'Cherokee', white semidouble, early; 'Jean May', light pink peony form, early; 'Orchid', rose-pink single, early; 'Sparkling Burgundy', rose-pink peony form, early; 'White Dove', white semidouble, early; 'Yuletide', red single, early.

Carissa grandiflora   (kar-ISS-ah grand-ih-FLOR-ah)   NATAL PLUM

Place of Origin	Zone	Plant Type	Mature Size
South Africa	10	Evergreen	6 by 5 ft.

Culture: Full sun to partial shade. Rich, well-drained, sandy soils. Will grow right along the ocean.

Comments: Thorns and density make this a fine barrier. Fruit and flowers often appear on the plant at the same time.

Cultivars: 'Green Carpet', to 1½ feet; 'Horizontalis', to 2 feet, spreading and dense; 'Tomlinson', to 2 feet, thornless.

Shrub Description	Season of Bloom	Flower Color	Flower Description
Fine-textured leaves make a medium-density shrub with a suckering habit and tall, vertical stems.	May–June	Reddish-brown	2-in., round, ruffled flowers with tight central heads fill the surrounding air with a sweet, Juicyfruit-gum scent.
Polished, leathery, dark green leaves, sometimes slightly bronzed, densely cover the many-branched, single or multitrunked woody scaffolding.	Oct.–Jan., early; Jan.–Mar., mid-season; Mar.–May, late.	White, pink, rose, and red cultivars	Camellia flowers range from 2 in. to over 5 in. wide, and come in single, semidouble, formal double, anemone form, and peony form.
Leathery, oval leaves are glossy, deep green, and form a dense mass on the upright, rounded, open, and thorny shrub.	All year	White	Jasmine-scented, star-shaped flowers open sporadically through-out the year, followed by edible, red, 1-2-in. fruits.

(continued)

Place of Origin	Zone	Plant Type	Mature Size

Carpenteria californica   (kar-pen-TEER-ee-ah kal-ih-FORN-ih-kah)   BUSH ANEMONE

| Western United States | 9 | Evergreen | 3-6 ft. by 3-6 ft. |

Culture: Full sun to partial shade. Well-drained, sandy garden soil. Prune after flowering to maintain shape, but don't shear. Tolerates drought.
Comments: Good shrub for unirrigated spots, although it also tolerates summer watering with positive drainage. Native of Sierra foothills.

Caryopteris ×*clandonensis*   'Heavenly Blue'   (care-ee-OP-ter-iss klan-doe-NEN-siss)   BLUE MIST

| Garden origin | 6 | Deciduous | 2½ by 2 ft. |

Culture: Full sun. Well-drained, sandy soil. Prune old growth to ground each spring to promote best flowering on new wood.
Comments: Wonderful blue effect in late summer, especially when planted in groups.

Ceanothus ×'Dark Star'   (see-an-OH-thuss)   CALIFORNIA LILAC

| Hybrid origin | 8 | Deciduous | 6 by 8 ft. |

Culture: Full sun. Well-drained, average soil.
Comments: Frequently seen along California highways. Many species available, from ground covers to tall shrubs.
Other Cultivars: 'Blue Buttons', medium lavender; 'Far Horizon', deep blue, 3-in. clusters; 'Frosty Blue', deep blue, with frosted petal margins; 'Gentian Plume', dark blue, 10-in. plumes; 'Joyce Coulter', large spikes of medium blue flowers; 'Julia Phelps', midnight blue, 1-in. clusters; 'Mountain Haze', medium blue, 3-4-in. clusters; 'Owlswood Blue', medium blue spikes to 6 in.; 'Ray Hartman', light blue, 3-5-in. spikes; 'Sierra Blue', bright blue, 6-8-in. spikes.
Species: *C. gloriosus*, Point Reyes ceanothus, light blue, 1-in. clusters on 1-1½-ft. plants; *C. griseus* var. *horizontalis*, Carmel creeper, light blue, 1-in. clusters on 2½-ft. plants; 'Santa Ana', indigo clusters; *C. impressus*, Santa Barbara ceanothus, large shrubs to 8 ft., beautiful, dark blue, 1-in. clusters.

Chaenomeles speciosa and hybrids   (kee-NOM-eh-lehz spee-see-OH-sah)   FLOWERING QUINCE

| Garden origin | 5 | Deciduous | 4-6 ft. by 6 ft. |

Culture: Full sun. Tolerates wide range of soils, except very alkaline.
Comments: The shrubs are gorgeous for 10 days early in the spring, serve as uninteresting barrier plantings the rest of the year.
Cultivars: 'Cameo', soft apricot, double flower form, compact growth; 'Low 'N White', soft white flowers, compact growth; 'Minerva', large, cherry red, velvety flowers; 'Pink Beauty', purplish pink; 'Toyo Nishiki', pink, white, red, and pink and white blossoms on the same plant.

Shrub Description	Season of Bloom	Flower Color	Flower Description
Thick, dark green, 2-4 in. leaves make dense foliage on slow-growing, multi-stemmed bush of erect branches.	June-Aug.	White	2-in., delicate white flowers with conspic-uous yellow stamens form in small clusters at the tips of the branches. Light, lemony fragrance.
3-in., gray-green, oval leaves on slender, low-growing branches.	Aug.-frost	Deep blue	Fringed flowers with protruding stamens emerge from leaf axils at tips of stems.
Tiny ¼-in., dark, glossy leaves on an open, irregular woody structure.	Mar.-Apr.	Blue	Many little, puffy flo-rets make 1½-in. clus-ters of deep cobalt blue with contrasting central dots of gold.
Shiny, oval leaves on densely branched, thorny stems that give a strong oriental appear-ance. A round and spread-ing bush.	Mar.	White, pink, red, apricot, salmon, or purple-red.	Delicate clusters of ¾-in., roselike flowers flock the stems early in the season. Many forms are double.

(continued)

Place of Origin	Zone	Plant Type	Mature Size

Chamelaucium uncinatum 'Vista'   (kam-el-AW-see-um un-sin-AH-tum)   GERALDTON WAXFLOWER

Place of Origin	Zone	Plant Type	Mature Size
Western Australia	10	Evergreen	6–8 ft. by 8–10 ft.

Culture: Full sun. Average soil with excellent drainage. Trim back by one-third each year to force best bloom.
Comments: Blooms for 3 months. Florists use sprays to fill cut flower bouquets.

Chimonanthus praecox   (ky-mo-NAN-thuss pree-koks)   WINTERSWEET

Place of Origin	Zone	Plant Type	Mature Size
China	7	Deciduous	12 by 8 ft.

Culture: Full sun in North to partial shade in South. Well-drained, moist soil.
Comments: Makes a fine standard when pruned to a single trunk, placed where people can enjoy its scent.

Choisya ternata   (SHOY-zee-ah ter-NAH-tah)   MEXICAN ORANGE

Place of Origin	Zone	Plant Type	Mature Size
Mexico	9	Evergreen	8 by 8 ft.

Culture: Full sun to partial shade in hot regions. Humusy, acid, well-drained soil.
Comments: Best along cooler coastal regions of California. Cut stems for indoor arrangements.

Cistus hybridus (also called *C. corbariensis*)   (SISS-tuss HY-brid-uss)   WHITE ROCK ROSE

Place of Origin	Zone	Plant Type	Mature Size
Mediterranean	8	Evergreen	2–4 ft. by 2–4 ft.

Culture: Full sun. Well-drained, average soil.
Comments: Drought-tolerant, good for dry banks. Looks best in a group.
Other Species: *C. ladanifer*, crimson spot rock rose, 3-in. flowers with crimson spots at the base of each petal; *C. ×purpureus*, 3-in., rose-purple flowers, petals have yellow base with maroon spots.

Clethra alnifolia   (KLETH-rah al-nih-FOAL-ee-ah)   SWEET PEPPERBUSH, SUMMER-SWEET

Place of Origin	Zone	Plant Type	Mature Size
Eastern United States	3	Deciduous	8–10 ft. by 4–5 ft.

Culture: Partial shade. Moist, even boggy, fertile soil.
Comments: Pruned to a single trunk, it makes a perfect little specimen tree.
Cultivar: 'Pinkspire', lovely pink flowers.

Shrub Description	Season of Bloom	Flower Color	Flower Description
Light green, very fine, needlelike leaves wave from open, sprawling shrub.	Dec.–Feb.	Pink to lavender	Waxy clusters of ½-in., long-lasting flowers appear along the ferny stems.
Tapering, medium green leaves on open, rangy, multistemmed shrub.	Feb.–Mar.	Yellow and reddish-brown	1-in. flowers appear well before leaves. Outer sepals are yellow, inner flower is red-brown. Noted for its spicy fragrance.
Shiny, bright green, 3-part, fan-shaped leaves have an elegant, oriental look. New wood is green.	Mar.–Apr.	White	Clusters of small, white, fragrant flowers, resembling orange blossoms, emerge between leaves at branch tips.
Crinkly, gray-green leaves form round mound on densely branched, slender-stemmed shrub structure.	June	White	Many 1½-in., crepe-papery petalled flowers with yellow centers.
Rich green foliage turns clear yellow in fall. Shrub is multistemmed, makes an upright, rounded, open bush.	July–Aug.	White	6-in. flower spikes at branch ends are composed of clusters of tiny florets. Long stamens protrude from the fragrant blooms.

(continued)

Place of Origin	Zone	Plant Type	Mature Size

Coleonema pulchrum   (ko-lee-oh-NEEM-ah pull-kruhm)   PINK BREATH OF HEAVEN

Place of Origin	Zone	Plant Type	Mature Size
South Africa	9	Evergreen	3-5 ft. by 2-4 ft.

Culture: Full sun to partial shade. Humusy, well-drained soil. Shear to shape after flowering.
Comments: A sweet little shrub with a springlike appearance in winter.
Other Species: *C. album*, white breath of heaven, white flowers.

Corylopsis pauciflora   (kor-ih-LOP-siss paw-sih-FLOR-ah)   BUTTERCUP WINTER HAZEL

Place of Origin	Zone	Plant Type	Mature Size
China, Japan	6	Deciduous	4-5 ft. by 4-5 ft.

Culture: Partial shade. Moist, well-drained soil. Protect from winds.
Comments: Gives a natural look in woodland settings. Mass several against darker evergreens for best effect. Cut stems for indoor bloom in late winter.
Other Species: *C. chinensis*, Chinese winter hazel, soft yellow flowers, 9 ft. tall.

Cotoneaster multiflorus   (ko-TONE-ee-ass-ter mul-tih-FLOR-us)   MANY-FLOWERED COTONEASTER

Place of Origin	Zone	Plant Type	Mature Size
China	6	Deciduous	6-12 ft. by 10-15 ft.

Culture: Full sun. Average, well-drained soil.
Comments: Cotoneaster is usually grown for berries, not flowers, but this one's grown for both.

Cytisus scoparius   'Lord Lambourne'   (SIT-ih-siss sko-PARE-ee-uss)   SCOTCH BROOM

Place of Origin	Zone	Plant Type	Mature Size
Scotland, Western Europe	6	Evergreen	6-8 ft. by 4-6 ft.

Culture: Full sun. Poor, sandy soil.
Comments: Although *C. scoparius* cultivars are not usually a weed problem, the species has invaded the coastal United States as a yellow-flowered weed.
Other Cultivars: 'Burkwoodii', red touched yellow; 'Butterfly', orange-yellow; 'Cornish Cream', cream; 'Hollandia', rose; 'Moonlight', pale yellow; 'Pomona', orange and apricot; 'St. Mary's', white; 'San Francisco', red.
Other Species: *C.×praecox*, Warminster broom, yellow and cream flowers on vertical, deciduous stems in May, rank odor.

Shrub Description	Season of Bloom	Flower Color	Flower Description
Small, narrow leaves, aromatic when crushed, form along the upright, slender, delicate stems.	Jan.-May	Pink	Little, ¼-in. stars of the softest pink are borne singly but freely over the bush.
3-in., oval leaves give a fine texture and yellow fall color. Shrub slowly spreads, sending up graceful, arching stems.	Mar.-Apr.	Yellow	2-3 fragrant, bell-shaped flowers hang in clusters from the bare branches.
Fine, blue-green foliage covers gracefully arching stems. Gives a weeping, moundlike appearance.	May	White	From 3 to 12, ½ in. wide, white flowers held in groups along the stems, followed by small red berries from Aug.-Oct.
Upright, slender, arching green twigs with flat stems carry inconspicuous leaves along their length.	May-June	Red and yellowish-white	Profusion of 1-in., pea-like scarlet-and-cream flowers borne on old wood.

(continued)

Place of Origin	Zone	Plant Type	Mature Size

Daphne cneorum   (DAF-nee nee-OR-um)   **GARLAND DAPHNE**

Europe	4	Evergreen	9-12 in. by 3 ft.

Culture: Full sun to partial shade. Sandy, well-drained, low-fertility soils sweetened with limestone. Shade or mulch roots to keep them cool in hot regions. Trimming back stems after flowering forces new bloom.

Comments: Matlike growth of this shrub makes it suitable to use as a ground cover.

Other Species: *D.* ×*burkwoodii,* Zone 5, very fragrant white flower clusters appear in June; *D. mezereum,* February daphne, Zone 4, purplish-pink flowers appear before new leaves on this deciduous species. *D. odora* 'Marginata', Zone 8, handsome foliage and heavy but heavenly scent from white flowers in Mar., grows to 3-4 ft.

Deutzia gracilis   (DOYT-zee-ah grah-SILL-iss)   **SLENDER DEUTZIA**

Japan	3	Deciduous	3 by 5 ft.

Culture: Full sun to partial shade. Humusy, well-drained soil. Easy to transplant. Prune 1 or 2 oldest stems to base each year. Trimming whole shrub reduces flowering.

Comments: Nondescript when not in flower, so mix with other shrubs in a border.

Other Species: *D.* ×*rosea*, pink flowers; *D. scabra*, to 7 ft., white to pink flowers in June; *D. scabra* 'Candidissima', double white flowers; 'Pride of Rochester', 4-in. clusters of double, frilly, purplish-pink flowers.

Echium fastuosum   (ECK-ee-um fast-yew-OH-sum)   **PRIDE OF MADEIRA**

Canary Islands	9	Evergreen	6 by 6 ft.

Culture: Full sun. Average, well-drained soil. Very drought-resistant. Good for coastal California. Remove faded flower spikes after bloom.

Comments: A gorgeous sight in bloom and quietly exotic when out of bloom.

Other Species: *E. wildpretii,* tower of jewels, a biennial echium worth noting. In its first year, makes a pretty mound of leaves. In its second year, sends up a huge 6-10 ft. stalk of rosy pink to red flowers. Self-sows.

Enkianthus campanulatus   (en-kee-AN-thus kam-pan-you-LAH-tus)   **RED VEIN, RED BELLS**

Japan	5	Deciduous	10-20 ft. by 4-10 ft.

Culture: Partial shade. Humusy, acid, well-drained, moist soil.

Comments: Likes conditions similar to those for azaleas and rhododendrons. Plant where it can be seen from below at close range.

Shrub Description	Season of Bloom	Flower Color	Flower Description
Low, spreading, slender branches covered with 1-in., narrow, dark green leaves.	Apr.–May	Rose	Dense clusters of fragrant, rosy pink flowers at branch ends cover plants in spring, and again in fall in warmer zones.
Finely toothed, 2-in., medium green leaves on many arching, slender stems that spread to 5 ft.	May	White	Pure white, ½-in. flowers cluster in 3-in. racemes along the graceful branches.
Gray-green leaves with pink center ribs make mounded sprays at tips of coarse, sprawling branches.	May–June	Blue	½-in., tubular, blue-purple florets form showy, erect, 1-ft. cones arising from leaf sprays.
Rich green leaves in whorls along layered, horizontal branches turn red to orange-red in fall. Tall, upright stems produce large, broad shrub.	May	Yellow and red	Pendulous clusters of yellow bells, tipped and veined in red, hang below leaves.

(continued)

Place of Origin	Zone	Plant Type	Mature Size

Escallonia exoniensis 'Frades' (ess-kall-AHN-ee-ah eks-ahn-ee-EN-sis) PINK PRINCESS ESCALLONIA

Chile	9	Evergreen	6 by 4 ft.

Culture: Full sun to partial shade. Tolerates drought, wind, most soils.
Comments: Fast-growing, pretty plant for difficult areas.
Cultivar: 'Balfouri', grows to 10 ft., dropping branches end in clusters of pinkish-white flowers.
Other Species: *E. rubra*, red escallonia, dense, round shrub grows to 10-15 ft., crimson flower clusters.

Exochorda ×macrantha 'The Bride' (eks-oh-KOR-dah ma-KRAN-thah) PEARL BUSH

Hybrid origin	6	Deciduous	4 by 4 ft.

Culture: Full sun. Average, well-drained soil.
Comments: 'The Bride' is the only cultivar available, superior to the species.
Other Species: *E. racemosa*, slender habit to 10-15 ft., small, white flowers.

Forsythia ×intermedia 'Spectabilis' (for-SITH-ee-ah in-ter-MEE-dee-ah speck-TAH-bill-iss) BORDER FORSYTHIA

Garden origin	5	Deciduous	7-12 ft. by 10-12 ft.

Culture: Full sun to light shade. Tolerates wide variety of soils.
Comments: Branches good for forcing indoors. The color is common, but so early that it's usually welcomed. Needs yearly pruning for best bloom.
Other Species: *F. suspensa*, weeping forsythia, long, weeping branches touch ground and root at the tips, less profuse bloomer than *F. ×intermedia*; *F. viridissima* 'Bronxensis', greenstem forsythia, dwarf form, 1-2 ft. tall.

Fothergilla gardenii (father-GILL-ah gar-DEEN-ee-eye) SMALL FOTHERGILLA

Southeastern United States	5	Deciduous	3 by 3 ft.

Culture: Full sun (in North) to partial shade. Humusy, acid soil with good drainage.
Comments: A pretty little shrub, good with woodsy plants. Fall color develops best in full sun. Named for John Fothergill, friend of Benjamin Franklin and John Bartram, who grew American plants in his English garden.
Other Species: *F. major*, grows to 10 ft., larger, more drought-tolerant than *F. gardenii*.

Shrub Description	Season of Bloom	Flower Color	Flower Description
Small, glossy, evergreen leaves on a compact shrub. Looks good pruned to just a few trunks.	Mar.-Nov.	Pink	Terminal clusters of pinkish-rose blossoms on erect stems are produced through most of the year.
2-in. oval leaves loosely cover this small, compact, weeping shrub.	Apr.-May	White	Profusions of pearl-like white buds open into loose panicles of 1½-in. flowers that emerge along branch ends.
Deep green, willowlike leaves along graceful, arching, long, slender stems that reach the ground, forming a rounded mass.	Mar.-Apr.	Yellow	When pruned back right after flowering, forsythia blooms profusely each year, with sulfur yellow flowers clustered along its slender stems before leaves appear.
Dark green leaves on slender, crooked branches turn brilliant yellow, orange, and scarlet in fall.	Apr.-May	White	Small, 1-2-in., brushy, white flower spikes have sweet honey scent, appear before leaves at branch tips.

(continued)

Place of Origin	Zone	Plant Type	Mature Size

Fuchsia hybrida (FEW-shah HY-brid-ah)   **HYBRID FUCHSIA**

Place of Origin	Zone	Plant Type	Mature Size
Hybrid origin	9	Varies by variety from deciduous to evergreen.	Varies from trailing to upright at 12 ft., and all sizes in between.

Culture: Light shade. Rich, moist, humusy soil. Prune in late winter to ground, or leave just a few buds on shortened stems of old wood.

Comments: Makes specimens, hedges, or container plants. Pinch early to increase bushiness. Pick spent flowers and berries as they appear to stimulate further flowering. Hybrid fuchsias come in hundreds of varieties.

Other Species: *F. magellanica,* hardy fuchsia, drooping red and violet flowers, hardy to Zone 6, where it acts as a herbaceous perennial.

Gardenia jasminoides 'August Beauty'   (gar-DEEN-ee-ah jaz-min-oh-EYE-deez)   **GARDENIA**

Place of Origin	Zone	Plant Type	Mature Size
Southern China	8	Evergreen	4-6 ft. by 4-6 ft.

Culture: Full sun in cool coastal areas, light shade elsewhere. Rich, humusy, acid, moist, well-drained soil.

Comments: Feed monthly with fish emulsion solution. Likes humid conditions, so moisten mulch frequently.

Other Cultivar: 'Mystery', 4-5 in. flowers, pinch for bushiness.

Genista tinctoria (jen-ISS-tah tink-TAWR-ee-ah)   **DYER'S GREENWOOD, BROOM**

Place of Origin	Zone	Plant Type	Mature Size
Europe, Western Asia	2	Deciduous	2-3 ft. by 2-3 ft.

Culture: Full sun. Tolerates poor, sandy, acid soil, but likes well-drained, limestone soil.

Comments: Doesn't like to be moved when established. Good for problem areas. Flowers make a yellow dye.

Other Species: *G. lydia,* hardy to Zone 7, 1½ ft. high spreading ground cover, yellow blossoms in June.

Shrub Description	Season of Bloom	Flower Color	Flower Description
Slender, arching branches and narrow, lancelike leaves.	June-frost	Pink, apricot, violet, red, blue, or white.	From single group of petals to very double masses of petals in pendulous, long-collared flowers with protruding stamens.
Attractive, shiny, dark green leaves make a dense shrub on stiffly branching, slender but strong stems.	May–Nov.	White	3-in., satiny, creamy white flowers prized for their sweet fragrance borne in leaf axils singly but lavishly over long growing season.
Vertical, sparse-leaved, green stems make a rounded, spiky shrub.	June, sporadically to Sept.	Yellow	Several pealike, yellow flowers in short racemes produced on new wood.

(continued)

Place of Origin	Zone	Plant Type	Mature Size

Grevillea ×'Robin Gordon'   (greh-VIL-ee-ah)

Australia	9	Evergreen	4-5 ft. by 7-9 ft.

Culture: Full sun. Dry, poor, well-drained soil. Care-free when established. Prune after spring flush.
Comments: Very attractive to birds. Very showy, low-growing shrub.
Other Cultivars: 'Ned Kelley', along with 'Robin Gordon', a top-rated grevillea.
Other Species: *G. banksii* var. *forsteri*, hardy to Zone 10, grows to 15-20 ft., dark red flowers; *G. lanigera*, woolly grevillea, tiny, gray-green leaves on 3-6-ft. plant, crimson and yellow flowers in Mar. attract hummingbirds, good for dry bank; *G. thelemanniana*, hummingbird bush, airy, open, 5-8 ft. shrub with fine, needlelike, dark green foliage, clusters of yellow-tipped red flowers appear throughout year at the ends of branches.

Hamamelis ×*intermedia*   'Arnold Promise'   (ham-ah-MEE-liss in-ter-MEE-dee-ah)
HYBRID WITCH-HAZEL

Garden origin	6	Deciduous	15 by 15 ft.

Culture: Full sun to light shade. Moist, humusy, well-drained soil.
Comments: Showy hybrid of *H. mollis*, Chinese and Japanese witch-hazels.
Other Cultivars: 'Diana', deep red flowers; 'Jelena', coppery orange flowers; 'Ruby Glow', coppery red flowers.

Hebe buxifolia   'Patty's Purple'   (HEE-bee buks-ih-FOAL-ee-ah)   BOXLEAF HEBE

New Zealand	8	Evergreen	3 by 3 ft.

Culture: Full sun. Average, well-drained soil. Prune heavily to maintain shape and foliage density.
Comments: Grown as much for precise leaf form as for flowers. Used as a dramatic low edging.
Other Cultivars: 'Alba', white flowers; 'Variegata', variegated leaves.

Hibiscus rosa-sinensis   'Hula Girl'   (hy-BISS-kus ROE-sah sy-NEN-siss)   CHINESE HIBISCUS

China	9	Evergreen	7 by 5 ft.

Culture: Full sun to partial shade. Moist, rich, well-drained soil. Protect from wind and hot afternoon sun.
Comments: Size of foliage, habit of hibiscus varies with the cultivar. Use as screen, specimen, or train to small, single-trunked tree. Prune back one-third growth yearly.
Other Cultivars: 'Agnes Gault', single, rose pink; 'Bride', single, white to pale pink; 'Brilliant', single, bright red; 'Butterfly', single, bright yellow; 'Cherie', single, tangerine with maroon throat; 'Diamond Head', single, dark red to red-black; 'Ecstasy', single, red with white rays; 'Fiesta', single, orange with crinkled edges; 'Full Moon', double, lemon yellow; 'Kona Improved', double, deep pink; 'President', single, red; 'Ross Estey', large, single, orange with rose centers; 'White Wings', single, white with ruby center.

Shrub Description	Season of Bloom	Flower Color	Flower Description
Open, arching, slender branches covered with big, stiff, lacy, fernlike leaves.	Intermittently through year, with spring and fall flushes.	Orange-red	Buds open yellow, change to orange-red. Brushy-looking flower clusters droop from the tips of the stems.
Dark gray-green leaves on slender branches with sparse, open, and rangy habit; yellow fall foliage.	Feb.-Mar.	Yellow	Reddish-brown calyxes hold spidery clusters of narrow, 1½-in. primrose yellow petals. Blooms appear sparsely on leafless branches very early in the year.
½-in., dark green leaves arranged regularly on dense branches of neat, rounded shrub.	July	Purple	Short, 1-in. spikes of purple flowers profusely borne over branch tips.
Large, glossy leaves give a coarse appearance; compact shrub.	June-Sept.	Yellow	6-in., light yellow, single bloom with cherry red center and protruding style with stamens attached.

(continued)

Place of Origin	Zone	Plant Type	Mature Size

Hibiscus syriacus 'Blue Bird'   (Hy-BISS-kus seer-ee-AH-kuss)   ROSE-OF-SHARON

China	5	Deciduous	6-10 ft. by 4-6 ft.

Culture: Full sun to partial shade. Moist, average soil. Tolerates city and seaside conditions.
Comments: One of Victorian farmsteads' mainstays, along with forsythia and hydrangea. Prune shoots to a few buds for larger bloom. Best massed in border.
Other Cultivars: 'Ann Arundel', pink; 'Diana', 6-in., waxy white; 'Red Heart', white with red eye; 'Woodbridge', rose red with dark red eye.

Hydrangea macrophylla 'Nikko Blue'   (hy-DRAIN-jee-ah mack-roe-FILE-ah)
BIG LEAF HYDRANGEA, GARDEN HYDRANGEA

Japan	6	Deciduous	4-6 ft. by 5-7 ft.

Culture: Full sun to partial shade. Rich, moist, humusy soil. Blue-flowered types must have an acid soil, turning mauve or pink in alkaline or neutral soils. Acidify soil with compost and/or gypsum.
Comments: Hydrangeas in florist shops are French hybrid dwarfs suited to containers, not the garden, so look for garden varieties in catalogs and nurseries.
Other Cultivars: 'Carmen', deep pink mophead type; 'Mariesii Variegata', cream-edged leaves, deep blue lacecap flowers in acid soil; 'Merritt's Beauty', carmine-red mophead type; 'Revelation', red mophead, long summer bloom season; 'Trophy', salmon-rose mophead type; 'White', white mophead type.
Other Species: *H. arborescens* 'Annabelle', wild hydrangea, Zone 4, cream to greenish-white flowers, cut off completely in winter; *H. paniculata* 'Grandiflora', peegee hydrangea, Zone 4, massive, 1-ft., white to pink flower heads in Aug., grows to 25 feet, needs a place by itself; *H. quercifolia* 'Snow Queen', oak leaf hydrangea, Zone 6, white flowers turn pink as pyramidal clusters mature in July, bold oaklike leaves turn burgundy, crimson, orange, or purple in fall, blooms on old wood.

Hypericum prolificum   (hy-PEER-ih-kum pro-LIF-ih-kum)   SHRUBBY ST.-JOHN'S-WORT

Eastern United States	5	Deciduous	3-4 ft. by 3-4 ft.

Culture: Full sun to partial shade. Tolerates poor, dry soils, city conditions.
Comments: Makes continuous show of bloom through most of the summer.
Other Species: *H. calycinum*, Aaron's beard or creeping St.-John's-wort, grows 1 ft. tall, dense evergreen ground cover with 3-in., yellow flowers; *H. elatum* 'Elsead', 3-4-in., yellow flowers, salmon-red berries in fall; *H. frondosum* 'Sunburst', 2-in. yellow flowers in profusion; *H.* ×*moserianum* 'Tricolor', Zone 7, 2½-ft. evergreen shrub, golden yellow flowers June-Oct., green and white foliage edged pink; *H. patulum* 'Sungold', 2-3-in. bright yellow flowers, semi-evergreen.

Ixora coccinea   (iks-OAR-ah cox-ih-NEE-ah)   FLAME OF THE WOODS

East Indies	9	Evergreen	4 by 4 ft.

Culture: Full sun. Fertile, moist, well-drained soil. Likes hot, humid weather.
Comments: Widely planted hedge in Florida. Makes wonderful everblooming houseplant.
Cultivars: 'Rosea', large, pink flower clusters; 'Super King', huge, orange-red clusters.

Shrub Description	Season of Bloom	Flower Color	Flower Description
Scalloped, medium green leaves on tall, stiffly branched shrub often trained to single trunk, making small tree.	Aug.	Blue	3½-in., very showy, shallow-cupped flowers with prominent centers last just one day.
5-9-in., oval, bright green, coarsely toothed leaves on mass of upright, un-branched stems. Spreads by suckering.	July-Sept.	Blue	'Nikko Blue' is a "mop-head" type hydrangea, with clusters of sterile florets forming large balls. "Lacecap" types (see other cultivars) have a ring of large outer petals surrounding tiny, inner florets, giving lacy effect.
Leaves, often spotted, thickly cover stiff, erect, densely branched stems, making a compact, rounded form.	July-Sept.	Yellow	¾-in., showy, 5-petalled flowers form mostly at branch tips.
Oblong, shiny green leaves on a compact, spreading bush.	All year	Coral-red	1½-in. tubular flowers form large, showy clusters in red, yellow, or orange-red.

(continued)

Place of Origin	Zone	Plant Type	Mature Size

Jasminum nudiflorum   (JAZ-min-um new-dih-FLOR-um)   WINTER JASMINE

China	6	Deciduous	3 by 10 ft.

Culture: Full sun to light shade. Average, well-drained soil.
Comments: In North, train it on a sunny south wall, where it will brighten the days of deep winter. Prune immediately after flowering season.
Other Species: *J. floridum*, Zone 7, ½-in. golden yellow flowers; *J. humile* 'Revolutum', Italian jasmine, Zone 7, evergreen, mounds rise to 10 ft., 1-ft. clusters of yellow, 1-in. florets have mild fragrance; *J. mesnyi*, primrose jasmine, Zone 8, 2-in. lemon yellow flowers in Nov.-Apr. during mild spells, good for holding steep banks; *J. sambac*, arabian jasmine, Zone 10, evergreen, white, 1-in. flowers carry heavy jasmine scent, fade to maroon.

Kalmia latifolia   (KAL-mee-ah lat-ih-FOAL-ee-ah)   MOUNTAIN LAUREL

Eastern United States	5	Evergreen	4-8 ft. by 4-6 ft.

Culture: Light shade. Rich, humusy, acid, moist, well-drained soil. Likes mulch.
Comments: Exquisite flower in form and color. Good for natural effect in eastern wooded glens. State flower of Connecticut and Pennsylvania.
Cultivars: 'Alba', pure white; 'Bullseye', white with reddish-purple markings; 'Fresca', lavender, with dark lavender markings; 'Ostbo Red', deep red buds open a light pink; 'Pink Frost', silvery frosted pink.

Kerria japonica   (CARE-ee-ah ja-PON-ih-kah)   GLOBEFLOWER

China, Japan	5	Deciduous	8 by 6 ft.

Culture: Partial shade, tolerates full sun. Average, well-drained soil in a protected spot. Feeding spurs rank growth. Remove suckers.
Comments: Plant so it has plenty of room to display its graceful green stems. Used as informal hedge, or in shrub border.
Cultivar: 'Pleniflora', double, orange-yellow, ball-like flowers.

Kolkwitzia amabilis   (kohl-KWIT-zee-ah ahm-AH-bil-iss)   BEAUTY BUSH

China	4	Deciduous	6 by 5 ft.

Culture: Full sun. Average soil. After bloom, thin out wood that bloomed the year before. Cut old, overgrown bushes to ground for renewal.
Comments: Place to the rear of the flower garden, as it gets leggy with age. Not much to look at when not in bloom.

Shrub Description	Season of Bloom	Flower Color	Flower Description
Groups of 3 little, dark green leaflets in oval shape cover long, willowy green stems that spread outward from central shrub.	Jan.–Mar.	Yellow	Clear, 1-in., scentless yellow flowers appear on leafless green stems during winter's mild spells.
Small, glossy, rhododendronlike leaves on graceful branches; dense when young, becoming open, irregular with age.	June	White to pink	Dainty, bell-shaped, 1-in. flowers that vary from white to deep pink; purple markings within. Flowers held in 6-in. clusters at branch tips.
2-4-in., toothed, medium green leaves along slim, yellow-green stems, forming an open, rounded shrub. Yellow fall foliage.	Apr.–May	Yellow	1½-in., roselike single flowers fill the bush in spring.
Dull, gray-green leaves on an upright, vase-shaped shrub with long, arching stems.	May–June	Pink	Clusters of pink, bell-shaped, yellow-throated flowers fall in profuse cascades from the top of the bush.

(continued)

Place of Origin	Zone	Plant Type	Mature Size

Lantana camara 'Radiation' (lan-TAN-ah ka-MAHR-ah) BUSH LANTANA

Central America	9	Evergreen	6 by 6 ft.

Culture: Full sun. Drought-tolerant but flowers best when given moist soil.
Comments: Good for steep banks, erosion-prone areas. Grows well in containers.
Other Cultivars: 'Christine', bright cherry-pink; 'Dwarf Pink', bright pink; 'Dwarf White', velvety white; 'Dwarf Yellow', bright yellow.

Leptospermum scoparium 'Ruby Glow' (lep-toe-SPUR-mum sko-PARE-ee-um) NEW ZEALAND TEA TREE

Australia, New Zealand	9	Evergreen	6-10 ft. by 6-8 ft.

Culture: Full sun. Average, well-drained soil.
Comments: A remarkable sight in full bloom. Pruning lower branches can enhance its appearance, as branches are interestingly arrayed. Good for hedges and screens.
Other Cultivars: 'Florepleno', double pink flowers; 'Keatleyi', grows to 10 ft., open habit, pale pink flowers; 'Red Damask', double, ruby red flowers, reddish leaves; 'Snow White', compact shrub with greenish-white flowers.

Leucothoe fontanesiana (loo-KO-tho-ee FON-tan-eez-ee-AN-ah) DROOPING LEUCOTHOE

Southeast United States	5	Evergreen	4-6 ft. by 4-6 ft.

Culture: Full to partial shade. Moist, acid, humusy soil.
Comments: Good for a woodsy spot, where it can serve as companion to rhododendrons and mountain laurels. Underground stems send up new shoots, forming a clump. Leaves turn bronze in shade.
Cultivars: 'Rainbow', green, yellow, and copper foliage variegations; 'Nana', dwarf form to 2-4 ft.

Lonicera tatarica (lah-NISS-er-ah tah-TARE-ih-kah) TATARIAN HONEYSUCKLE

Central Asia	4	Deciduous	9-12 ft. by 10 ft.

Culture: Full sun to partial shade. Average soil. Prune its vigorous growth after flowering.
Comments: Mix with evergreens in a shrub border so its straggly winter appearance will be hidden.
Cultivars: 'Arnold Red', red flowers; 'Grandiflora', large, white flowers; 'Lutea', yellow berries; 'Nana', dwarf form to 3 ft., pink flowers; 'Rosea', flowers rose outside, pale pink inside; 'Sibirica', deep pink flowers.
Other Species: *L. fragrantissima,* winter honeysuckle, Zone 5, semi-evergreen, 6-10 ft. tall, richly fragrant, white blossoms in Apr.; *L. korolkowii,* blueleaf honeysuckle, Zone 5, bluish to gray-green leaves, ¾-in. deep rose flowers in May; *L. nitida,* box honeysuckle, Zone 7, evergreen, turns bronze in winter, ½-in., fragrant white flowers in June; *L. morrowii* 'Xanthocarpa', Zone 4, makes dense, ground-hugging mound, ½-in., creamy white flowers in May.

Shrub Description	Season of Bloom	Flower Color	Flower Description
Wrinkly, dark green, 1–3-in. leaves have strong, even objectionable odor when crushed, densely cover compact, multibranched stems.	All year	Orange-red	2-in. clusters of squarish petals resemble round mosaics of red and yellow tiles. Produces masses of color in all seasons.
Tiny, dark green, needlelike leaves cover densely branched, very shrubby bush.	Feb.–Apr.	Red	¾-in., deep ruby red flowers cover the bush in late winter and spring.
4-6-in. leathery, dark bronze-green leaves along slender, spreading branches form elegant, medium-textured shrub.	Mar.–May	White	2-3-in. racemes of white, fragrant, lily-of-the-valley-like flowers hang from under leaves along length of stems.
2½-in., oval, bluish-green leaves cover the slender stems of this arching, upright shrub.	May	White, pink, or red	Profusions of 1-in., trumpet-shaped flowers ranging from white through pink to red. Red berries in June favored by birds.

(continued)

Place of Origin	Zone	Plant Type	Mature Size

Mahonia aquifolium   (mah-HONE-ee-ah ack-wih-FOAL-ee-um)   **OREGON GRAPE**

Place of Origin	Zone	Plant Type	Mature Size
Pacific Northwest	5	Evergreen	3-6 ft. by 3-5 ft.

   Culture: Partial shade to full shade. Moist, acid, humusy soil. Protect from winter sun and winds; likes a northern exposure.
   Comments: Excellent as an evergreen ground cover in shady spots. Spreads by underground stolons.
   Other Species: *M. repens*, creeping mahonia, Zone 6, a dwarf form, to 1 ft.

Mahonia bealei   (Mah-HONE-ee-ah BEE-lee-eye)   **LEATHERLEAF MAHONIA**

Place of Origin	Zone	Plant Type	Mature Size
China	6	Evergreen	10-12 ft. by 10 ft.

   Culture: Partial shade. Rich, moist, well-drained soil in a protected spot.
   Comments: Dramatic when grown against a house wall and lit at night.

Nandina domestica   (nan-DEE-nah doe-MESS-tik-ah)   **HEAVENLY BAMBOO, NANDINA**

Place of Origin	Zone	Plant Type	Mature Size
China	7	Evergreen	6-8 ft. by 4-6 ft.

   Culture: Partial to full shade. Average soil.
   Comments: Not a spectacular plant, but beloved for its delicacy and color. Good filler near entranceways, walkways, and grouped with other shrubs.

Nerium oleander   'Calypso'   (NEER-ee-um OH-lee-an-der)   **OLEANDER**

Place of Origin	Zone	Plant Type	Mature Size
Mediterranean region	8	Evergreen	8-12 ft. by 8-12 ft.

   Culture: Full sun. Tolerates any soil, most conditions.
   Comments: All parts of the plant are poisonous. Good for difficult areas. Commonly used in California and Florida along highways. Tip prune for density. Prune to a few stems to form treelike shapes.
   Other Cultivars: 'Algiers', single, deep red, 6-8 ft. tall; 'Casablanca', single, white, 6-8 ft. tall; 'Hardy Pink', single, salmon-pink; 'Hardy Red', single, red; 'Hawaii', single, salmon-pink with yellow throat; 'Mrs. Roeding', double salmon-pink; 'Petite Pink', dwarf, single, pink; 'Petite Salmon', dwarf, single, salmon; 'Ruby Lace', large, red blooms, 6-8 ft. tall; 'Sister Agnes', single, white; 'Tangier', single, soft pink, 6-8 ft. tall.

Shrub Description	Season of Bloom	Flower Color	Flower Description
Lustrous, spiny, hollylike leaves are bronze when new, turning dark green, then purplish-bronze in fall. Open, upright habit, thick stems.	Apr.–May	Yellow	Showy, 3-in. clusters of bright yellow flowers followed by blue berries in June.
Tropical-looking, spiny, large, compound leaves held horizontally from strong vertical stems.	Mar.–Apr.	Lemon-yellow	Buds at branch tips burst into highly fragrant yellow bells, followed by clusters of blue-black berries in July.
Fine-textured foliage in whorls on long, slender, bamboolike stems. Some leaves turn partially or entirely brilliant red in cold weather.	June	White	Creamy white, 6-12-in. flower clusters form at branch tips, followed by bright red berries that hang in sprays among reddish foliage all winter.
Narrow, gray-green leaves on tall, rangy stems give a coarse effect.	June–Oct.	Red	Clusters of large, single, cherry red flowers reach June peak, but continue through the summer.

(continued)

Place of Origin	Zone	Plant Type	Mature Size

Paeonia suffruticosa   'Kinkaku' (also called *'Golden Palace'*)   (pee-OH-nee-ah suff-roo-tih-KOH-sah keen-KAH-koo)   **TREE PEONY**

Northwest China	5	Deciduous	4 by 6 ft.

Culture: Full sun to partial shade.

Comments: Familiar motif in Chinese art and embroidery. Double forms may need staking. Excellent specimen plant. Choose site carefully, as it lives for many years but resents being moved.

Other Cultivars: 'Godaishu', also called 'Large Globelike', pure white, double; 'Hanadaijin', also called 'Minister of Flowers', deep reddish-purple, semidouble; 'Hana Kisoi', also called 'Floral Rivalry', ruffled, pink, semidouble; 'Hohdai', also called 'Emperor's Reign', rose red, double; 'Taiyo', also called 'Great Emperor', red, semidouble.

Philadelphus coronarius   (fil-ah-DEL-fis kor-oh-NAH-ree-us)   **MOCK ORANGE**

Southeastern Europe	5	Deciduous	10-12 ft. by 10-12 ft.

Culture: Full sun to partial shade. Likes moist, well-drained soil; tolerates dry soil.

Comments: Free-flowering species that perfumes the June air deliciously.

Other Species: *P. ×lemoinei* cultivars owe their fragrance to *P. microphyllus*, a native of the United States, in their heritage, bloom in June; 'Avalanche', grows to 4 ft., very fragrant, single, white flowers; 'Belle Etoile', grows to 6 ft., single, fringed, showy, white flowers with maroon blush at base; 'Boule d'Argent', grows to 5 ft., double, white flowers; 'Innocence', grows to 8 ft., single, white flowers nearly 2 in. across; 'Mont Blanc', grows to 4 ft., single, white flowers nearly 1½ in. across; *P. ×virginalis* cultivars tend to be semidouble to double white flowers, with a less pervasive fragrance than other types, bloom in June; 'Enchantment', grows to 5 ft., double; 'Frosty Morn', grows to 4 ft., double; 'Miniature Snowflake', grows to 3 ft., single; 'Minnesota Snowflake', grows to 8 ft., 2-in., double; 'Virginal', grows to 9 ft., 2½-in., semidouble, popular.

Photinia ×fraseri   (foh-TIN-ee-ah FRAY-zer-eye)   **RED LEAF PHOTINIA**

Parents from China, Japan	8	Evergreen	10-12 ft. by 15 ft.

Culture: Full sun. Fertile, humusy, well-drained soil. Withstands summer droughts with occasional water. Prune each summer to keep bushy and compact. Grow as hedge, or prune to one or few stems.

Comments: A mildew-resistant shrub that serves well as a hedge.

Other Species: *P. serrulata*, Chinese photinia, Zone 7, 15-30 ft. tall. Showy, off-white flowers followed by red berries. Large, leathery leaves.

Shrub Description	Season of Bloom	Flower Color	Flower Description
Deeply lobed, typical peony leaves held elegantly on stiff, open branches.	May	Yellow	Gorgeous, 6-12-in., silky-petalled, semi-double, golden yellow flowers produced over a 10-day blooming period.
Dark green leaves borne outward on stiff, slender, gently arching stems that freely sucker, forming a rounded, somewhat leggy shrub.	Late May-Early June	White	1½-in., single, pure white flowers carry a delightful citrus-jasmine scent.
Spring growth is bright, bronzy-red, turning dark green above, lighter green beneath. Multistemmed, upright, vigorous, slender trunks.	Mar.-Apr.	White	Attractive but not showy 4-in. clusters of small, ivory white flowers.

(continued)

Place of Origin	Zone	Plant Type	Mature Size

Pieris japonica   'Dorothy Wyckoff'   (py-AIR-iss ja-PON-ih-kah)   JAPANESE PIERIS

Place of Origin	Zone	Plant Type	Mature Size
Japan	6	Evergreen	10 by 6 ft.

Culture: Partial shade to full shade. Moist, acid, humusy, well-drained soil in a protected spot. Plant with rhododendrons and azaleas.

Comments: Perfectly suited for a woodsy walk. Select plants in late Apr. from the nursery so you can evaluate flowers and fragrance.

Other Cultivars: 'Mountain Fire', white flowers; 'Valley Valentine', rosy red flowers; 'Variegata', variegated leaves blush pink when young, white flowers; 'Wada's Pink', deep pink buds, clear pink flowers; 'White Cascade', white flowers.

Other Species: *P. formosa* 'Forrestii', Chinese pieris, Zone 7, to 12 ft. tall, showy scarlet young leaves and white flowers; *P. floribunda*, mountain pieris, Zone 4, to 6 ft. tall, erect flower clusters.

Pittosporum tobira   (pit-oh-SPOR-um toh-BY-rah)   JAPANESE PITTOSPORUM

Place of Origin	Zone	Plant Type	Mature Size
Japan	8	Evergreen	6-12 ft. by 8-15 ft.

Culture: Full sun to partial shade. Likes fertile, moist, humusy soil, but tolerant of dry conditions.

Comments: Good as a screening hedge, massed with other shrubs, and along foundation.

Cultivar: 'Variegata', grows to 5 ft., gray-green leaves are edged in white.

Potentilla fruticosa   'Primrose Beauty'   (po-ten-TIL-ah froo-tih-KOH-sah)   BUSH CINQUEFOIL

Place of Origin	Zone	Plant Type	Mature Size
Northern Europe, Asia	2	Deciduous	2 by 3 ft.

Culture: Full sun to partial shade. Likes well-drained loam, but tolerates heat, cold, drought, poor soil.

Comments: Most beautiful when massed in groups. Good low plant for front of shrub border. Trouble-free and prolific bloomer.

Other Cultivars: 'Abbottswood', blue-green foliage, large, white flowers; 'Gold Star', 2-in., rich golden yellow flowers; 'Katherine Dykes', silvery foliage, 1-in., light lemon yellow flowers; 'Princess', pale pink flowers; 'Red Ace', 1½-in., bright red flowers that fade quickly to yellow; 'Tangerine', pale orange flowers.

Prunus glandulosa   'Rosea'   (PROO-nuss gland-you-LOH-sah rose-EE-ah)   DWARF FLOWERING ALMOND

Place of Origin	Zone	Plant Type	Mature Size
China, Japan	4	Deciduous	4-6 ft. by 4-6 ft.

Culture: Full sun. Moist, humusy, well-drained soil. Prune hard after flowering.

Comments: Pretty in bloom, inconspicuous in leaf. Mix with other shrubs.

Other Cultivar: 'Alboplena', double, white flowers.

Shrub Description	Season of Bloom	Flower Color	Flower Description
New leaves form red tufts in spring, resembling flowers. Mature leaves are dark green, glossy, held in tiers over upright, densely branched stems. Leaves turn reddish in winter.	Apr.	Pink	Shrub festooned with strings of flower buds over winter, which open as small pink florets in 6-in. hanging panicles. Light fragrance.
Whorls of dark green, leathery, lustrous leaves cluster at ends of dense, stiff, broadly spreading stems.	Apr.–May	White	Clusters of small, yellowish, creamy white flowers appear above leaves at twig ends. Fragrance similar to orange blossoms.
Tiny, gray-green leaves borne thickly along short, dense, shrubby branches, making a fine-textured mound.	June–Oct.	Yellow	1½-in., pale yellow, single, roselike flowers borne continually from summer to frost.
Narrow, light green foliage has no autumn coloring. Stems form clumps with few branches in upright, open form.	May	Pink	Masses of double pink blossoms flock bare branches, followed by ½-in. red fruit.

(continued)

Place of Origin	Zone	Plant Type	Mature Size

Prunus tomentosa   PROO-nuss toe-men-TOE-sah)   NANKING CHERRY

Place of Origin	Zone	Plant Type	Mature Size
Himalayas, Northwest China	2	Deciduous	6-8 ft. by 10 ft.

Culture: Full sun. Average, well-drained soil. Tolerates heat, cold, drought.
Comments: Use massed with other shrubs in the border. Valuable as early bloomer for gardens in far North.

Punica granatum   'Wonderful'   (POON-ih-kah grah-NAY-tum)   POMEGRANATE

Place of Origin	Zone	Plant Type	Mature Size
Southeastern Europe to Himalayas	8	Deciduous	8-10 ft. by 5-8 ft.

Culture: Full sun. Tolerates dry, alkaline soil, but water regularly for best fruit production.
Comments: If grown without irrigation, fall rains may split ripening fruit. Doesn't fruit well in cool regions along California coast.
Other Cultivars: 'Chico', grows to 2-3 ft., double, orange flowers, no fruit; 'Nana', grows to 3 ft., excellent dwarf pomegranate for container culture.

Raphiolepis indica   (raf-ee-OH-lep-iss IN-dih-kah)   INDIAN HAWTHORN

Place of Origin	Zone	Plant Type	Mature Size
Southern China	7	Evergreen	4-5 ft. by 4-5 ft.

Culture: Full sun to partial shade. Average, well-drained soil. Tolerates drought, seacoast conditions. Easy to care for, needs little pruning.
Comments: Useful in front of a shrub border for off-season flowers; nice appearance.
Cultivars: 'Enchantress', deep rose pink; 'Snow White', white; 'Spring Rapture', deep pink.
Other Species: *P.* ×'Majestic Beauty', grows to 15 ft., forms small tree when pruned to standard, soft pink flowers.

RHODODENDRONS (See the chart, Rhododendrons and Azaleas, on page 236.)

Ribes odoratum   (RY-beez oh-door-AH-tum)   CLOVE CURRANT

Place of Origin	Zone	Plant Type	Mature Size
Midwestern United States	4	Deciduous	6 by 8 ft.

Culture: Full sun. Rich, moist, well-drained soil. Remove 3-year-old wood.
Comments: Old-fashioned garden favorite with a strong scent of cloves in spring. Very effective trailing over a garden wall.
Other Species: *R. sanguineum* 'King Edward VII', Zone 5, red flowers from Mar.-June.

Shrub Description	Season of Bloom	Flower Color	Flower Description
Medium green leaves are woolly underneath, arrayed on broad, spreading, irregular shrub with densely branched twigs. Shiny, red-brown bark of winter interest.	Apr.	White	Pink-blushed buds open to white, nearly 1-in., fragrant flowers, followed by edible red fruits in June and July.
Slender, lustrous, bright green leaves turn yellow in fall. Dense mass of arching stems makes a fountain-shaped shrub.	July–Aug.	Orange-red	4-in., waxy, single flowers are followed by typical, large pomegranate fruits that ripen in Oct.
Shiny bronze new growth turns dark green, leathery, forming a neat, dense, round shrub.	Dec.–May	White to pink	1-in. flowers in profuse clusters at branch tips vary with environmental conditions from white with pink blush to pink.
Pendulous, gray-green leaves on a loose, open shrub with old stems and younger suckers around outside.	Apr.–May	Yellow and red	Very spicily fragrant, yellow tubular flowers tinged red at their bases hang in racemes of 5-10 blossoms. Black berries follow if both sexes are planted.

(continued)

Place of Origin	Zone	Plant Type	Mature Size

ROSES "Roses" include all sorts of related plants, including tiny miniatures and climbing and vining sorts, the latter covered separately in the chart, Climbing and Rambling Roses, on page 273. The bushy and shrubby roses form the two major categories of most roses. Bush roses include hybrid teas, grandifloras, floribundas, and polyantha types. These are discussed in more detail under June in Chapter 2 (see page 57). "Shrub roses" is a catch-all phrase including many old hybrids and some species. The shrub-form species roses described in this chart are old garden favorites that are still planted for their beauty and function.

Rosa hugonis   (ROE-sah HOO-gawn-iss)   FATHER HUGO ROSE

China	5	Deciduous	6–8 ft.

   Culture: Tolerates poor soil. Needs sunny, warm site. Prune older canes to encourage new, floriferous growth.
   Comments: Suitable for a woodland planting.

Rosa rubrifolia (also called *R. glauca*)   (ROE-sah roo-brih-FOAL-ee-ah)   REDLEAF ROSE

Europe	2	Deciduous	6 ft.

   Culture: Tolerates poor soil. Somewhat tolerant of shady location.
   Comments: Beautiful fall display of foliage and hips, can be more spectacular than summer bloom.

Rosa rugosa   (ROE-sah roo-GO-sah)   RUGOSA ROSE

Japan, Western Asia	2	Deciduous	6–7 ft.

   Culture: Tolerates poor soil. Somewhat tolerant of shady location.
   Comments: Big red hips chock full of vitamin C.

Rosa spinosissima (also called *R. pimpinellifolia*)   (ROE-sah spy-no-SISS-ih-mah)   SCOTCH ROSE

Europe	4	Deciduous	3 ft.

   Culture: Tolerates most soils. Somewhat tolerant of shady location.
   Comments: An excellent rose for holding erosion-prone banks. Now naturalizing in the eastern United States.

Shrub Description	Season of Bloom	Flower Color	Flower Description
Upright, arching canes form a mound. Leaves turn bronze-orange in fall. Small, dark red fruit appear in late summer.	Late May	Soft yellow	Masses of medium single blooms cover bush. Incomparably beautiful in bud.
Mature foliage gains a red-purple cast that forms a beautiful color harmony with its orange-red hips in fall.	Mid-June-July	Mauve-pink	Small, single flowers appear in clusters.
Forms tall barrier of thorny canes. Dark green, rough-textured, handsome foliage.	Peak in spring, continues lightly all summer.	Rosy pink	Single, fragrant flowers with prominent yellow stamens.
Small, fernlike leaves, stems covered with long, thin prickles.	Early June	Pink, yellow, or white	Available in single and double forms. Carries a light fragrance.

(continued)

Place of Origin	Zone	Plant Type	Mature Size

Rosa wichuraiana (ROE-sah witch-oor-ee-AN-ah) MEMORIAL ROSE

China	6	Deciduous	1½ ft.

Culture: Tolerates poor soil. Somewhat shade tolerate.
Comments: Good for erosion control. Dense growth prevents weeds. Hips are favored by birds.

Spiraea prunifolia (spy-REE-ah proon-ih-FOAL-ee-ah) SHOE BUTTON SPIRAEA, BRIDAL-WREATH SPIRAEA

Korea, China	5	Deciduous	4-6 ft. by 6 ft.

Culture: Full sun. Average, well-drained soil. Thin out old canes and weak branches immediately after flowering.
Comments: Victorian in look and elegantly beautiful, especially as a hedge.
Other Species: S. ×*arguta*, garland spiraea, Zone 4, early, free-flowering, with flat clusters of white flowers along arching, bare, 4-ft. stems of previous year's wood, quite showy; S. ×*bumalda* 'Anthony Waterer', flat umbels of crimson-pink florets appear in June and July, with sporadic bloom thereafter on 2-ft. stems, blooms on new growth; S. *nipponica* 'Snow Mound', neat 5-ft. shrub, one of the prettiest spiraeas in bloom and out; S. *thunbergii*, baby's breath spiraea, 4-6 ft., very bushy, short lived shrub with narrow leaves gives fine-textured look. Single flowers appear in small clusters in Apr. on previous year's growth. S. ×*tanhouttei*, bridal-wreath, Zone 4, upright, vase-shaped shrub with long branches of previous year's wood arching to ground, profusely covered with precise clustes of white florets in late May.

Syringa ×*chinensis* (sy-RING-gah chy-NEN-siss) CHINESE LILAC

Garden origin	3	Deciduous	8 by 15 ft.

Culture: Full sun. Rich, moist, humusy soil. Prune out excess suckers, older stems.
Comments: More profuse bloom and a more elegant appearance than *Syringa vulgaris*, below, make this shrub best choice for landscaping.
Cultivar: 'Alba', white flowers.
Other Species: S. *laciniata*, cutleaf lilac, graceful, arching stems carry ferny foliage, 3-in., lilac clusters have perfumy fragrance; S. *microphylla* 'Superba', little leaf lilac, Zone 4, grows to 6 ft., twice as wide. 3-in. clusters of rosy lilac florets appear in May, again in Aug.-Sept; S. *meyeri* 'Miss Kim', dwarf Korean lilac, dainty, to 5 ft., pink buds open, then fade to ice-blue clusters in June; S. ×*persica*, persian lilac, Zone 5, graceful, rounded shrub measures 6 ft. tall, same width, bears profusions of fragrant lilac clusters in May.

Shrub Description	Season of Bloom	Flower Color	Flower Description
Dark, glossy foliage evergreen in warmer regions. A tough, low-growing, spreading rose. Produces dark red hips.	Mid-June–July	White	2-in., fragrant flowers borne in clusters of 2-10.
Glossy, dark green, oval leaves turn bronzy, reddish-orange in fall. Graceful, slender stems make an open, fine-textured form.	Mid-May	White	Sprays of button-sized, double flowers resembling miniature roses cover the long, bare branches of the previous year's wood.
Fine-textured leaves cover vase-shaped mass of long, limber stems, giving a billowing appearance.	May	Lilac	Large, loose, sweetly scented panicles of fine florets make slender stems arch gracefully under their weight.

(continued)

Place of Origin	Zone	Plant Type	Mature Size

Syringa vulgaris   'Alphonse Lavallée'   (sy-RING-gah vul-GARE-iss)   **LILAC**

Place of Origin	Zone	Plant Type	Mature Size
Southeastern Europe	3	Deciduous	20 by 15 ft.

Culture: Full sun. Rich, moist, humusy soil. Prune out all suckers arising from roots except a few for vigorous stems.

Comments: Place within shrub borders; doesn't offer much interest when out of bloom.

Other Cultivars: 'Jan Van Tol', single, white; 'Mme. Lemoine', double, white; 'President Lincoln', single, blue; 'President Grevy', double, blue; 'Jacques Collot', single, lilac; 'Charm', single, pink; 'Mme. Antoine Buckner', double, pink; 'Congo', single, magenta; 'Charles Joly', double, magenta; 'Ludwig Spaeth', single, purple; 'Angel White', for Zones 8-9, single, white, doesn't require deep winter freeze as do other *S. vulgaris* cultivars; 'Lavender Lady', for Zones 8-9, single, lavender, doesn't require deep winter freeze as do other *S. vulgaris* cultivars.

Tamarix hispida   (TAM-ar-iks HISS-pid-ah)   **KASHGAR TAMARISK**

Place of Origin	Zone	Plant Type	Mature Size
Central Asia	5	Deciduous	4 by 6 ft.

Culture: Full sun. Poor, well-drained soil. Cut back hard each year, even to ground, as it blooms on new growth.

Comments: Most compact and neatest-looking tamarisk. Doesn't like to be transplanted. Site it where it won't be seen in winter, when it turns red-brown like a dead Christmas tree. Good for desert, coastal sites.

Other Species: *T. ramosissima* 'Rosea', summer glow tamarisk. Zone 2, grows to 10-15 ft., rose pink flower spikes.

Tibouchina urvilleana   (tih-boo-CHEE-nah ur-vill-ee-AN-ah)   **PRINCESS FLOWER**

Place of Origin	Zone	Plant Type	Mature Size
Brazil	10	Evergreen	8-10 ft. by 8-10 ft.

Culture: Full sun to partial shade. Acid, humusy, well-drained soil. Pinch stems after flowering to create a bushy plant, especially in containers.

Comments: A very showy subtropical plant. Popular in California among those who love the color purple. Likes head in sun, feet in shade.

Viburnum carlesii   (vy-BURN-um kar-LEEZ-ee-eye)   **SPICE VIBURNUM**

Place of Origin	Zone	Plant Type	Mature Size
Korea	5	Deciduous	5 by 8 ft.

Culture: Full sun to partial shade. Moist, humusy, well-drained soil.

Comments: Flowers last only 10-14 days; plant inconspicuous at other times, so mix into a shrub border rather than using as a specimen.

Cultivar: 'Compactum', dwarf form to 3 ft.

Other Species: The following have *V. carlesii* as one of their parents; *V. ×burkwoodii*, semi- to fully evergreen, taller than *V. carlesii*, but with a similar sweet scent; *V. ×carlcephalum*, larger than *V. carlesii*, with 6-in. flower clusters, carries spicy fragrance, good fall color; *V. ×juddii*, Zone 4, hardier, but not as fragrant as *V. carlesii*.

Shrub Description	Season of Bloom	Flower Color	Flower Description
Heart-shaped leaves often covered by mildew in mid-summer. Freely suckering stems make large, upright, irregular shrubs.	May	Lilac	Upright panicles of fragrant, double florets scent the late spring mornings.
Feathery, light green, lacy foliage on fast-growing, loose, wispy, and open stems.	Aug.-Sept.	Pink	Tiny florets form 7-9-in. panicles at branch tips, covering shrub with a cloud of bright pink flowers.
3-6-in., bronzy-green, felty leaves appear sparsely over large, open, treelike shrub. Branch tips, buds covered with reddish fuzz.	May, intermittently through Feb.	Purple	Pretty, 3 in. wide, royal purple flowers borne singly or in clusters.
Dull green leaves turn reddish-purple in autumn. Shrub is upright, rounded.	Apr.-May	White	Pink buds open to 3½-in., blushing white clusters of very fragrant flowers. The scent is floral and spicy, like cloves and gardenias.

(continued)

Place of Origin	Zone	Plant Type	Mature Size

Viburnum davidii (vy-BURN-um da-VID-ee-eye)   DAVID VIBURNUM

China	7	Evergreen	2-3 ft. by 4-5 ft.

Culture: Partial shade to full shade. Moist, humusy, well-drained soil.
Comments: Showy fruit sets best when 2 or more shrubs massed together. Makes an excellent ground-covering shrub in the foreground of ferns and rhododendrons in shady, woodsy spots.
Other Species: *V. rhytidophyllum*, leatherleaf viburnum, Zone 6, corrugated leaves droop in winter. Off-white, 8-in. clusters of flowers in May, fruits vary from red to black, reaches 15 ft., gives coarse effect in the border.

Viburnum macrocephalum var. *macrocephalum*   (vy-BURN-um MACK-roe-SEFF-ah-lum)   CHINESE SNOWBALL

Garden origin	7	Deciduous in Zone 7; evergreen in warmer zones.	6-12 ft. by 6-12 ft.

Culture: Partial shade. Rich, moist, well-drained soil.
Comments: Good drainage is imperative for this variety, which has the largest flowers of any viburnum.
Cultivar: 'Sterile', sterile white blossoms.

Viburnum plicatum var. *tomentosum*   'Mariesii' (vy-BURN-um plih-KAHT-um toe-men-TOE-sum)   DOUBLE FILE VIBURNUM

China, Japan	5	Deciduous	10-12 ft. by 12-14 ft.

Culture: Full sun. Moist, humusy, well-drained soil.
Comments: The flower display is quite unusual and showy.
Other Cultivar: 'Shasta', grows to 6 ft., compact form with large, white flowers, good horizontal effect.

Viburnum sieboldii (vy-BURN-um see-BOLD-ee-eye)   SIEBOLD VIBURNUM

Japan	4	Deciduous	20 by 15 ft.

Culture: Full sun to light shade. Moist, humusy, rich, well-drained soil.
Comments: Bold, striking plant because of multicolored fruits. One of the showiest viburnums for northern gardens.
Other Species: *V. trilobum*, American cranberry, edible cranberry fruit hangs on shrub through winter, likes boggy conditions; *V. opulus*, European cranberry, similar to *V. trilobum*, but fruit is not edible.

Shrub Description	Season of Bloom	Flower Color	Flower Description
Grooved, dark green, leathery, narrowly oval leaves held horizontally over short, mounded, compact shrub.	June	White	3-in., flat clusters of small, dull white flowers followed by shiny, metallic blue, pea-sized fruit later in the year.
Oval, dark green, pointed leaves on upright, rounded, and spreading shrub gives a dense effect.	May-June	Green to white	Huge, 8-12-in. snowball flower clusters open chartreuse, fade to pure white.
Pleated, 4-in., oval, leathery, dull, dark green leaves held along tiered, horizontal branches. Brownish to purplish-red color in fall.	May-June	White	Lace cap effect given by large, white petals surrounding smaller petals in 3-in. clusters, followed by red berries that turn black by fall. Flowers carried in orderly double files along horizontal branches.
6-in., dark green, polished leaves on a tall, wide spreading, open shrub or small tree. Leaves bronze with fall frosts.	May	White	3-4-in., flat clusters of creamy white flowers with a rather unpleasant odor borne profusely in midspring, followed by red to black berries on red cluster stalks.

(continued)

Place of Origin	Zone	Plant Type	Mature Size

Viburnum tinus   (vy-BURN-um TY-nuss)   LAURUSTINUS

Place of Origin	Zone	Plant Type	Mature Size
Mediterranean	7	Evergreen	6-12 ft. by 7-10 ft.

Culture: Full sun to full shade. Tolerates wide range of soils, most conditions.

Comments: Dense habit and tolerance of poor conditions make it ideal for screening and hedges in hot and dry southern and western gardens. Dwarf forms make good container plants.

Vitex agnus-castus   'Latifolia'   (VY-teks AHN-yus-CASS-tus lat-ih-FOAL-ee-ah) CHASTE TREE

Place of Origin	Zone	Plant Type	Mature Size
Southern Europe, Western Asia	7	Deciduous	10-15 ft. by 10-20 ft.

Culture: Full sun. Ordinary, even poor, soil.

Comments: Similar to *Buddleia* spp. in appearance and culture. Heavy freezes will nip it to ground in cold zones. Spiky look softens at a distance.

Other Cultivars: 'Alba', white flowers; 'Rosea', pink flowers; 'Variegata', leaves variegated cream and green.

Weigela florida   (wy-GEEL-ah FLOR-ih-dah)   WEIGELA

Place of Origin	Zone	Plant Type	Mature Size
Northern China, Japan, Korea	5	Deciduous	6-9 ft. by 9-12 ft.

Culture: Full sun to partial shade. Fertile, humusy, well-drained soil. Prune annually after flowering.

Comments: Best massed with other shrubs in the border, where it's partially hidden when not in bloom.

Cultivars: 'Variegata Nana', grows to 4-5 ft., cream-colored leaf margins, soft pink flowers; 'Folis-purpureis', grows to 4 ft., dark purple leaves, pink flowers.

Other Species: *W. hybrida* 'Bristol Ruby', ruby red flowers beloved by hummingbirds; 'Bristol Snowflake', white flowers fading to pink blush; 'Vanicek', violet-red flowers.

Shrub Description	Season of Bloom	Flower Color	Flower Description
2-3-in., oval, dark green leaves on an upright, dense shrub. New growth is burgundy red.	Feb.-Apr.; second fall bloom in warm zones.	White	Pink buds open to white flowers in 3-in., flat clusters. Metallic blue fruit and flowers can be on shrub at same time.
Narrow leaves are held in fans of 5, giving a pleasing foliage form to the stiff, open, spreading branch and trunk structure.	July-Oct.	Lavender-blue	1 ft. long, slender flower spikes carry a sweet scent and are produced freely at branch ends over the shrub.
2-4-in., oval, light green leaves on spreading branches that arch to the ground make a coarse, rounded, awkward shrub.	May	Pink	Small groups of 1¼-in., tubular, rosy pink flowers produced freely on previous year's wood.

What is a rhododendron? Most of us think of medium to large shrubs with leathery, evergreen leaves and big floral puffs in white, pink, red, lavender, or purple in June. Those who know the genus better realize that rhododendrons range from miniature forms just a few inches high to tree-sized forms 80 feet tall. Some are deciduous, some evergreen.

Over 900 species of rhododendron are known, and there are over 10,000 named cultivars, 2,000 of which are in commerce! The genus includes not only what we usually call rhododendrons, but also the azaleas. Azaleas are not precisely defined. Like rhododendrons in general, some are deciduous and some are evergreen, and some azaleas are larger than some rhododendrons. Put most simply, azaleas are an undefined subset of the genus rhododendron.

Rhododendrons have a reputation for being finicky and hard to grow. They're finicky, but if you cater to their needs, they'll grow quite nicely. To understand their needs, you should know that this group of plants grows wild in moist, shady forests. Here shafts of sunlight reach through the trees to play over the finely formed leaves of the wild rhododendrons. On the cool forest floor, years of fallen leaves have built a thick duff that serves as a reservoir of nutrients released by decay organisms and moisture made slightly acidic from the decayed leaves. The duff also serves as a thick, protective mulch for the roots of the rhododendrons, which lie close to the surface. Reproduce conditions like these at home and you should have success.

Translating those conditions from the wild to the home garden, make sure to give rhododendrons an acid soil, very well drained and yet moisture retentive. A soil very rich in organic matter supplies this, so mix finished compost 50-50 with existing soil and mulch thickly with an organic mulch. In regions where the soil is alkaline or full of dissolved salts, such as parts of the desert and the West, you may need to make the soil more acid. Rhododendrons can take acidity down to pH 4.5, and prefer a soil between 5.5 and 6.0. You can further acidify finished compost, which usually has a pH of 6.5, by adding pine needle duff from a coniferous forest floor, gypsum, or ferrous sulfate. This latter salt supplies iron, which may be in short supply at higher pHs.

Rhododendrons need protection from summer's baking heat, and prefer a cool, misty, semishaded, sheltered spot. Conifers nearby help produce these conditions by trapping moist air under their boughs during summer's dry sunny days, which benefits any rhododendrons planted around them. In the winter, when the leaves of the deciduous forests are gone, evergreen rhododendrons are revealed to the piercing sun. Again, nearby conifers will give shade and also protect the rhododendrons from the wind.

The following chart describes some of the best species and classes of hybrid rhododendrons. Check with your local nurseries for cultivars fitted to your region in colors you prefer.

More than any other garden shrub, rhododendrons are climate-specific—that is, they thrive in the regions they hail from, but aren't very adaptable in other climates. The best hybrid for you is the one that proves itself by growing well in your region. Always make sure that the rhododendrons you buy in the colder regions aren't frost-tender kinds shipped up north by the tens of thousands by suppliers anxious to cash in on the springtime markets.

Zone	Plant Description	Flower Description	Season of Bloom
Rhododendron arborescens (ROE-doe-DEN-dron AR-boar-ESS-ens) **SWEET AZALEA**			
4	Deciduous 10-ft. native of eastern Appalachians.	1-in., white to light pink, fragrant, funnel-shaped flowers.	June
R. arboreum (ar-BOAR-ee-um) **TREE RHODODENDRON**			
9	Reaches 40 ft. tall. Green, glossy, 8-in., evergreen leaves. Native of Himalayas.	2-in., scarlet flowers held in 6-8 in. trusses.	Nov.-Jan.

Zone	Plant Description	Flower Description	Season of Bloom

R. calendulaceum (cal-EN-jue-LACE-ee-um) **FLAME AZALEA**

Zone	Plant Description	Flower Description	Season of Bloom
5	5–10-ft. deciduous plants. Appalachian native.	Vividly colored (varying from yellow to orange to scarlet) trusses of 5–7 funnel-shaped, 2-in. flowers with conspicuous stamens.	June

R. carolinianum (care-oh-LIN-ee-AH-num) **CAROLINA RHODODENDRON**

Zone	Plant Description	Flower Description	Season of Bloom
6	Grows to 6 ft. high and as wide. Evergreen, oval, 3-in., semiglossy leaves curl at temperatures below 30°F. North Carolina native.	Pale rose-purple, 1½-in., funnel-shaped flowers held in groups of 5–10.	May

R. catawbiense (cah-TAW-bee-ENS) **CATAWBA RHODODENDRON**

Zone	Plant Description	Flower Description	Season of Bloom
5	6–10-ft., lightly branched plants. 3–6 in. glossy and handsome evergreen leaves. Native to Blue Ridge.	Profuse flowering can cover the shrub completely in lilac to lavender 2-in. funnels held in 6-in. trusses.	May–June

_R._ 'Gable Hybrids' **GABLE HYBRID AZALEA**

Zone	Plant Description	Flower Description	Season of Bloom
6	Hardiest of the evergreen azaleas. Short, shrubby, dense plants from 2–4 ft. tall and as wide. Developed in Pennsylvania.	Cultivars available in pink, purple and white. Flowers cluster profusely over plants.	May

_R._ ×gandavensis (GAN-dah-VEN-siss) **GHENT AZALEA**

Zone	Plant Description	Flower Description	Season of Bloom
4	Upright, shrubby group of plants of variable but modest height. Deciduous, with rich fall foliage colors.	2-in. typical azalea flowers range from yellow to orange to red, with many pink shades.	May

R. kaempferi (CAMP-fer-eye) **TORCH AZALEA**

Zone	Plant Description	Flower Description	Season of Bloom
6	Taller and more open than the 'Gable Hybrids', with small, glossy, evergreen leaves.	1½-in., flared funnels are orange-red in the true species, and vary from red to salmon to rose and white in the Kaempferi hybrids, which are derived from the species Floriferous.	Apr.

(continued)

Zone	Plant Description	Flower Description	Season of Bloom

R. 'Knap Hill-Exbury Hybrids'   EXBURY HYBRID AZALEA

| 6 | This group of deciduous azaleas shows a generally upright form, with a loose, open habit and small leaves clustered near branch tips. Grows from 4-8 ft. tall. | Flowers are wide-mouthed, flaring trumpets 2-3 in. wide in huge trusses of 15-30 flowers. Exquisite mixes of several color combinations. | May-June |

R. ×kosteranum   (koss-ter-AH-num)   MOLLIS HYBRID AZALEA

| 6 | Grows 3-6 ft. tall and as wide in an upright rounded form. Coarse, deciduous foliage clusters at branch tips, colors nicely in fall. | 2½ in. wide flowers appear in clusters of from 5-7 in a range of colors from yellow and gold to pink, red, and white. | May |

R. macrophyllum   (MACK-roe-FY-lum)   WEST COAST RHODODENDRON, CALIFORNIA ROSEBAY

| 7 | Thick-trunked shrub with 3-8-in., deep green, evergreen leaves, reaches from 4-12 ft. tall and as wide. The native West Coast rhododendron is the state flower of Washington. | Red buds open to 2½ in., rose-purple flowers held in trusses of 20 flowers. | June |

R. maximum   (MAX-ih-mum)   ROSEBAY RHODODENDRON

| 4 | 15 ft. tall, loose and open shrub with glossy, evergreen leaves from 6-10 in. long. Native from Nova Scotia to Georgia. | Rose-pink and white flowers in 4-in. trusses partially hidden by new foliage. | June-July |

R. mucronulatum   (MEW-crow-new-LAH-tum)   KOREAN AZALEA

| 4 | Upright, compact, oval form of deciduous azalea, with clean-looking character, nice foliage. Plant in shaded spot out of sun. | Bright rosy purple, 1 ¾-in. wide flowers held in clusters of 6 or less. 'Cornell Pink' is a favored pink form. | Blooms well before foliage in Mar.-Apr. in Northeast, as early as Jan. on West Coast. |

Zone	Plant Description	Flower Description	Season of Bloom

R. 'P.J.M. Hybrids'   P.J.M. HYBRID RHODODENDRON

5	3-6 ft. shrubs form a rounded, dense mound of small, evergreen leaves that may be deciduous in northernmost range. Leaves turn plum purple in fall.	Lavender-pink flowers vary in color intensity.	Apr.

R. schlippenbachii   (SHLIP-en-BOCK-ee-eye)   **ROYAL AZALEA**

5	Native to Manchuria and Japan. Upright, rounded form, to 8 ft. tall and just as wide. Deciduous foliage is dark green, turning orange and red in fall. One of the finest of the hardy azaleas.	Fragrant, 3-in. wide, flaring bells are pale rose, held in groups of 3 to 6.	May

R. vaseyi   (VASE-ee-eye)   **PINK-SHELL AZALEA**

5	Native to Blue Ridge Mountains, adapted to wet or dry soils. Upright, slender stems produce deciduous leaves that color red in fall.	Pale pink to rose flowers with red-brown spotting held in clusters of 5-7 atop the thin branches before the leaves appear.	May

R. viscosum   (viss-COE-sum)   **SWAMP AZALEA**

3	Native to swamps from Maine to South Carolina. An open, loose, and spreading shrub that grows from 3-8 ft., depending on conditions. Deciduous 2½-in. dark green leaves turn bronze in fall.	White to pale pink, heavily clove-scented flowers are 1-in. funnels, cluster in groups of 4-9.	Late June-July

R. yakusimanum   (yack-KOO-see-MAH-num)   **YAKUSIMANUM RHODODENDRON**

6	Dense, spreading shrub to 3 ft. tall and as wide. 3-in., evergreen leaves are dark green above, gray to tan or white and woolly underneath. Native to Yakusima Island, Japan. One of the most charming and elegant of all rhododendrons. New foliage is gray, suedelike.	Bright coral buds open to pink bells that soon turn white, are carried 12 to a truss.	May

Place of Origin	Zone	Mature Size	Plant Description	Season of Bloom	Flower Color

***Allamanda cathartica* 'Williamsii'** (al-ah-MAN-dah kah-THART-ick-ah)
  YELLOW ALLAMANDA

Place of Origin	Zone	Mature Size	Plant Description	Season of Bloom	Flower Color
Guiana	10	15 ft.	Profusely covered with large, trumpet-shaped flowers. Carries leathery leaves in whorls. Evergreen. Tie to supports.	June–Sept.	Yellow

Culture: Full sun to light shade. Rich, well-drained loam.
Comments: A good potted vine for a humid greenhouse that stays above 55°F. Prune in late winter to within 2–3 nodes of old wood. Let plant rest during the winter; water sparingly and don't fertilize.

Anemopaegma chamberlaynii (also called ***Bignonia chamberlaynii***)
  (ah-nee-mo-PIG-mah chame-ber-LAYN-ee-eye)   **YELLOW TRUMPET VINE**

Place of Origin	Zone	Mature Size	Plant Description	Season of Bloom	Flower Color
Brazil	9	20 ft.	3-in., trumpet-shaped flowers appear in clusters. Evergreen, climbs by tendrils.	All summer	Pale yellow with purple and white markings in the throat

Culture: Full sun to partial shade. Average soil.
Comments: Spreads by underground roots, so keep it confined. Creates a thick screen. Needs support.

Anredera cordifolia (also called ***Boussingaultia baselloides***)
  (an-RED-er-ah cord-ih-FOAL-ee-ah)   **MADEIRA VINE**

Place of Origin	Zone	Mature Size	Plant Description	Season of Bloom	Flower Color
Paraguay	9	20 ft.	Stems with 2–3-in. oval leaves produce 1 ft. long clusters of tiny, fragrant flowers. Foliage covers the vine densely. Evergreen and twining.	Aug.–Oct.	White

Culture: Full sun. Rich, sandy soil.
Comments: Produces aerial tubers in leaf axils that are planted for new vines. In cold regions, store roots over winter in a root cellar. A favorite porch and pergola cover in the South.

Place of Origin	Zone	Mature Size	Plant Description	Season of Bloom	Flower Color

Antigonon leptopus (an-TIG-oh-non lep-TOE-pus) **ROSA DE MONTANA, CORAL VINE, LOVE VINE**

Place of Origin	Zone	Mature Size	Plant Description	Season of Bloom	Flower Color
Mexico	9	25 ft.	Chains of flowers trail over dark green, heart-shaped leaves. Climbs using tendrils. Evergreen in Zone 10; deciduous in areas of light frosts.	Aug.–Oct.	Bright pink

Culture: Full sun. Average to poor soil.
Comments: A beloved, fast-growing vine of the southeastern United States, used to cover verandas. Excellent potted climber in the northern winter greenhouse. Prune hard after flowering.
Cultivar: 'Album', white flowers.

Beaumontia grandiflora (bo-MONT-ee-ah grand-ih-FLOR-ah) **EASTER LILY VINE, HERALD'S TRUMPET**

Place of Origin	Zone	Mature Size	Plant Description	Season of Bloom	Flower Color
Nepal	9	30 ft.	Broad, oval, tropical-looking leaves cover sturdy branches. Hundreds of large, fragrant trumpets are borne on previous year's wood. An evergreen twiner.	Apr.–Sept.	White

Culture: Full sun. Deep, rich soil.
Comments: Likes a warm, sheltered spot away from prevailing winds. Prune after flowering. Greenhouse plants must be given lots of rooting room and temperatures no lower than 60°F.

Bignonia capreolata (also called ***Anisostichus capreolatus***) (big-NOAN-ee-ah cap-ree-oh-LAH-tah) **CROSS VINE**

Place of Origin	Zone	Mature Size	Plant Description	Season of Bloom	Flower Color
Southeastern United States	7	40–60 ft.	A rampant vine with deep green leaves spaced evenly along its stems. 2-in. flower trumpets appear in midspring. Evergreen climber.	Apr.–May	Orange to red with red throats

Culture: Full sun to partial shade. Average soil.
Comments: Clings to stone, brick, or concrete walls, covering them quickly with rampant growth. Give it lots of room.

(continued)

Place of Origin	Zone	Mature Size	Plant Description	Season of Bloom	Flower Color

---

Bougainvillea buttiana hybrids   (boo-gain-VEE-lee-ah but-ee-AN-ah) HYBRID BOUGAINVILLEA

| South America | 10 | 15 ft. | The flamboyantly colored bracts are displayed among broad, oval leaves carried on flimsy branches. Evergreen, climbs using hooked spines. | All summer | Yellows, reds, and white |

Culture: Full sun. Rich, humusy loam.
Comments: Needs a spot sheltered from the wind. Tie to trellising to keep it in place. Prune in spring before growth starts.
Cultivars: 'Barbara Karst', red flowers; 'California Gold', yellow flowers; 'Jamaica White', white flowers; 'San Diego Red', red flowers; 'Texas Dawn', pink flowers.

Bougainvillea spectabilis   (boo-gain-VEE-lee-ah speck-TAH-bill-iss) PURPLE BOUGAINVILLEA

| Brazil | 9 | 20 ft. | Hardy, vigorous vine. Foliage mingles with huge clusters of flower bracts, creating spectacular effect. Evergreen, climbs using hooked spines. | All year | Purple |

Culture: Full sun. Rich, humusy loam.
Comments: Blooms well even in cool summers. Hardier by 10° than the hybrids. A tropical look for the patio in summer. Prune before new growth starts. Repot in late winter, taking care not to break fragile roots.

Campsis grandiflora   (CAMP-siss grand-ih-FLOR-ah)   CHINESE TRUMPET CREEPER

| China | 7 | 30 ft. | 3-in.-diameter trumpets appear in clusters of 6-9 flowers. Rough-looking leaves are divided into 7-9 coarse leaflets, each 2½ in. long. Deciduous, climbs by aerial rootlets. | Aug. | Scarlet |

Culture: Full sun. Rich soil.
Comments: Showiest of the trumpet vines. Good for rapidly covering walls or trellis. Loved, as are all campsis, by hummingbirds.

Place of Origin	Zone	Mature Size	Plant Description	Season of Bloom	Flower Color

Campsis radicans (CAMP-siss RAD-ih-cans) **COMMON TRUMPET VINE**					
Eastern United States	5	40 ft.	A rampant vine. Trumpets, 2-in. in diameter, appear in clusters among the coarsely toothed leaflets. Deciduous, climbs by aerial rootlets.	July–Sept.	Orange-red

Culture: Full sun. Average soil.
Comments: This vigorous grower can tear its support—whether stone or wooden wall—to pieces, and must be kept in check.
Cultivar: 'Flava', the yellow version of the common orange-red trumpet.

Campsis ×tagliabuana 'Mme. Galen' (CAMP-siss tag-lee-ah-boo-AH-nah)					
Hybrid origin	5	30 ft.	Dark green foliage is more handsome than most campsis types. Flowers showier than *C. radicans*. Deciduous climber.	July–Sept.	Salmon-red

Culture: Full sun. Average soil.
Comments: A cross between *C. grandiflora*'s showy flowers and *C. radicans*' winter hardiness.

Clematis alpina 'Pamela Jackman' (CLEM-ah-tiss al-PINE-ah) **ALPINE VIRGIN'S BOWER**					
Southern Europe	4	6 ft.	Small, bushy plant bearing a profusion of 2-in., nodding, satiny blue bells on single stalks. Deciduous, climbs by twisting leaf stems.	Apr.–May	Blue

Culture: Foliage likes full sun; roots like the shade. Rich, moist soil.
Comments: A fine feature in a small garden. Likes to trail over rock walls.
Other Cultivars: 'Ruby', rose red flowers; 'White Moth', blooms are double, white.

(continued)

Place of Origin	Zone	Mature Size	Plant Description	Season of Bloom	Flower Color

Clematis armandii (CLEM-ah-tiss ar-MAN-dee-eye) **EVERGREEN CLEMATIS**					
South and Central China	7	20 ft.	1-2 in. fragrant, star-like flowers cluster among the arrays of 6-8 in. long leaves. Evergreen, climbs by twisting leaf stems.	Mar.-Apr.	White

Culture: Full sun to light shade. Rich, moist, well-drained soil.
Comments: Trailing vines with cascades of dark green leaves give a tropical effect. Interplant with deciduous clematis for better look in winter.
Cultivars: 'Hendersoni Rubra', pink flowers; 'Apple Blossom', pale pink blossoms.

Clematis chrysocoma var. **_sericea_** (also called **_C. spooneri_**) (CLEM-ah-tiss cry-so-KOHM-ah sir-EE-see-ah) **HAIRY CLEMATIS**					
China	4	20 ft.	A vigorous clematis with bronzy, downy stems and an ability to cover itself with flowers. Deciduous, vigorous climber.	May-June	Creamy white

Culture: Full sun to light shade. Rich, moist soil.
Comments: Cut back after flowering to keep this variety in its alloted space. _C. spooneri_ 'Rosea' of the catalogs is a _C. chrysocoma-C. montana_ 'Rubens' hybrid.

CLEMATIS LARGE-FLOWERED HYBRIDS (See the chart, Clematis Large-Flowered Hybrids, on page 268.)

Clematis macropetala (CLEM-ah-tiss mack-roe-peh-TAL-ah) **DOWNY CLEMATIS**					
China	4	10 ft.	Nodding, semidouble, bell-shaped flowers 2-3 in. across resemble ballerinas' skirts. Deciduous, climbs by twisting leaf stems.	May-June	Lavender-blue

Culture: Full sun for foliage, roots need shade. Rich, moist soil.
Comments: Happily scrambles over rocks, low walls, and fences. Prune after flowering, if pruning is necessary.
Cultivar: 'Rose O'Grady', delicate pink flowers.

Place of Origin	Zone	Mature Size	Plant Description	Season of Bloom	Flower Color

Clematis montana 'Alba'   (CLEM-ah-tiss mon-TAN-ah)   ANEMONE CLEMATIS

Place of Origin	Zone	Mature Size	Plant Description	Season of Bloom	Flower Color
Himalayas	4	20 ft.	Masses of white, 2-3 in., anemonelike flowers with frilly, yellow stamens. Deciduous, climbs by twisting leaf stems.	May-June	White

Culture: Full sun for foliage, roots need shade. Rich, moist soil.
Comments: A vigorous climber ideal for covering outbuildings. Prune directly after flowering.
Other Cultivars: 'Elizabeth', soft pink flowers; 'Rubens', rosy pink blooms; 'Tetra-Rose', lilac pink blossoms; 'Wilsonii', white, fragrant flowers appear in July-Aug.

Clematis paniculata (also called *C. dioscoreifolia*)   (CLEM-ah-tiss pan-IK-you-LAH-tah)   SWEET AUTUMN CLEMATIS

Place of Origin	Zone	Mature Size	Plant Description	Season of Bloom	Flower Color
Japan	5	30 ft.	Panicles of fragrant, 1-in. flowers smother this easy-to-grow, robust climber late in the season. Evergreen in the warmest zones. Climbs using twisting leaf stems.	Sept.-Oct.	White

Culture: Full sun to light shade. Rich, moist soil.
Comments: Drops its dark green leaves in the North. Prune after flowering. Plant on an arbor with spring and summer bloomers for continuous flowering.

Clematis tangutica   (CLEM-ah-tiss tang-you-TEEK-ah)   GOLDEN CLEMATIS

Place of Origin	Zone	Mature Size	Plant Description	Season of Bloom	Flower Color
Northwestern China	3	15 ft.	Twining stems produce masses of fine leaves and nodding flowers. Deciduous, climbs by twisting leaf stems.	June	Bright yellow

Culture: Full sun to partial shade. Rich, moist soil.
Comments: Silky seed heads make this plant decorative from June right through frost. Prune after flowering.

(continued)

Place of Origin	Zone	Mature Size	Plant Description	Season of Bloom	Flower Color

Clematis texensis   (CLEM-ah-tiss tex-EN-siss)   **SCARLET CLEMATIS**

Place of Origin	Zone	Mature Size	Plant Description	Season of Bloom	Flower Color
Southwestern United States	4	8 ft.	Little flowers, urn-shaped and narrow at the mouth, hang among dark blue-green leaves. Deciduous, climbs by twisting leaf stems.	July–Oct.	Carmine red

Culture: Full sun to light shade. Rich, moist soil.
Comments: This showy native American often dies back to the ground in winter, but puts out flowers on new spring growth. Tolerates drought.

Clerodendrum thomsoniae   (kleer-oh-DEN-drum tom-SOHN-ee-eye)   **BLEEDING-HEART, GLORY BOWER**

Place of Origin	Zone	Mature Size	Plant Description	Season of Bloom	Flower Color
West Africa	9	6–10 ft.	Panicles of small flowers adorn the dark green, deeply ribbed foliage. Evergreen, climbs by twining stems.	Aug.–Oct.	White with crimson star

Culture: Full sun. Humusy, well-drained soil.
Comments: Because of its modest size and free-flowering habit, makes a fine potted plant, indoors in a sunny room or outdoors on a sunny patio. Prune after flowering.

Clianthus puniceus   (klee-AN-thus pew-NEE-see-us)   **PARROT'S BEAK**

Place of Origin	Zone	Mature Size	Plant Description	Season of Bloom	Flower Color
New Zealand	9	6–8 ft.	3-in. flowers resembling a parrot's beak are borne in clusters forming in the leaf axils. Foliage is feathery, dark green. Evergreen, nonclimbing sprawler.	June–July	Crimson

Culture: Full sun. Rich, sandy soil.
Comments: Best trained to a trellis to show off beautiful leaves. Thin and prune out dead wood in spring.

Place of Origin	Zone	Mature Size	Plant Description	Season of Bloom	Flower Color

Clytostoma callistegioides (also called *Bignonia violacea*) (kly-toe-STOH-mah kal-ih-STEE-jee-oh-EYE-deez) VIOLET TRUMPET VINE, LOVE CHARM VINE

Place of Origin	Zone	Mature Size	Plant Description	Season of Bloom	Flower Color
Brazil	9	15 ft.	Glossy, dark green leaflets cover this vigorous grower. Lifts profuse masses of 3-in. trumpets aloft for the Easter season in warm areas. Evergreen, climbs using tendrils.	Mar.–Apr.	Lavender

Culture: Sun or shade. Average soil.
Comments: Tops get nipped back at 20°F, but roots withstand frosts to 10°F. A sturdy grip allows it to climb over anything. Prune in late winter.

Cobaea scandens (KO-bee-ah SKAN-dens) CUP-AND-SAUCER VINE

Place of Origin	Zone	Mature Size	Plant Description	Season of Bloom	Flower Color
Mexico	10	30 ft.	The 2½-in., bell-shaped flowers open green, then turn violet, then purple. They're surrounded by a green calyx. Flowers appear singly on the vine. Deciduous, climbs using tendrils.	May–Oct.	Purple and green

Culture: Full sun. Average soil.
Comments: Fast-growing. Treated as an annual in all but the warmest zones. Makes an excellent sunscreen in the greenhouse, sun room. Prune in late fall to contain growth.
Cultivar: 'Alba', white and green flowers.

Decumaria barbara (day-koo-MAIR-ee-ah bar-BEAR-ah) CLIMBING HYDRANGEA VINE

Place of Origin	Zone	Mature Size	Plant Description	Season of Bloom	Flower Color
Southeastern United States	6	30 ft.	Small, fragrant flowers cover the vine's glossy foliage in high summer. Deciduous in the North; semi-evergreen in the Sun Belt. Climbs using aerial roots.	June–July	White

Culture: Sun or shade. Average soil.
Comments: An excellent vine to train up into a tree. Resembles *Hydrangea anomala* (below), but less showy and earlier blooming.

(continued)

Place of Origin	Zone	Mature Size	Plant Description	Season of Bloom	Flower Color

Distictis buccinatoria   (diss-TIK-tuss BUCK-sin-ah-TOR-ee-ah)   **BLOOD RED TRUMPET VINE**

| Mexico | 9 | 20-30 ft. | Clusters of variably sized flower trumpets (2-6 in.) appear among dark green, oblong leaves. Evergreen, climbs using tendrils. | Peaks in June | Red with golden throat |

Culture: Full sun to partial shade. Average soil.
Comments: Flowers form on tips of new growth, so prune after peak bloom. Lightly prune vine tips in late fall. Can be rampant.
Other Species: *Distictis laxiflora,* has vanilla-scented trumpets, a rampant grower.

Distictis × 'Riversii'   (diss-TIK-tuss RIV-er-zee-eye)   **ROYAL or RIVER'S TRUMPET VINE**

| Mexico | 9 | 20-30 ft. | This hybrid distictus carries gorgeous flower trumpets. Evergreen, climbs using tendrils. | Peaks in June | Purple with orange throat |

Culture: Full sun to partial shade. Average soil.
Comments: In Zone 10 it will bloom most of the year. In Zone 9, its peak is June, but it will flower lightly during the whole growing season.

Gelsemium sempervirens   (gel-SEM-ee-um sem-per-VY-rens)   **CAROLINA YELLOW JESSAMINE**

| Southeastern United States | 7 | 20 ft. | Shiny, 4-in. leaves along the twining stems give a delicate appearance. Early in the year it produces clusters of fragrant, funnel-shaped flowers. Evergreen, climbs by twining. | Feb.-Mar. | Yellow |

Culture: Sun or shade. Roots like cool, rich soil.
Comments: A good vine for growing up small trees since its roots like to be shaded. In winter the leaves turn red. All parts of the plant are toxic. Prune after flowering.

Place of Origin	Zone	Mature Size	Plant Description	Season of Bloom	Flower Color
Gloriosa rothschildiana (glor-ee-OH-sah roth-child-ee-AN-ah) **GLORY LILY**					
Africa	9	10-15 ft.	Large, lily-shaped flowers are set against pretty, bright green, recurved leaves. Deciduous, climbs by tendril-like, elongated leaf tips.	June-Aug.	Scarlet, edged with yellow

Culture: Full sun to light shade. Moist soil.
Comments: The gloriosa grown for accent or on posts in greenhouse or outside in containers. After tops die, store in cool cellar in pot. Withhold water until Jan.

Hardenbergia violacea (hard-en-BER-jee-ah vy-oh-LAY-see-ah) **LILAC VINE, CORAL PEA**					
Australia	9	10 ft.	Clusters of pealike flowers emerge from leaf axils. Slender leaves trace pretty patterns on the trellis. Evergreen, climbs by twining.	Feb.-Apr.	Violet-blue

Culture: Partial shade to full shade. Rich, peaty loam.
Comments: Vine grows with a lovely, compact habit that makes it just right for training on a porch, low fence, or wall. Prune after flowering.

Hibbertia scandens (also called **_H. volubilis_**) (hy-BERT-ee-ah SKAN-dens) **GUINEA GOLD VINE**					
Australia	10	10-30 ft.	A low climber with dark, waxy leaves and single flowers. Evergreen, climbs by twining.	May-Oct.	Bright yellow

Culture: Partial shade. Moist, humusy soil.
Comments: Although it will grow in full sun, prefers light shade. Good plant for a fence or trellis where it can be seen. Prune in early spring to thin out thick growth.

(continued)

Place of Origin	Zone	Mature Size	Plant Description	Season of Bloom	Flower Color

Hoya carnosa   (HOY-ah car-NO-sah)   WAX FLOWER

Southeastern Asia	10	10 ft.	Perfect little waxy, five-pointed stars hang in fragrant clusters. 2-3-in. oval leaves are leathery, glossy. Evergreen, climbs by stem rootlets.	June–July	Creamy white

Culture: Semishade when grown outdoors; sun indoors. Humusy, sandy soil.
Comments: Nice plant for trimming a sunny window. Likes to be potbound. Let it dry out between waterings. Needs no pruning.
Cultivars: 'Exotica', yellowish-pink leaves edged in green; 'Variegata', green leaves have white margins.

Hydrangea anomala   (hy-DRAIN-jee-ah ahn-AHM-ah-lah)   CLIMBING HYDRANGEA

Japan	4	50 ft.	Lacy clusters of flowers 6-10 in. across bloom on long stems held above coarse, heart-shaped leaves. Deciduous, climbs by aerial rootlets.	June	White

Culture: Shade to full sun. Rich, moist, well-drained soil.
Comments: Prune in winter to keep it within bounds. Good cover for a large, partially shaded stone or brick wall.

Jasminum grandiflorum (also called *J. officinale 'Grandiflorum'*)   (JAZ-min-um grand-ih-FLOR-um)   ROYAL JASMINE

China	7	12 ft.	Fragrant clusters of small flowers form on shrubby-looking vines. Semi-evergreen in warm zones; deciduous in colder regions. Not a climber; needs support.	June–Sept.	White

Culture: Full sun to partial shade. Average soil.
Comments: Flowers open all summer, perfuming the area around them. The vine looks nice on walls, fences, or on a trellis. Thin to shape after flowering.

Place of Origin	Zone	Mature Size	Plant Description	Season of Bloom	Flower Color

Jasminum nitidum (JAZ-min-um NIT-ih-dum)   ANGEL-WING JASMINE

Place of Origin	Zone	Mature Size	Plant Description	Season of Bloom	Flower Color
Admiralty Islands	10	20 ft.	Beautiful, pinwheel-shaped, fragrant flowers appear in groups of 3 over handsome, evergreen, glossy foliage. Not a climber; needs support.	May–Aug.	White

Culture: Full sun to partial shade. Average soil.
Comments: This vine will run, but happily forms a shrubby plant if kept pruned back. An excellent plant for a patio container.

Jasminum nudiflorum   (JAZ-min-um new-dih-FLOR-um)   WINTER JASMINE

Place of Origin	Zone	Mature Size	Plant Description	Season of Bloom	Flower Color
China	6	15 ft.	Flowers appear early, before the leaves. Stems are slender and willowy. Hardiest of the jasmines, but unfortunately not fragrant. Deciduous. Not a climber, needs support.	Jan.–Mar.	Bright yellow

Culture: Full sun to full shade. Average soil.
Comments: Can be grown as a ground cover if not staked up. Best grown along a wall or fence where graceful branches can hang down. Prune after flowering.

Jasminum officinale   (JAZ-min-um off-ish-in-AL-ee)   POET'S JASMINE

Place of Origin	Zone	Mature Size	Plant Description	Season of Bloom	Flower Color
Himalayas	7	30 ft.	A vine with deeply divided leaves, sprinkled all summer with small, heavily fragrant flowers. The scent is the essence found in jasmine perfume. Semi-evergreen to deciduous; climbs by twining, but requires support.	Mar.–Nov.	White

Culture: Full sun to partial shade. Average soil.
Comments: This species jasmine doesn't mind being potbound; grow indoors in a sunny spot. Thin after flowering.
Cultivar: 'Grandiflorum', larger flowers than species.

(continued)

Place of Origin	Zone	Mature Size	Plant Description	Season of Bloom	Flower Color

Jasminum polyanthum (JAZ-min-um polly-AN-thum) **PINK JASMINE**

Place of Origin	Zone	Mature Size	Plant Description	Season of Bloom	Flower Color
Western China	9	20 ft.	Panicles of rose pink buds open to clusters of fragrant white flowers among dark green leaves, each with 5 to 7 leaflets. Evergreen, climbs by twining.	Feb.–June	White

Culture: Full sun to partial shade. Average soil.
Comments: A free-flowering vine that needs a trellis and supports for upright growth. Good also as a ground cover or in a pot in a cool greenhouse. Prune after flowering.

Lapageria rosea (lap-ah-JEER-ee-ah roe-ZEE-ah) **CHILEAN BELLFLOWER**

Place of Origin	Zone	Mature Size	Plant Description	Season of Bloom	Flower Color
Southern Chile	10	10–20 ft.	Very showy vine that produces waxy flower bells, 3 in. long, singly and in small clusters. Slender stems carry dark green, leathery leaves. Evergreen, climbs by twining.	July–Oct.	Rosy red

Culture: Partial shade. Rich, humusy, well-drained soil.
Comments: Chile's national flower likes a mix of compost, peat, and sand when grown in a 10-in. pot indoors. Will not tolerate too much heat or frost. Prune to desired shape in early spring.
Cultivar: 'Alba', flowers are white with pink blush.

Lathyrus latifolius (LATH-ih-russ lat-ih-FOAL-ee-us) **PERENNIAL PEA**

Place of Origin	Zone	Mature Size	Plant Description	Season of Bloom	Flower Color
Europe	3	6–10 ft.	A vine that dies back to the roots each year. Clambers among shrubs and over banks and low walls, throwing out clusters of 7-9 pealike flowers as it goes. Herbaceous perennial vine, climbs by tendrils.	June–Sept.	Deep to light rose or white.

Culture: Full sun. Moist, rich soil.
Comments: Lathyrus has escaped to the wild, where it is familiar in many parts of the country. Cut back regularly to promote continued blooming.
Cultivar: 'White Pearl', a white bloomer.

Place of Origin	Zone	Mature Size	Plant Description	Season of Bloom	Flower Color

Lonicera flava (lo-NISS-er-ah FLAH-vah) YELLOW HONEYSUCKLE					
Southeastern United States	6	20-30 ft.	A deciduous climbing vine, native to the mid-South, that produces its fragrant honeysuckle flowers in whorls.	May–June	Yellow

Culture: Full sun to partial shade. Average soil.
Comments: This species's color is best described as yellow-orange.

Lonicera heckrottii (lo-NISS-er-ah heck-ROT-ee-eye) EVERBLOOMING HONEYSUCKLE, GOLD FLAME HONEYSUCKLE					
United States	4	15 ft.	2-in. flowers appear in clusters on this viny shrub. Deciduous, needs support.	May–frost	Yellow inside; purplish outside

Culture: Full sun to partial shade. Average soil.
Comments: Its chief feature is its long period of bloom. Thin to shape during dormancy.

Lonicera hildebrandiana (lo-NISS-er-ah hil-dih-brand-ee-AN-ah) GIANT BURMESE HONEYSUCKLE					
Burma	10	50-60 ft.	Fragrant, 6-7-in. flower tubes open creamy white, then turn reddish-orange. The glossy evergreen leaves are borne on fast-growing twining stems.	June	Reddish-orange

Culture: Full sun. Rich, moist soil.
Comments: In the Burmese jungle, this vine will grow to nearly 100 ft. Showy plant for a large greenhouse. Prune out old wood occasionally.

(continued)

Place of Origin	Zone	Mature Size	Plant Description	Season of Bloom	Flower Color

Lonicera japonica 'Halliana'   (lo-NISS-er-ah ja-PON-ih-kah)   HALL'S HONEYSUCKLE

East Asia	4	30 ft.	Rampant vine with heavily fragrant flowers. Evergreen to semi-evergreen, climbs by twining.	June	White and creamy yellow

Culture: Full sun to partial shade. Any soil.
Comments: A pest in the mid-Atlantic states. Good ground cover. Grown for its sweet scent. Prune severely to keep it within bounds each dormant period.
Cultivar: 'Aureo-reticulata', slower-growing garden favorite with gold-veined leaves.

Lonicera periclymenum   (lo-NISS-er-ah pare-ih-cly-MEE-num)   WOODBINE HONEY-SUCKLE

Europe	4	20 ft.	Fragrant, whorled flowers decorate the slender, deciduous stems of this twining vine.	June–Aug.	Light yellow with purple-red blush

Culture: Partial shade. Any soil.
Comments: This is the famed woodbine of Shakespeare and of European lore. Makes excellent progress on trees. A good screen. Prune older stems to ground in winter.
Cultivars: 'Belgica', known as early Dutch honeysuckle, blooms May–June; 'Serotina', called late Dutch honeysuckle, blooms July–Oct.

Lonicera sempervirens   (lo-NISS-er-ah sem-per-VY-rens)   TRUMPET HONEYSUCKLE

Eastern United States	3	50 ft.	Stems grow to make a big plant with bluish-green leaves. Flowers are 1½–2-in. trumpets with no fragrance. Deciduous, climbs by twining.	June–Aug.	Scarlet outside, yellow inside

Culture: Full sun to partial shade. Good soil.
Comments: A very hardy vine to cover fences, walls, other structures. Flowers are followed by red berries. Prune out old wood in late winter.
Cultivars: 'Dropmore Scarlet', bright red blooms; 'Sulphurea', yellow flowers; 'Superba', scarlet blossoms.

Place of Origin	Zone	Mature Size	Plant Description	Season of Bloom	Flower Color

Macfadyena unguis-cati (mack-fad-ee-EN-ah UNG-wiss CAT-eye)
CAT'S-CLAW, YELLOW TRUMPET VINE

Place of Origin	Zone	Mature Size	Plant Description	Season of Bloom	Flower Color
Argentina	8	25-40 ft.	Showy, 2½-in., trumpet-shaped flowers decorate this fast-growing vine that clings by means of clawlike tendrils (hence the common name). Deciduous to semi-evergreen.	Apr.–May	Yellow

Culture: Full sun. Average soil.
Comments: Its tenacious, hooked claws give this vine the ability to cover and cool walls facing the hot sun. Prune to shape after bloom; trim some stems to ground level to force new stems each year.

Mandevilla 'Alice du Pont' (man-dih-VILL-ah)   **BIG CHILEAN JASMINE**

Place of Origin	Zone	Mature Size	Plant Description	Season of Bloom	Flower Color
Brazil	10	20-30 ft.	2-4-in. morning-glory-like flowers of the purest pink are borne singly on vines covered with rumply leaves. Evergreen, climbs by twining.	June–Nov.	Pink

Culture: Partial shade. Rich, humusy soil.
Comments: One of the prettiest greenhouse plants. Grows to 10 ft. in a large pot. Refuses to bloom in hot temperatures, likes California coastal areas. Trim stems back by a third in late winter.

Mandevilla laxa (also called *M. suaveolens*)   (man-dih-VILL-ah LAKS-ah)   **CHILEAN JASMINE**

Place of Origin	Zone	Mature Size	Plant Description	Season of Bloom	Flower Color
Argentina	9	15 ft.	2-in., ruffled flowers open in clusters of 5 or 6, pouring a wonderful fragrance into the air. Vine twines in an open, loose shower of long, heart-shaped leaves. Deciduous.	June–Aug.	White

Culture: Full sun. Rich soil.
Comments: May need some support as it twines up a tree, fence, or post. Loses its leaves in winter. Blooms on new growth, so feel free to keep it trimmed. Great in heated sunroom.

(continued)

Place of Origin	Zone	Mature Size	Plant Description	Season of Bloom	Flower Color

Manettia cordifolia   (man-ET-ee-ah kor-dih-FOAL-ee-ah)   **FIRECRACKER VINE**

| Brazil | 10 | 3–6 ft. | Dainty little herbaceous climber with striking, 1-in., tubular flowers, tipped yellow at their slightly flared open ends. Evergreen, climbs by twining. | All year | Scarlet-red with yellow edging |

Culture: Full sun to partial shade. Rich, moist, well-drained soil.
Comments: In a sunny, warm location, it flowers in all seasons. A very tender vine, it doesn't like greenhouse temperatures below 55°F. Prune in spring to promote more blooms.

Millettia reticulata   (mill-ET-ee-ah reh-tick-you-LAH-tah)   **EVERGREEN RED WISTERIA**

| China | 8 | 10–15 ft. | Rich, deep carmine, pealike blossoms appear in clusters at the tips of the vine's branches. Leaves are leathery, bright green. Evergreen. Climbs by twining but needs some support. | July–Sept. | Violet-red |

Culture: Full sun. Humusy, moist, well-drained soil.
Comments: Deeply colored flowers are nicely set off by the pretty leaves. Will survive in sheltered parts of Zone 7.

Pandorea jasminoides   (pan-DORE-ee-ah jaz-min-oh-EYE-deez)   **BOWER VINE**

| Australia | 9 | 20 ft. | Shiny, dark green leaves on slender stems form a backdrop for the 2 in. wide trumpets that appear in clusters of 4–8 blooms. Evergreen, climbs by twining. | June–Oct. | White and pink |

Culture: Full sun. Rich soil.
Comments: Shiny foliage and blushing pink flowers give this vine a quiet beauty. Good in the greenhouse. Prune annually in spring to promote a thicker growth.
Cultivars: 'Alba', pure white flowers; 'Rosea', flowers are pink with maroon throats.

Place of Origin	Zone	Mature Size	Plant Description	Season of Bloom	Flower Color

Pandorea pandorana (pan-DORE-ee-ah pan-dore-AHN-ah) **WONGA-WONGA VINE**

| Australia | 9 | 20 ft. | The lush, shiny foliage of this exotic vine tends to obscure the clustered sprays of small, 1-in. trumpets. Evergreen, climbs by twining. | Apr. | Creamy white with brown to purple spots in throat |

Culture: Full sun to partial shade. Rich soil.
Comments: Makes a fence-covering screen or a ground cover. Give it room to grow and use in combinations with more exuberant flowers. Prune annually after bloom.

Passiflora ✕alatocaerulea (also called **P. pfordtii**)
(pass-ih-FLOR-ah ah-LAHT-oh-see-REW-lee-ah) **HYBRID PASSIONFLOWER**

| Hybrid origin | 8 | 15–30 ft. | Bears fragrant, 4-in. flowers. 3-lobed leaves distinguish it from P. caerulea, which has 5 lobes. Semi-evergreen, climbs by tendrils. | June–Oct. | White and pink with bluish-purple crown |

Culture: Full sun to partial shade. Rich to average soil.
Comments: Most commonly grown passionflower in California. Grows well in a cool greenhouse or sunny room in the house, as do all the species of passionflowers listed here. Prune back excess growth in late winter.

Passiflora caerulea (pass-ih-FLOR-ah see-REW-lee-ah) **BLUE CROWN PASSIONFLOWER**

| Brazil | 8 | 15–30 ft. | 5 blue, showy petals surrounded by green sepals appear singly on the vines. Evergreen, climbs by tendrils. | June–Oct. | Bluish-purple |

Culture: Full sun to partial shade. Rich to average soil.
Comments: Trim in late winter to keep it looking good. Excellent for an unheated greenhouse.
Cultivar: 'Constance Elliott', white flowers.

(continued)

Place of Origin	Zone	Mature Size	Plant Description	Season of Bloom	Flower Color

Passiflora edulis   (pass-ih-FLOR-ah ED-you-lus)   PURPLE GRANDADILLA, PASSION FRUIT

Place of Origin	Zone	Mature Size	Plant Description	Season of Bloom	Flower Color
Brazil	9	6-10 ft.	Showy flowers, 2-3 in. across, adorn compact, semi-evergreen vines, and are followed by small edible fruits. Climbs by tendrils.	June-Sept.	White with purple and white crowns

Culture: Full sun to partial shade. Rich, moist, sandy loam.
Comments: A favorite for growing on fences. Needs pruning of old, dead growth in late winter. Purple grandadilla is the source for passion fruit and juice.

Passiflora incarnata   (pass-ih-FLOR-ah in-kar-NAH-tah)   MAYPOP, WILD PASSION-FLOWER

Place of Origin	Zone	Mature Size	Plant Description	Season of Bloom	Flower Color
Southeastern United States	7	20 ft.	Spreads rapidly by underground rhizomes. Covered with pretty, 2-in. flowers. A herbaceous perennial, climbs by tendrils.	July-Oct.	White with purplish-pink crowns

Culture: Full sun. Well-drained but moist soil.
Comments: Outside, it can decorate a fence, arbor, or trellis. Inside, it makes a fine potted plant. Thin overgrown plants in late winter. This vine is the state flower of Tennessee.

Passiflora jamesonii   (pass-ih-FLOR-ah jaym-SOHN-ee-eye)   CORAL-RED PASSIONFLOWER

Place of Origin	Zone	Mature Size	Plant Description	Season of Bloom	Flower Color
Peru	9	20 ft.	Showy, 4-in. blooms sport elongated crowns of purplish tubes in their centers. Leaves are deeply cut and glossy. Evergreen, climbs by tendrils.	June-Oct.	Bright coral-red

Culture: Full sun. Rich to average soil.
Comments: The vine is a strong grower. Prune excess growth in late winter.

Place of Origin	Zone	Mature Size	Plant Description	Season of Bloom	Flower Color

Passiflora mollissima		(pass-ih-FLOR-ah moll-ISS-im-ah)		**BANANA PASSION VINE**	
Andes	9	30 ft.	3-in. flowers have long (4-5-in.) green tubes in their centers, and hang downward from the vines. Evergreen, climbs by tendrils.	June-Oct.	Rosy pink

Culture: Full sun. Rich to average soil.
Comments: Flowers are followed by 2-in. yellow fruits, hence the common name of this pretty vine. Can be rampant, so prune back annually to keep it within bounds.

Petrea volubilis		(peh-TREE-ah vol-OO-bill-us)		**PURPLE WREATH**	
West Indies	10	10 ft.	9-in. racemes of small starlike, lilac florets have rich purple centers. When petals fall, blue calyx holds color. Vine itself is open, scraggly, with rough, leathery leaves. Evergreen, climbs by twining.	Intermittent from Apr.-July	Purple

Culture: Sun to partial shade. Rich, moist, well-drained soil.
Comments: Lends a striking note to any warm greenhouse, where it will bloom over winter. Prune lightly after the main flower display to keep the vine shaped.

Pileostegia viburnoides		(PIL-ee-oh-STEE-jee-ah vy-burn-oh-EYE-deez)		**CLINGING VINE, TANGLEHEAD**	
Himalayas	7	45 ft.	Flowers are borne in panicles that hang among dark green leaves. Evergreen vines attach to walls using rootlets.	Aug.-Oct.	Creamy white

Culture: Full shade to sun. Moist, humusy soil.
Comments: Profusely covered with showy flowers in autumn. Slow-growing, tenacious climber. Likes shade. Good on a north wall. Prune out old or out-of-place wood in winter.

(continued)

Place of Origin	Zone	Mature Size	Plant Description	Season of Bloom	Flower Color

Plumbago auriculata (also called **P. capensis**)   (plum-BAY-goh aw-rik-you-LAH-tah)
CAPE PLUMBAGO

Place of Origin	Zone	Mature Size	Plant Description	Season of Bloom	Flower Color
South Africa	9	10 ft.	1-2-in. tubular flowers produced all year in warmer parts of Zones 9 and 10. Shrubby vine with light green, semi-evergreen leaves. Not a true climber. Train to vine shape.	Mar.-Dec.	Sky blue

Culture: Full sun. Well-drained, sandy soil.
Comments: Covers low walls and fences, functions as a ground cover on bare soil, and tolerates summer drought once it's established. Prune hard in spring.

Polygonum aubertii   (pol-IG-oh-num aw-BER-tee-eye)   **SILVER LACE VINE**

Place of Origin	Zone	Mature Size	Plant Description	Season of Bloom	Flower Color
Western China	4	40 ft.	A perennial vine with loose panicles of small flowers and sparse leaves, giving an open, airy appearance. Deciduous, climbs by twining.	Aug.-Sept.	White

Culture: Full sun. Average soil.
Comments: This rapid grower can extend itself up to 25 ft. over a growing season, and should be kept in check. Prune hard in fall.

Pyrostegia venusta (also called **Bignonia venusta**)   (pie-roh-STEE-jee-ah ven-OO-stah)
FLAME VINE

Place of Origin	Zone	Mature Size	Plant Description	Season of Bloom	Flower Color
Brazil	10	20 ft.	3 in. long flowers cluster in massed groups over this evergreen vine. Climbs by tendrils.	Summer, again in winter	Hot, tropical orange

Culture: Full sun to partial shade. Rich soil.
Comments: A favorite vine for shading walls if grown on a trellis, or outdoor patios if grown on an arbor. Won't tolerate frost. Does well in a greenhouse. Prune hard after flowering.

ROSES (See the chart, Climbing and Rambling Roses, on page 273.)

Place of Origin	Zone	Mature Size	Plant Description	Season of Bloom	Flower Color

Schisandra chinensis (sky-SAN-drah chy-NEN-siss) **MAGNOLIA VINE**

China	5	25 ft.	1-in. typical magnolia flowers appear singly on long, drooping stems. If both sexes are present, scarlet berries follow the flowers. Deciduous, climbs by twining.	Apr.-May	White to pale pink

Culture: Sun to semishade. Average soil.
Comments: Fragrant vine that likes its roots cool. If growing both a male and a female, train them to intertwine for nice effect. Prune when dormant.

Schizophragma hydrangeoides (skiz-oh-FRAG-mah hy-drain-jee-oh-EYE-deez)
JAPANESE HYDRANGEA VINE

Japan	5	30 ft.	4-in. clusters of florets, each with a single calyx lobe. Leaves are toothed like an actual hydrangea. Deciduous, climbs by aerial rootlets.	June	Creamy white

Culture: Sun to semishade. Rich, moist soil.
Comments: Needs to be tied to upright supports when young. Two different kinds of blooms: showy single petals are sterile, smaller creamy clusters are fertile. Prune in late winter. Closely resembles *Hydrangea anomala.*

Schizophragma integrifolium (skiz-oh-FRAG-mah in-teg-rih-FOAL-ee-um)
CHINESE HYDRANGEA VINE

China	7	12 ft.	Although the vine reaches only to 12 ft., it bears large, 10-in. clusters of hydrangea-like flowers. Petals of sterile florets can reach 3½ in. across. Deciduous, climbs by aerial rootlets.	July-Aug.	White

Culture: Sun to semishade. Rich, moist soil.
Comments: "The most elegant deciduous vine I've ever seen," said Marshall Olbrich, a renowned nurseryman and horticulturist. Prune only to train.

(continued)

Place of Origin	Zone	Mature Size	Plant Description	Season of Bloom	Flower Color

Senecio confusus (sen-EE-see-oh con-FEW-suss)   MEXICAN FLAME VINE

Place of Origin	Zone	Mature Size	Plant Description	Season of Bloom	Flower Color
Mexico	9	10 ft.	Daisylike flowers have orange-red rays and yellow centers, appear in clusters. Evergreen in areas of no frost. Climbs by twining.	All season	Orange-red

Culture: Sun to semishade. Moist, sandy soil.
Comments: Frosts will nip it back to the ground, but it regrows swiftly each year. Gives a striking splash of color in the greenhouse.

Solandra maxima (soh-LAN-drah MAX-ih-mah)   CUP-OF-GOLD

Place of Origin	Zone	Mature Size	Plant Description	Season of Bloom	Flower Color
Mexico	9	20–40 ft.	Chalice-shaped, 9-in. flowers are striped down the centers of the petals. Evergreen. Needs support.	Feb.–Apr.	Yellow with brownish-purple stripes

Culture: Full sun for foliage, roots need shade. Tolerates poor soil.
Comments: Makes quick, even rampant growth. In Zone 10, blooms all winter. Needs frost protection in Zone 9. Good greenhouse vine. Prune annually to induce new shoots.

Solanum jasminoides (soh-LAN-um jaz-min-oh-EYE-deez)   POTATO VINE

Place of Origin	Zone	Mature Size	Plant Description	Season of Bloom	Flower Color
Brazil	9	30 ft.	A wiry-looking vine with profuse clusters of small, nightshade-shaped flowers on thin stems. Deciduous in areas with frost. Climbs by twining.	Mar.–June; Aug.–Nov.	Pale blue to white with yellow stamens

Culture: Full sun to partial shade. Average soil.
Comments: Useful but not spectacular for covering fences. Keep it pruned to the area desired, as it can grow wantonly. Prune hard at any time to promote new growth or keep in check.
Cultivars: 'Album', white flowers; 'Grandiflorum', a cultivar with larger flowers the same color as the species.

Place of Origin	Zone	Mature Size	Plant Description	Season of Bloom	Flower Color

Solanum wendlandii (soh-LAN-um wend-LAND-ee-eye) **COSTA RICAN POTATO VINE, COSTA RICAN NIGHTSHADE**

Costa Rica	10	50 ft.	Large flower clusters make spectacular displays on long, coarse stems. Deciduous, climbs by twining.	July–Oct.	Lilac-blue

Culture: Full sun. Well-drained average soil.
Comments: Extremely attractive vine when used on pergolas and buildings. Prune during winter.

Stephanotis floribunda (stef-in-OH-tiss flor-ih-BUN-dah) **MADAGASCAR JASMINE**

Madagascar	10	15 ft.	Clusters of waxy, sweet-smelling blossoms contrast beautifully with the dark green, thick, leathery leaves. Evergreen, climbs by twining.	May–Oct.	White

Culture: Partial shade. Rich, moist, cool soil.
Comments: Usually grown under glass, needs 4 hours of direct sun daily for bloom. Stop feeding in Sept., allow soil to dry between waterings. Prune to refresh plant.

Stigmaphyllon ciliatum (stig-mah-FY-lon sill-ee-AH-tum) **BUTTERFLY VINE, ORCHID VINE**

Brazil	10	10-20 ft.	Umbels of 3-6 orchid-like flowers among sparse, heart-shaped leaves. Vines tender and evergreen, climb by twining.	July–Sept.	Golden yellow

Culture: Full sun to partial shade. Humusy, acid soil.
Comments: Produces bloom from late spring to winter, with a chief flush in the hot months. Prune annually in winter. A good greenhouse plant; prefers ample root space.

(continued)

Place of Origin	Zone	Mature Size	Plant Description	Season of Bloom	Flower Color

---

Tecomaria capensis   (tek-oh-MAIR-ee-ah cap-EN-siss)   CAPE HONEYSUCKLE

Place of Origin	Zone	Mature Size	Plant Description	Season of Bloom	Flower Color
South Africa	9	15–20 ft.	Clusters of 2-in., tubular flowers create colorful splashes among glistening leaves. Evergreen, tie to support.	Oct.–May	Orange-red

Culture: Full sun. Rich, moist, well-drained soil.
Comments: The foliage looks nice through the year. Prune annually just after flowering to force new growth.

Thunbergia alata   (thun-BER-jee-ah ah-LAH-tah)   BLACK-EYED SUSAN VINE

Place of Origin	Zone	Mature Size	Plant Description	Season of Bloom	Flower Color
South Africa	10	6 ft.	Flaring petals are set off by deep purple-black centers. Blooms appear amid triangular leaves of the evergreen, twining vines.	June–Sept.	Creamy orange with purplish-black centers

Culture: Full sun. Rich, moist, well-drained soil.
Comments: Often grown in a hanging pot as an annual in the colder climates. Adds an unusual color scheme to the greenhouse.

Thunbergia grandiflora   (thun-BER-jee-ah grand-ih-FLOR-ah)
BLUE TRUMPET VINE, CLOCK VINE, SKY FLOWER

Place of Origin	Zone	Mature Size	Plant Description	Season of Bloom	Flower Color
India	10	20–50 ft.	3-in., cup-shaped flowers appear alone or in clusters on the tender evergreen vine. Climbs by twining.	Fall, winter, spring	Pure, pale blue

Culture: Full sun to light shade. Rich, moist, well-drained soil.
Comments: Casts a heavy shade, so it is a good choice to cover an open fence, where its flowers can be admired. Prune annually in early spring to keep it in trim.

Place of Origin	Zone	Mature Size	Plant Description	Season of Bloom	Flower Color

Thunbergia gregorii	(thun-BER-jee-ah greg-OR-ee-eye)			**ORANGE CLOCK VINE**	
Africa	10	6 ft.	2-in., flat, flared flowers borne profusely on hairy stems. Evergreen, climbs by twining.	June–Sept.	Orange

Culture: Full sun. Average, well-drained soil.
Comments: Thrives in a generous-size pot. Can be grown as an annual. Orange color is very intense. Prune the spent shoots in winter.

Trachelospermum asiaticum	(track-el-oh-SPUR-mum aiz-ee-AT-ih-kum)			**YELLOW STAR JASMINE**	
Japan	8	15 ft.	Fragrant blossoms dangle from shrubby climbing stems. Evergreen, climbs by twining.	Apr.–July	Whitish-yellow

Culture: Prefers partial shade, tolerates full sun. Average soil.
Comments: Somewhat smaller than *T. jasminoides*. Versatile vine that works well on the patio, or in a pot inside. Prune as needed, in fall.

Trachelospermum jasminoides	(track-el-oh-SPUR-mum jaz-min-oh-EYE-deez)				
STAR JASMINE					
China	9	20 ft.	Sprays of heavily scented, starlike flowers produced in small clusters among the attractive, shiny, dark, evergreen leaves. Climbs by twining.	Apr.–Aug.	White

Culture: Full sun to shade. Average soil.
Comments: Allowed to trail, it forms a thick, fragrant ground cover. Tied up to supports, it will turn a porch post into a jasmine pillar. Prune as needed, in fall.
Cultivar: 'Variegatum', flowers are variegated green with reddish tinge.

(continued)

Place of Origin	Zone	Mature Size	Plant Description	Season of Bloom	Flower Color

Tropaeolum speciosum (tro-pee-OH-lum spee-see-OH-sum) **FLAME FLOWER, FLAME CREEPER**

Place of Origin	Zone	Mature Size	Plant Description	Season of Bloom	Flower Color
Chile	7	10 ft.	1-in. flowers produced amid bright green leaves. Deciduous, climbs by coiling stalks.	July–Sept.	Bright red

Culture: Sun for foliage, shade for roots. Moist, cool, humusy soil.
Comments: Delicate roots must be grown in shade, but the vines like to climb into evergreens and shrubs to find the sun. Dies back to the ground in winter.

Vigna caracalla (also called **Phaseolus giganteus**) (VIG-nah kare-ah-KAL-ah) **SNAIL VINE**

Place of Origin	Zone	Mature Size	Plant Description	Season of Bloom	Flower Color
South America	10	20 ft.	Flowers resemble those of the pea, with the tails curled like snail shells. Blooms in pendant clusters. Deciduous, climbs by twining.	All year	Light lavender

Culture: Full sun. Average soil.
Comments: Loses its visual appeal late in the season when it enters rest period. Compensate by growing late-flowering vines like morning-glory. Prune to ground after first frosts.

Wisteria floribunda (wiss-TEER-ee-ah flor-ih-BUN-dah) **JAPANESE WISTERIA**

Place of Origin	Zone	Mature Size	Plant Description	Season of Bloom	Flower Color
Japan	4	35 ft.	Woody vine that attains a great height from which to hang its long, fragrant clusters of flowers. Deciduous, climbs by twining.	Apr–May	Violet

Culture: Full sun. Rich soil.
Comments: This species's long clusters give a cascading effect as they open from the top down. Prune when dormant.
Cultivars: 'Longissima', also called 'Macrobotrys', violet flower clusters measure up to 3 ft. long; 'Longissima Alba', fragrant, white clusters range from 15-24 in. long; 'Rosea', 15-18 in. long, pink flower clusters are very fragrant; 'Violacea Plena', violet clusters of double flowers.

Place of Origin	Zone	Mature Size	Plant Description	Season of Bloom	Flower Color

Wisteria sinensis (wiss-TEER-ee-ah sy-NEN-siss) **CHINESE WISTERIA**					
China	5	80-100 ft.	This familiar wisteria, with dense clusters of slightly fragrant flowers, creates a spectacular effect in early spring. Deciduous, climbs by twining.	Apr.–May	Blue-violet

Culture: Full sun. Rich, well-drained soil.
Comments: Will keep growing for many years, reaching great lengths. 6-12 in. long clusters of florets appear before the leaves. Prune when dormant.
Cultivar: 'Alba', white, fragrant clusters.

Wisteria venusta (wiss-TEER-ee-ah ven-OO-stah) **SILKY WISTERIA**					
Japan	5	30 ft.	Large clusters of big flowers hang pendulously from vines carrying silky, downy leaves. Deciduous, climbs by twining.	Apr.–May	White

Culture: Full sun. Rich, well-drained soil.
Comments: Very profuse bloomer. The best of the white wisterias. Prune annually in winter to keep to the form you want.
Cultivar: 'Violacea', fragrant, bluish-purple clusters.

These hybrid, giant-flowered clematises are typically hardy to Zone 4. They bloom best with 8 hours of sunshine per day, and good, neutral to slightly acid garden loam. Like most other types of clematis, they like their roots shaded, preferably by a deep mulch. Most range between 8 and 12 feet in length when mature.

PRUNING CODE: Some clematis vines flower on 1-year-old wood, others on new growth. How you prune is determined by the plant's flowering habit.

Those that flower on 1-year-old wood don't need pruning to make good bloom, but may require it to stay within bounds. These types are best pruned after flowering is finished. This allows new shoots to grow and mature in time for next season's floral display. Varieties in this category are given a pruning code of A.

Those that flower on new growth need an annual trimming back to just a few feet of old wood in order to stimulate the production of as much new growth each year as possible. This pruning should be done before these deciduous vines burst their buds for the new year's growth. Varieties in this category are given a pruning code of B.

Cultivar Name	Flower Description	Season of Bloom	Pruning Code
'Barbara Jackman'			
	Lavender sepals ("petals") marked with crimson stripes. 5-7 in. wide.	May-June	A
'Belle of Woking'			
	Silvery blue double flowers. 6-8 in. wide.	May-June	A
'Capitaine Thuilleaux'			
	Creamy sepals with red-pink bars. 6-8 in. wide.	May-June	A
'Comtesse de Bouchard'			
	Rosy pink sepals with cream stamens. 4-6 in. wide.	June -Sept.	B
'Crimson King'			
	Big crimson blooms, double on old wood, single on new growth. 6-8 in. wide.	June-Sept.	A

Cultivar Name	Flower Description	Season of Bloom	Pruning Code
'Dr. Ruppel'			
	8 ruffled pink sepals have wide carmine bars. 6-8 in. wide.	May-June	A
'Duchess of Edinburgh'			
	Very double white rosettes with yellow stamens. 4-6 in. wide.	May-June; Sept.	A
'Ernest Markham'			
	Hot magenta sepals with golden stamens. 4-6 in. wide.	Aug.-Oct.	B
'Etoile Violette'			
	Deep purple, with golden stamens. 4-5 in. wide.	July-Sept.	B
'Gillian Blades'			
	Big, ruffled white sepals with yellow stamens. 7-9 in. wide.	May-June; Sept.	A
'Hagley Hybrid'			
	Shell pink cupped sepals with dusky purple stamens. 5-6 in. wide.	June-Sept.	B

(continued)

Cultivar Name	Flower Description	Season of Bloom	Pruning Code
'Henryi'			
	Handsome, pure white sepals with creamy bar, reddish stamens. 6-8 in. wide.	June-Sept.	A
'Jackmanii'			
	4 velvety purple sepals; profuse bloom. 4-6 in. wide.	June-Sept.	B
'John Warren'			
	8 overlapping soft pink sepals with carmine edges and midribs. 6-8 in. wide.	June-Sept.	A
'Lady Betty Balfour'			
	Violet-blue sepals with yellow stamens. 6-8 in. wide.	Sept.-Oct.	B
'Lincoln Star'			
	Raspberry pink sepals with pale edges and maroon center. 6-8 in. wide.	May-June; Sept.	A
'Marcel Moser'			
	Soft lavender sepals with dark red bars. Reddish-purple stamens. 7-9 in. wide.	May-June; Sept.	A

Cultivar Name	Flower Description	Season of Bloom	Pruning Code
'Mrs. N. Thompson'			
	Long, graceful, violet-blue sepals with deep red bars and red stamens. 4-6 in. wide.	May-June; Sept.	A
'Nelly Moser'			
	Large, pale pink sepals carry bars of darker pink. 7-9 in. wide.	May-June; Sept.	A
'Niobe'			
	Sepals open dark red, mature to a rich ruby. Golden stamens. 4-6 in. wide.	June-Sept.	B
'Ramona'			
	Lavender-blue sepals with dark stamens. 6-8 in. wide.	June-Sept.	A
'Red Cardinal'			
	Gracefully curved, crimson sepals with yellow stamens. 6-8 in. wide.	June-Sept.	B
'Ruby Glow'			
	Ruby red sepals with dark stamens. 4-6 in. wide.	June-Sept.	A
'Star of India'			
	Plum-colored sepals with red bars. 4-6 in. wide.	June-Sept.	B

(continued)

Cultivar Name	Flower Description	Season of Bloom	Pruning Code
'Ville de Lyon'			
	Velvety carmine sepals shade to deep crimson on the edges. Golden stamens. 4-6 in. wide.	July-Oct.	B
'Violet Charm'			
	Long, pointed sepals of deep violet. 7-9 in. wide.	June-Sept.	A
'Vyvyan Pennell'			
	Double deep violet sepals with reddish-purple centers. 6-8 in. wide.	May-June	A
'Will Goodwin'			
	Frilled, lavender-blue, deeply veined sepals with golden stamens. 6-8 in. wide.	June-Sept.	A

Natural climbing roses are classified as "large-flowered climbers," and usually carry stiff, vigorous stems that grow to 15 feet and more. Most flowers are large (4 to 6 inches), and occur at a peak season, although some bloom usually appears after the peak is finished. They are a disease-resistant group, ordinarily, and relatively hardy to 0°F if mulched or mounded with soil so the crowns are protected. They like to grow upright so you should plan on providing some sort of support.

Climbing sports of familiar bush roses such as hybrid teas, floribundas, and polyanthas are mutations with a penchant for long, vigorous stems. 'Climbing Peace', for instance, is a sport, or mutation, of the familiar 'Peace' hybrid tea rose that is grown as a bush. Although some cultivars are hardy, most of these climbers are tender in Zone 8 and colder, and will need protection. Climbing sports are recognized by the word "climbing" in front of the name of a familiar rose. These types bloom best if bent and tied to a trellis, fence, railing or other horizontal support.

'Lady Banks' roses (sometimes simply called Banksian roses) are evergreen in Zone 10, deciduous in areas of frost, and not reliably hardy in areas colder than Zone 7. They're thornless, with small flowers, and grow to 20 or 30 feet, or even more in favored spots. This type is disease-resistant.

Rambling roses are old-fashioned, very hardy, disease-resistant types with long, slender stems. They are excellent for covering pergolas, arbors, walls, trees, or roofs. Roses used as trailing vines are included in this category.

Flower Color	Season of Bloom	Remarks
Large-flowered Climbing Roses		
'America'		
Salmon	June–Sept.	Blossoms very double, profuse. Easy-to-grow, hardy, and disease-resistant. Called "the perfect climber." Fragrant.
'Blossomtime'		
Pink	June–Sept.	Compact form, reaching only 6 ft. Lovely pink flowers borne 3 to a cluster appear all season. Fragrant.
'Don Juan'		
Deep red	June–Sept.	4-5 in. wide blooms perfume the air with a strong damask scent. Perfect for growing on a post near a doorway. Disease-resistant. Not hardy in Zone 7 and north.
'Dortmund'		
Bright cherry	June, with repeats	Single flowers form large clusters over its compact (to 10 ft.) frame. Hardy and disease-resistant, with a light fragrance.

(continued)

Flower Color	Season of Bloom	Remarks
'Handel'		
Light pink edged with rose	June–Sept.	Beautiful blooms appear over whole plant. Best on a fence, up a post, or across a railing.
'Joseph's Coat'		
Cardinal red, yellow, or orange	All seasons	Double, 4 in. wide blossoms range from yellow to red, even in the same cluster. Hardy to Zone 8. Reaches 12-15 ft.
'Madame Alfred Carriere'		
White	June–Aug.	4 in. wide, double, mildly fragrant blossoms are produced all summer. Hardy only to Zone 8. Pest-free. Reaches 15 ft.
'Mermaid'		
Ivory yellow	June–Sept.	Blossoms are single and carry bouquets of golden stamens in their centers. Grows 15-30 ft. Disease-free, mildly fragrant, and hardy to Zone 7.
'New Dawn'		
Pink, turning silver	June–Sept.	Little (2 in. wide) blossoms appear in small clusters on long stems. Very hardy, vigorous. Reaches 15 ft.
'Royal Flush'		
White with pink edges	June–Aug.	This hardy, compact little rose has few thorns and a light floral scent. The blooms turn light lavender before petals fall. Grows to 6-8 ft.
'Royal Sunset'		
Orange to cream	June–Aug.	A beautiful apricot hue and a pretty scent are offered by the 4-5 in. wide double blossoms. Grows to 6 ft. Disease-resistant. Needs deep winter mulching.

Flower Color	Season of Bloom	Remarks
'White Dawn'		
White	June-Sept.	Very double blossoms are 2-3 in. across in massed, pure white clusters. Grows to 15 ft. Hardy. Lightly fragrant.

Climbing Sports

'Climbing Cecile Brunner'		
Light pink	May peak	This is a climbing 'Sweetheart' rose that can reach 25 ft. or more, blooming profusely over its entire length. Hardy to Zone 7. Light scent.
'Climbing Charlotte Armstrong'		
Deep pink	May-June	A climbing hybrid tea rose with crimson buds and well-formed, very double blooms. Will cover an arbor or large trellis. Needs winter protection. Strong floral scent.
'Climbing Chrysler Imperial'		
Dark red	May-June	Large (5 in. wide) very double blossoms on thick canes carry a rich fragrance. Needs winter protection.
'Climbing Crimson Glory'		
Deep crimson	May-June	Grows to 10-12 ft. on vigorous stems. Blossoms are heavily fragrant with a strong damask scent. Hardy to Zone 6.
'Climbing Dainty Bess'		
Light pink with red centers	May-June	Exquisitely pretty, dainty pink flowers with cherry red stamens in the cups. Petal edges are scalloped. Flowers are single. Disease-resistant. Reaches 10 ft. Needs winter protection.

(continued)

Flower Color	Season of Bloom	Remarks
'Climbing Elegance'		
Yellow	May-June	Hardy to Zone 6, it carries a strong fragrance, and makes a fine cut flower.
'Climbing Etoile de Hollande'		
Red	May-June	Not very hardy, but a superior climbing rose in Zones 8-10. Flowers borne on long stems, so they are good for cutting. Grows to 20 ft. in warm areas. Needs protection in cold-winter areas. Damask scent.
'Climbing First Prize'		
Deep pink	May-June	Large (6 in. wide) blossoms are impressive. Grows to 12-15 ft. Hardy to Zone 7.
'Climbing Mrs. Sam McGredy'		
Salmon pink	May-June	Repeats bloom during the season. Flowers are 4-5 in. wide, double, fragrant.
'Climbing Peace'		
Gold with pink edges	May-June	The climbing version of the world's favorite rose. A vase of cut flowers of this kind is simply gorgeous. Grows to 15 ft., but train horizontally for best bloom. Protect in winter.
'Climbing Snowbird'		
Pale yellow to cream	May-June	Grows to 6-8 ft. Hardy in Zones 8 and 9 only. Classed as a white rose, but color is rich cream. Fragrant.

'Lady Banks' Roses

Rosa banksiae **'Alba Plena'** (ROE-sah BANK-sih-ah)		
White	May-June	This is the white form of 'Lutea', and carries the bonus of a sweet, violet scent.

Flower Color	Season of Bloom	Remarks
R. banksiae 'Lutea'		
Yellow	May–June	Masses of very double, scentless, small flowers cover the long (20-30 ft.), thornless, slender stems. Hardy to Zone 7. Evergreen in Zone 10.

Rambling Roses

'Chevy Chase'		
Red	June	Small red flowers are produced in profusion during flowering season. Disease-resistant and hardy. Keep older canes pruned out.
'Evangeline'		
Pink with white and yellow centers	June	Will cover large areas. Hardy to Zone 6. Disease-resistant and fragrant. Keep 2- and 3-year-old wood pruned out.
Rosa laevigata (ROE-sah lee-vih-GATE-ah)		
White	May	Naturalized from Georgia to Texas. Fragrant. 3 in. wide blooms ramble over sheds and trees.

Height	Flower Color	Plant Description

Clitoria ternatea   (clih-TOR-ee-ah ter-NAH-tee-ah)   **BUTTERFLY PEA**

10-15 ft.	Blue	Blooms in just 4 months. Pinch to keep the vine bushy. Climbs by twining.

Cultivar: 'Blue Sails' carries deep blue, semidouble flowers.

Cobaea scandens   (KO-bee-ah SKAN-dens)   **CUP-AND-SAUCER VINE**

10-25 ft.	Purple and green	Fast-growing. 2½-in. single bells turn from green to purple as they mature. Climbs by tendrils. Because of a rather dull appearance, best used behind showier plants as a screen.

Dolichos lablab   (DOLL-ih-kohs LAB-lab)   **HYACINTH BEAN**

15-25 ft.	Purple to white	Bright green leaves and scented, 1-in., pea-shaped flowers add a cheery note to a sunny post or trellis. Flowers followed by purple seedpods.

Eccremocarpus scaber   (ek-REEM-oh-KAR-pus SKAH-ber)   **CHILEAN GLORY FLOWER**

6-12 ft.	Red-orange	Huge, showy clusters of 1-in. tubular flowers appear at tips of this dense vine. Perennial in areas of mild winter temperatures. Tolerates sun or partial shade.

Ipomoea alba   (ih-po-MEE-ah AL-bah)   **MOONFLOWER**

20-30 ft.	Satiny white	6-in., sweetly scented flowers open in early evening, close next morning. Good for growing up a post near a patio where folks spend their evenings.

Ipomoea nil   'Scarlet O'Hara'   (ih-po-MEE-ah NIL)   **JAPANESE IPOMOEA**

10-20 ft.	Scarlet	4 in. wide trumpets with fringed or fluted petals. The species has yielded hybrids with red, pink, blue, lavender, and violet flowers.

Cultivar: 'Flying Saucer' comes in sky blue and white.

Height	Flower Color	Plant Description

Ipomoea quamoclit (ih-po-MEE-ah KWAM-oh-clit)   **CYPRESS VINE**

| 10-20 ft. | Scarlet, pink, or white | 1½-in., star-shaped flowers open in the evening and morning, close during the sunny hours. Feathery foliage is attractive along fences or on latticework. |

Ipomoea tricolor 'Heavenly' (ih-po-MEE-ah TRY-color)   **MORNING-GLORY**

| 10-20 ft. | Sky blue | Large, heavenly trumpets of the purest sky blue carry a sunny golden yellow in their throats. Plant wilts in hot sun, even when given ample water, recovers in evening. |

Lathyrus odorata (LATH-ih-russ oh-door-AH-tah)   **SWEET PEA**

| 5-8 ft. | Blue, rose, purple, carmine, white, or pink | Sweet-smelling, pea-blossom-shaped flowers in shades of blues and pinks add color and fragrance to trellis or netting. Remove spent blooms or flower production will cease. Excellent in the greenhouse. Poisonous. |

Phaseolus coccineus (fay-zee-OH-luss cox-ih-NEE-us)   **SCARLET RUNNER BEAN**

| 15-30 ft. | Rich scarlet | A true bean whose pods are perfectly edible, this vine produces pendulous clusters of 12 or more 1-in. flowers. |

Thunbergia alata (thun-BER-jee-ah ah-LAH-tah)   **BLACK-EYED SUSAN VINE**

| 5-8 ft. | Pale yellow-orange with black centers | Blooms with 2-in., flat flowers. Likes a cool greenhouse and thrives in a hanging basket in the summer. |

Tropaeolum majus (troh-pee-OH-lum MAY-jus)   **NASTURTIUM**

| 5-10 ft. | Maroon, orange, yellow, or white | Although usually allowed to trail over the ground, nasturtium will climb up to 6 ft., providing lots of colorful, edible buds and flowers. There is a dwarf form just 15 in. tall. |

Tropaeolum peregrinum (troh-pee-OH-lum pair-eh-GRY-num)   **CANARY-BIRD FLOWER**

| 10-15 ft. | Canary yellow | The 1-in. frilly flowers carry green spurs. A pretty vine that does best in dappled shade and moist soil. Good for a cool greenhouse. |

Chapter 5
Maintaining the Garden's Beauty

The three most important areas where gardeners get to apply their aesthetic sense are in selecting the plants, siting them in the garden, and maintaining them artistically. We've already discussed the first two areas in Chapters 1 and 2. Now we need to look at the artistic maintenance of the garden.

Too many gardeners simply plant their trees and shrubs and then allow them to grow rampantly, following their own plant growth imperatives. But beauty is about quality, not quantity. Just as intensive gardening has become the standard for vegetable gardening because it produces the most food for the effort, so the strongest, deepest aesthetic experiences are to be gained in intensively cultivated and maintained ornamental gardens, like those of Japan, not in extensive landscapes full of unkempt specimen trees and shrubs.

Keep your plantings limited to a number that you can maintain intensively; don't set yourself garden tasks so herculean that you're bound to fail. Success and satisfaction can be achieved in a 10-by-10-foot outdoor "room," where a 3-acre plot would cause only chaos and frustration.

Maintenance involves the standard work of the garden: improving the soil, mulching, watering, trellising, controlling pests, pruning out old and dead wood, renewing and dividing plants, heading back unruly growth, disentangling vines, tip pruning for a bushier, fresher appearance, and general tidying up. There are many excellent garden guides that tell you how to carry out these necessary tasks. But in this book *artistic* maintenance centers around three main ways to maintain the living beauty of the garden: pruning for character and beauty (a concept that is seldom, if ever, discussed), proper watering, and proper spacing between mixed plants in a grouping.

Pruning Artistically

Probably the most neglected task in American ornamental gardening is pruning for beauty, and yet for a minimum of effort it pays enormous dividends in the artistic appearance of the garden. There's no way to teach art, but by careful observation and application and an unrelenting insistence on the highest standards of quality, ordinary gardeners become creators of horticultural art. When properly applied, such pruning exposes the multiple trunks and

What if common trees growing in the ground were pruned like bonsai, to reveal more pleasing shapes in both wood and foliage? An evergreen chamaecyparis, top left, could be opened to reveal branches and background. A pomegranate, top right, is given the bonsai treatment, as are the Japanese maple at lower left and the old pink crabapple at lower right.

lower branches of shrubs that wouldn't otherwise be seen, revealing and enhancing the natural movements and rhythms of the plants. These exposed parts can be quite attractive if pruned conscientiously.

The best example of conscientious pruning is bonsai. There's something ultimately satisfying about the asymmetrical forms that develop under the clippers of bonsai masters. They have a grace that comes from their balance—a dense area of compact foliage here balanced by a thin, extended branch with bits of foliage there. Always the shape of the trunk and branches is an integral part of the pleasure one gets from looking at the plant.

Now visualize your whole garden—annuals, perennials, vines, shrubs, and trees—as a bonsai on a full-size scale. Again it is the asymmetrical balance of forces that makes the whole garden beautiful—while certain areas of trunk are exposed, other areas are hidden behind foliage; an especially sensuous curve of a branch is revealed; the sinuous form of a vine, with bushels of flowers tumbling over it all, is called out from the foliage by the sun and the urges of nature.

Pruning for Character

The best plants to prune for character are those with small or finely textured leaves—species of leptospermum, clethra, prunus and barberry—or those with outstanding bark, such as stewartia, franklinia, red-barked *Cornus alba* 'Sibirica', paperbark maple, Persian parrotia, and amelanchier, among others. Large-leaved plants, such as magnolias and abutilons, are best allowed to grow as they will, for they know how best to display their leaves in the optimum way. If low branches are removed to expose the wood, large-leaved plants tend to look top-heavy.

Start your artistic pruning program when the plants are young, but prune very lightly for the first few years to allow the plants a chance to display as much leaf area as possible and build up a strong root system. From there, apply some of the techniques of bonsai to appropriate trees and shrubs. Try to avoid the purely symmetrical shape unless you want to feature such a shape—as with the perfect symmetry of *Metasequoia glyptostroboides,* the dawn redwood.

With shrubs, especially conifers, remove some branches to allow open places where branches and trunk may be seen. The effect is one of aesthetically contrasting areas of dense foliage and open, woody structure. Old and low-growing conifers can go from undistinguished lumps of green needles to extremely attractive plants when their old wood is displayed by judicious pruning of lower and side branches.

Among flowering woody plants, you'll find that azaleas, species of hawthorn and prunus, shrubby cotoneasters, *Pittosporum tobira,* and the syringas lend themselves to artistic pruning. Among nonflowering plants, boxwood, pines, hemlocks, spruces, hollies, and various hedges are all improved by judicious pruning.

Encouraging More Rose Blooms

Roses are a special case. It's possible to train roses to standard (tree) forms, but most so-called tree roses are floribunda types grafted to the top of a trunk of *Rosa rugosa* or other strong grower, and need a lot of extra care to remain a standard. More frequently, the gardener will want to prune shrub roses, climbers, and ramblers for best bloom rather than to achieve a certain shape.

With hybrid tea roses, that means taking out two-year-old canes and any that might

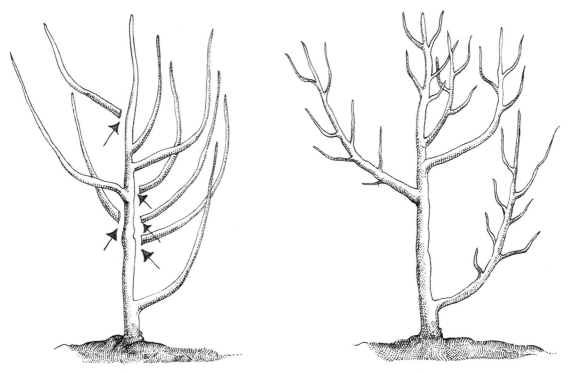

Rather than allowing many little branches to grow, prune shrubs when young to establish several main branches. This gives a more pleasing flower display when the plants mature.

be even older, and nipping back the tips of year-old canes. Roses bloom on new shoots from one-year-old wood, and so pruning means cutting back older wood and allowing the flowering canes to remain. With shrubby roses like grandifloras and floribundas, prune to a simple shrub shape, removing most of the older wood each year. Rambling and climbing roses should be kept to the three to five strongest canes each year. All dead and diseased canes should be cut back with sharp shears disinfected in bleach between cuts. Prune rambling and climbing roses after flowering, prune shrub roses in spring before budburst in cold winter areas, or in fall in mild winter areas.

Pruning Guidelines

There's no way to give complete pruning instructions for all the plants listed in this book. But we can give some general principles that, if understood and followed, will allow you develop great expertise as a pruner.

Prune Lightly at Planting

When planting bare-root ornamental trees, prune back broken roots to fresh tissue, cut away broken branch tips to a healthy bud, and take out any crowded or crossed branches. Prune as little as possible at

Oriental horticulturists liken this effect to clouds in the sky. Removal of selected branches that aren't central to the composition gives a nice contrast between foliage, branch structure, and background.

planting time for maximum leaf production the first year. Some say to cut the central leader or growing point back by a third to compensate for root loss, but that may be too severe a rule. If the plant can't support all the leaves produced the first year, it will simply die back to a level it can handle, and you can prune away the dead tips next winter. If given enough water, good drainage so it doesn't sit in a bog, and an adequate root system, most trees will do just fine. As for shrubs, the same pruning rules apply to the roots, but often you'll find these are a tangled mass. Take your spade and separate the roots a bit so they splay outward evenly all around. This pushing around in the root ball with the spade will lightly prune a lot of small roots, forcing the plant to produce new growing root tips and generally hastening the plant's settling in period.

Unless it's absolutely necessary to do otherwise, transplant trees and shrubs when they're dormant. If you've pruned to give them a generous root system, prepared a large planting hole, and made sure they didn't dry out, most will wake up and hardly notice they've been moved. Vigorous growth, however, won't start in most species until the root system has grown to penetrate the soil to the plant's satisfaction. Only then will top growth take off.

Plants then tend to reach an equilibrium between leaf area and root structure. Prune off too much wood and the root system will shrink. Prune off too many roots, and the tops die back to restore equilibrium. Wood is the plant's storehouse for food and scaffolding for leaf and flower display. Don't remove it without good reason.

Understand How the Plant Grows and Flowers

It's folly to prune anything unless you thoroughly understand what you're doing.

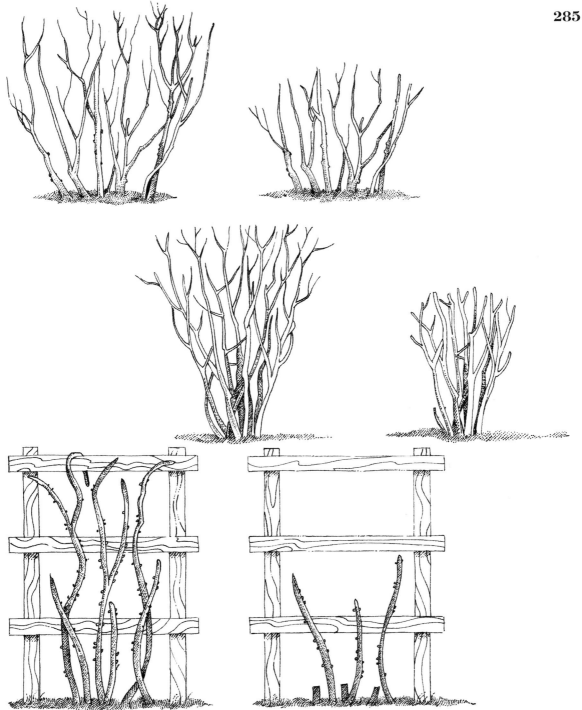

At top, a hybrid tea rose has been topped back for the winter. This bush is just 2 years old. Next season, 2- and 3-year-old wood will be taken out completely. In center, a shrub rose has been pruned back and older wood removed. At bottom, ramblers that threaten to outgrow their trellis are heavily pruned; they're vigorous enough to withstand it.

And that means understanding how the plant came to grow as it did, the consequences of the pruning cut, and what will happen if you don't prune. And that means understanding the growth of the plant through time.

One of the best ways to grasp the growth of a plant through time is to mark several limbs with colored tape, make various kinds of cuts on them, then study what happens to subsequent buds, flowers, and vegetative growth over several years. Keep a notebook of the original intention or theory you were investigating when making each pruning cut. That way you can refer back to refresh your memory each year. If you do this with an azalea, for instance, you'll notice that next year's flowers arise on buds just below the attachment point of this year's flowers, and that if you shear the plant, you'll shear off most of next year's flowers. As you begin to grasp how each plant reacts to a particular kind of pruning cut, record the information in the notebook on the page devoted to that cut.

Prune for Health and Wealth

Pruning for health means cutting out crossed limbs, diseased tissue, and dead wood. It can mean opening up the center of a tree to allow better air circulation, thus cutting down on mildew problems. It can mean removing suckers from the base that will turn your specimen into an overgrown shrub patch if left unchecked.

Pruning for wealth means pruning for a maximum number, or maximum size, of fruit or flowers. Blue-ribbon-sized roses, for instance, can be produced by removing all clusters from a shoot except for the big terminal cluster, and removing all buds except the largest terminal bud. On the other hand,

shearing a plant like forsythia means stimulating side shoot production, with an attendant profusion of blooms from the side shoots next year.

Watering to Keep the Garden's Beauty Alive

As you expand your garden, or install one to begin with, give a thought to how you will water it during dry spells. After all, water is one of the essential ingredients for good plant growth; without enough of this liquid asset during times of drought, your investment in a yard full of beautiful, blooming plants could be ruined.

Here in California and other semiarid regions, watering has been brought to a high art, with flowering gardens entirely underlaid with a system of delivery pipes and various kinds of sprinkler heads. Some throw fine sprays of water over circles about 20 feet in diameter, others pop out of the ground and drench everything quickly, then sink out of sight. Many of the systems are connected to a computerized board that automatically waters each section of the garden as the gardener wishes.

In semiarid regions, most garden centers carry plastic irrigation systems of varying quality. If you're contemplating buying an irrigation system, speak with someone who has the system in operation. If it works well for them, it will probably work for you, too. You can also write for a catalog of up-to-the-minute irrigation equipment from Harmony Farm Supply (see Mail-Order Sources for Ornamental Trees, Shrubs, and Vines on page 295 for the address).

In more well-watered portions of the country, the worst that happens is that you have to drag the hose up the hill during the hot, rainless days of midsummer. It may not

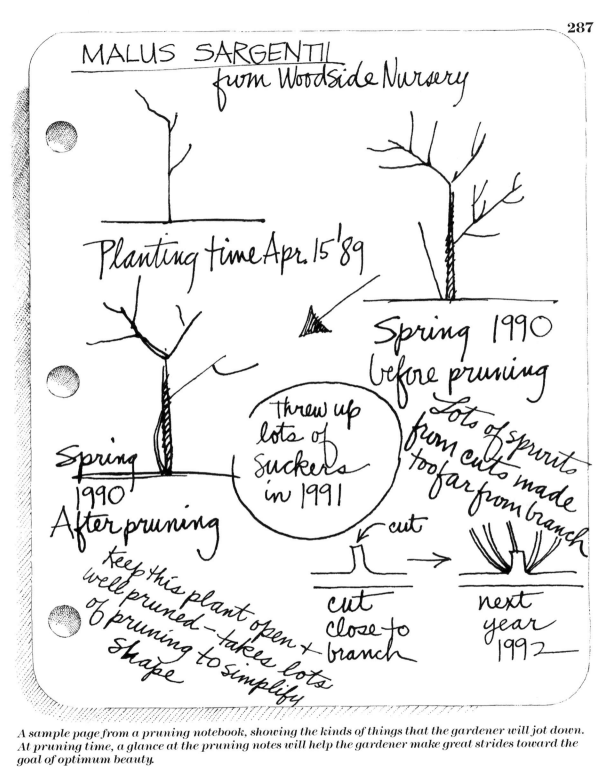

MALUS SARGENTII
from Woodside Nursery

Planting time Apr. 15 '89

Spring 1990
before pruning

Spring
1990
After pruning

threw up
lots of
suckers
in 1991

Lots of spruits
from cuts made
too far from branch

cut

cut
close to
branch

next
year
1992

keep this plant open +
well pruned — takes lots
of pruning to simplify
shape

A sample page from a pruning notebook, showing the kinds of things that the gardener will jot down. At pruning time, a glance at the pruning notes will help the gardener make great strides toward the goal of optimum beauty.

be worth it to install an elaborate sprinkler system for ornamentals. It's better to water ornamentals on the ground so their leaves don't get wet and possibly mildewy. What may be perfectly useful is a single water line with a garden spigot from which you can draw water and to which you can attach a soaker hose. A length of soaker hose laid down the center of a bed of perennials, or snaking through the choice shrubbery, may be all the irrigation equipment you need east of the Rockies.

Overwatering can be very detrimental to the health and good looks of gardens with poor drainage. Most plants can't stand wet feet. Plants grow best when they are slightly stressed between waterings—this causes the roots to reach out for water and makes for a sturdier plant. But the stress should be slight—almost every plant does its best when it gets adequate water.

Plants spaced closely in a garden draw more water per square foot of soil than plants spaced more sparsely, and may be more in need of supplemental summer watering. Keep these increased watering needs in mind as you plan a mixed garden in which different kinds of plants, from trees to shrubs to perennials and annuals, share close quarters.

Spacing for a Good-Looking and Healthy Garden

Spacing of garden plants has a direct effect on how easy it will be for you to maneuver in the garden with your annual rounds of pruning, shearing, dividing, digging, renewing, and planting new stock. And how easy your access is has a direct relation to how good the plants will look. Plants spaced too close together may inhibit your best intentions, with the result that they won't look their best.

Always plant for the mature size of the tree or shrub—that is, the size it will reach in ten years. A decade seems like such a long time, until the decades seem to come as swiftly as the years once did, and your tiny sapling is suddenly high overhead, and exploding with flowers. A spacing approach that gives young plants plenty of room to grow will also give you plenty of room to tend to their needs. Plus it will make sure enough air and sunlight reach the young plants to give them a good, healthy start.

When trees and shrubs mature, they look good just touching, rather than just not touching. If our chart, Flowering Trees, gives a dimension of 20 by 15 feet for a mature plant, then the young plant should be placed 20 feet from the nearest plant anywhere near its size. In the early days of the garden, fill all the resulting empty space with perennials, strawberries, annuals, herbs, and vegetables.

Whether the plant is a tiny alyssum or a giant horse-chestnut, spacings that are too close may cause problems with air circulation and fungus growth, and cause deep shading that kills off understory branches. However, in some cases you may want this latter effect, so you would prune out the dead branches to create a shady bower.

Appendix A
Common Name Index

Flowering Trees

Common Name	Latin Name	Common Name	Latin Name
Apple serviceberry	*Amelanchier grandiflora*	Fragrant snowbell	*Styrax obassia*
Australian flame tree	*Brachychiton acerifolius* 'Majestic Beauty'	Franklin tree	*Franklinia alatamaha*
		Fringe tree	*Chionanthus virginicus*
Australian tea tree	*Leptospermum laevigatum*	Gold medallion tree	*Cassia leptophylla*
BB tree	*Evodia danielii*	Golden-chain tree	*Laburnum ×watereri* 'Vossii'
Bailey's acacia	*Acacia baileyana*		
Bee tree	*Evodia danielii*	Golden trumpet tree	*Tabebuia chrysotricha*
Black locust	*Robinia pseudoacacia*	Golden-rain tree	*Koelreuteria paniculata*
Callery pear	*Pyrus calleryana*		
Cape chestnut	*Calodendrum capense*	Hally Jolivette cherry	*Prunus ×*'Hally Jolivette'
Carolina silverbell	*Halesia carolina*	Handkerchief plant	*Davidia involucrata*
Common catalpa	*Catalpa bignonioides*	Hong Kong orchid tree	*Bauhinia blakeana*
Crape myrtle	*Lagerstroemia indica*	Indian bean tree	*Catalpa bignonioides*
Dove tree	*Davidia involucrata*	Jacaranda	*Jacaranda mimosifolia*
Eastern redbud	*Cercis canadensis*	Japanese flowering cherry	*Prunus serrulata* 'Shogetsu'
Empress tree	*Paulownia tomentosa*	Japanese flowering crabapple	*Malus floribunda*
English hawthorn	*Crataegus laevigata*	Japanese flowering dogwood	*Cornus kousa*
Epaulette tree	*Pterostyrax hispidus*	Japanese pagoda tree	*Sophora japonica*
		Japanese snowbell	*Styrax japonicus*
European mountain ash	*Sorbus aucuparia*	Japanese stewartia	*Stewartia pseudo-camellia*
Evergreen pear	*Pyrus kawakamii*		
Firewheel tree	*Stenocarpus sinuatus*	Japanese tree lilac	*Syringa reticulata*
		Kaffirboom coral tree	*Erythrina caffra*
Flame eucalyptus	*Eucalyptus ficifolia*	Korean evodia	*Evodia danielii*
		Korean mountain ash	*Sorbus alnifolia*
Flaxleaf paperbark	*Melaleuca linariifolia*	Little Girl hybrid magnolia	*Magnolia ×*'Betty'
Floss silk tree	*Chorisia speciosa*	Merrill's magnolia	*Magnolia ×loebneri* 'Merrill'
Flowering dogwood	*Cornus florida*		

Flowering Trees—continued

Common Name	Latin Name	Common Name	Latin Name
Mimosa	*Albizia julibrissin*	Smoke tree	*Cotinus coggygria*
Myrobalan plum	*Prunus cerasifera* 'Thunder-cloud'	Snow-in-summer	*Melaleuca linariifolia*
Okame cherry	*Prunus* ×'Okame'	Sourwood	*Oxydendrum arboreum*
Pacific dogwood	*Cornus nuttallii*	Southern catalpa	*Catalpa bignonioides*
Pagoda dogwood	*Cornus alternifolia*		
Persian parrotia	*Parrotia persica*	Southern magnolia	*Magnolia grandiflora*
Poinciana	*Delonix regia*		
Purple plum	*Prunus cerasifera* 'Thunder-cloud'	Star magnolia	*Magnolia stellata*
		Sweet bay magnolia	*Magnolia virginiana*
Red Jade crabapple	*Malus* ×'Red Jade'	Tea crabapple	*Malus hupehensis*
Redbud crabapple	*Malus* ×*zumi* 'Calocarpa'	Ussurian pear	*Pyrus ussuriensis*
		Weeping bottlebrush	*Callistemon viminalis*
Rowan tree	*Sorbus aucuparia*		
Ruby horse-chestnut	*Aesculus* ×*carnea*	Weeping Higan cherry	*Prunus subhirtella* 'Pendula'
Sargent cherry	*Prunus sargentii*		
Sargent crabapple	*Malus sargentii*	Yellow wood	*Cladrastis lutea*
Saucer magnolia	*Magnolia* ×*soulangiana*	Yellowhorn	*Xanthoceras sorbifolium*
Siberian crabapple	*Malus baccata* var. *mandshurica*	Yoshino cherry	*Prunus yedoensis*
		Yulan magnolia	*Magnolia heptapeta*
Silk oak	*Grevillia robusta*		
Silk tree	*Albizia julibrissin*		
Silver frost weeping pear	*Pyrus salicifolia* 'Pendula'		

Flowering Shrubs

Common Name	Latin Name	Common Name	Latin Name
		Bush anemone	*Carpenteria californica*
Beauty bush	*Kolkwitzia amabilis*	Bush arbutus	*Abelia* ×*grandiflora*
Big leaf hydrangea	*Hydrangea macrophylla* 'Nikko Blue'	Bush cinquefoil	*Potentilla fruticosa* 'Primrose Beauty'
Blue hibiscus	*Alyogyne huegelii*		
Blue mist	*Caryopteris* ×*clandonensis* 'Heavenly Blue'	Bush lantana	*Lantana camara* 'Radiation'
Border forsythia	*Forsythia* ×*intermedia* 'Spectabilis'	Buttercup winter hazel	*Corylopsis pauciflora*
		Butterfly bush	*Buddleia davidii*
Bottlebrush	*Callistemon citrinus*	California lilac	*Ceanothus* ×'Dark Star'
Bottlebrush buckeye	*Aesculus parviflora*	California rosebay	*Rhododendron macrophyllum*
Boxleaf hebe	*Hebe buxifolia* 'Patty's Purple'	Carolina allspice	*Calycanthus floridus*
Bridal-wreath spiraea	*Spiraea prunifolia*	Carolina rhododendron	*Rhododendron carolinianum*
Broom	*Genista tinctoria*		

Flowering Shrubs—continued

Common Name	Latin Name	Common Name	Latin Name
Red bells	*Enkianthus campanulatus*	Summer-sweet	*Clethra alnifolia*
Red leaf photinia	*Photinia ×fraseri*	Swamp azalea	*Rhododendron viscosum*
Redleaf rose	*Rosa rubrifolia*	Sweet azalea	*Rhododendron arborescens*
Red vein	*Enkianthus campanulatus*	Sweet pepperbush	*Clethra alnifolia*
Rosebay rhododendron	*Rhododendron maximum*	Tatarian honeysuckle	*Lonicera tatarica*
Rose-of-Sharon	*Hibiscus syriacus* 'Blue Bird'	Torch azalea	*Rhododendron kaempferi*
Royal azalea	*Rhododendron schlippenbachii*	Tree peony	*Paeonia suffruticosa* 'Kinkaku' (also called 'Golden Palace')
Rugosa rose	*Rosa rugosa*		
Scotch broom	*Cytisus scoparius* 'Lord Lambourne'	Tree rhododendron	*Rhododendron arboreum*
Scotch heather	*Calluna vulgaris* 'J. H. Hamilton'	Weigela	*Weigela florida*
Scotch rose	*Rosa spinosissima*	West Coast rhododendron	*Rhododendron macrophyllum*
Shoe button Spiraea	*Spiraea prunifolia*	White forsythia	*Abeliophyllum distichum*
Shrubby St.-John's-wort	*Hypericum prolificum*	White rock rose	*Cistus hybridus* (also called *C. corbariensis*)
Siebold viburnum	*Viburnum sieboldii*		
Slender deutzia	*Deutzia gracilis*	Winter jasmine	*Jasminum nudiflorum*
Small fothergilla	*Fothergilla gardenii*	Wintersweet	*Chimonanthus praecox*
Spice viburnum	*Viburnum carlesii*	Yesterday-today-and-tomorrow	*Brunfelsia pauciflora* 'Floribunda'
Strawberry tree	*Arbutus unedo*		

Flowering Evergreen and Deciduous Vines

Common Name	Latin Name	Common Name	Latin Name
Alpine virgin's bower	*Clematis alpina* 'Pamela Jackman'	Blood red trumpet vine	*Distictis buccinatoria*
Anemone clematis	*Clematis montana* 'Alba'	Blue crown passionflower	*Passiflora caerulea*
Angel-wing jasmine	*Jasminum nitidum*	Blue trumpet vine	*Thunbergia grandiflora*
Banana passion vine	*Passiflora mollissima*	Bower vine	*Pandorea jasminoides*
Big Chilean jasmine	*Mandevilla* 'Alice du Pont'	Butterfly vine	*Stigmaphyllon ciliatum*
Black-eyed Susan vine	*Thunbergia alata*	Cape honeysuckle	*Tecomaria capensis*
Bleeding-heart	*Clerodendrum thomsoniae*	Cape plumbago	*Plumbago auriculata* (also called *P. capensis*)

Common Name	Latin Name	Common Name	Latin Name
Carolina yellow jessamine	*Gelsemium sempervirens*	Glory bower	*Clerodendrum thomsoniae*
Cat's-claw	*Macfadyena unguis-cati*	Glory lily	*Gloriosa rothschild-iana*
Chilean bellflower	*Lapageria rosea*	Golden clematis	*Clematis tangutica*
Chilean jasmine	*Mandevilla laxa* (also called *M. suaveolens*)	Gold flame honeysuckle	*Lonicera heckrottii*
		Guinea gold vine	*Hibbertia scandens* (also called *H. volubilis*)
Chinese hydrangea vine	*Schizophragma integrifolium*		
Chinese trumpet creeper	*Campsis grandiflora*	Hairy clematis	*Clematis chrysocoma* var. *sericea* (also called *C. spooneri*)
Chinese wisteria	*Wisteria sinensis*		
Climbing hydrangea	*Hydrangea anomala*		
Climbing hydrangea vine	*Decumaria barbara*	Hall's honeysuckle	*Lonicera japonica* 'Halliana'
Clinging vine	*Pileostegia viburnoides*	Herald's trumpet	*Beaumontia grandiflora*
Clock vine	*Thunbergia grandiflora*	Hybrid bougainvillea	*Bougainvillea buttiana*
Common trumpet vine	*Campsis radicans*	Hybrid passionflower	*Passiflora ×alatocaeru-lea* (also called *P. pfordtii*)
Coral pea	*Hardenbergia violacea*		
Coral-red passionflower	*Passiflora jamesonii*		
Coral vine	*Antigonon leptopus*	Japanese hydrangea vine	*Schizophragma hydrangeoides*
Costa Rican potato vine	*Solanum wendlandii*	Japanese wisteria	*Wisteria floribunda*
Costa Rican nightshade	*Solanum wendlandii*	Lilac vine	*Hardenbergia violacea*
Cross vine	*Bignonia capreolata* (also called *Anisostichus capreolatus*)	Love charm vine	*Clytostoma callistegioides* (also called *Bignonia violacea*)
Cup-and-saucer vine	*Cobaea scandens*	Love vine	*Antigonon leptopus*
Cup-of-gold	*Solandra maxima*		
Downy clematis	*Clematis macropetala*	Madagascar jasmine	*Stephanotis floribunda*
Easter lily vine	*Beaumontia grandiflora*	Madeira vine	*Anredera cordifolia* (also called *Bous-singaultia baselloides*)
Everblooming honeysuckle	*Lonicera heckrottii*		
Evergreen clematis	*Clematis armandii*	Magnolia vine	*Schisandra chinensis*
Evergreen red wisteria	*Millettia reticulata*		
Firecracker vine	*Manettia cordifolia*	Maypop	*Passiflora incarnata*
Flame creeper	*Tropaeolum speciosum*	Mexican flame vine	*Senecio confusus*
Flame flower	*Tropaeolum speciosum*	Orange clock vine	*Thunbergia gregorii*
Flame vine	*Pyrostegia venusta* (also called *Bignonia venusta*)	Orchid vine	*Stigmaphyllon ciliatum*
		Parrot's beak	*Clianthus puniceus*
Giant Burmese honeysuckle	*Lonicera hildebrand-iana*		

Flowering Evergreen and Deciduous Vines—continued

Common Name	Latin Name	Common Name	Latin Name
Passion fruit	*Passiflora edulis*	Woodbine honeysuckle	*Lonicera periclymenum*
Perennial pea	*Lathyrus latifolius*		
Poet's jasmine	*Jasminum officinale*	Yellow allamanda	*Allamanda cathartica 'Williamsii'*
Potato vine	*Solanum jasminoides*		
Purple bougainvillea	*Bougainvillea spectabilis*	Yellow honeysuckle	*Lonicera flava*
		Yellow star jasmine	*Trachelospermum asiaticum*
Purple grandadilla	*Passiflora edulis*	Yellow trumpet vine	*Anemopaegma chamber-laynii* (also called *Bignonia chamber-laynii*)
Purple wreath	*Petrea volubilis*		
River's trumpet vine	*Distictis ×'Riversii'*		
Rosa de Montana	*Antigonon leptopus*		
Royal jasmine	*Jasminum grandiflorum* (also called *J. officinale* 'Grandi-florum')		
		Yellow trumpet vine	*Macfadyena unguis-cati*
Royal trumpet vine	*Distictis ×'Riversii'*		
Scarlet clematis	*Clematis texensis*		
Silky wisteria	*Wisteria venusta*		
Silver lace vine	*Polygonum aubertii*		

Flowering Annual Vines

Common Name	Latin Name	Common Name	Latin Name
Sky flower	*Thunbergia grandiflora*	Black-eyed Susan vine	*Thunbergia alata*
Snail vine	*Vigna caracalla* (also called *Phaseolus giganteus*)	Butterfly pea	*Clitoria ternatea*
		Canary-bird flower	*Tropaeolum peregrinum*
Star jasmine	*Trachelospermum jasminoides*	Chilean glory flower	*Eccremocarpus scaber*
Sweet autumn clematis	*Clematis dioscorei-folia* (also called *C. paniculata*)	Cup-and-saucer vine	*Cobaea scandens*
		Cypress vine	*Ipomoea quamoclit*
		Hyacinth bean	*Dolichos lablab*
Tanglehead	*Pileostegia viburnoides*	Japanese ipomoea	*Ipomoea nil* 'Scarlet O'Hara'
Trumpet honeysuckle	*Lonicera sempervirens*		
Violet trumpet vine	*Clytostoma callistegioides* (also called *Bignonia violacea*)	Moonflower	*Ipomoea alba*
		Morning-glory	*Ipomoea tricolor*
		Nasturtium	*Tropaeolum majus*
		Scarlet runner bean	*Phaseolus coccineus*
Wax flower	*Hoya carnosa*	Sweet pea	*Lathyrus odorata*
Wild passionflower	*Passiflora incarnata*		
Winter jasmine	*Jasminum nudiflorum*		
Wonga-wonga vine	*Pandorea pandorana*		

Appendix B
Mail-Order Sources for Ornamental Trees, Shrubs, and Vines

These represent some of the more comprehensive catalogs. We only wish we could have listed every one, for some of the small catalogs contain hard-to-find treasures. This group of nurseries, however, gives you access to almost all of the plants mentioned in this book.

The Antique Rose Emporium
    Route 5, Box 143
    Brenham, TX 77833
    (Old-fashioned roses)

Armstrong Roses
    P.O. Box 1020
    Somis, CA 93066
    (Roses)

Busse Gardens
    Route 2, Box 238
    Cokato, MN 55321
    (Perennials)

Carlsons Gardens
    Box 305
    South Salem, NY 10590
    (Rhododendrons and azaleas)

Fiore Enterprises
    P.O. Box 67
    Prairie View, IL 60069
    (Trees, shrubs, evergreens)

Forest Farm
    990 Tetherow Road
    Williams, OR 97544
    (Natives, West Coast ornamentals)

Greer Gardens
    1280 Goodpasture Island Road
    Eugene, OR 97401
    (Rhododendrons and azaleas)

Harmony Farm Supply
    P.O. Box 451
    Graton, CA 95444
    (Irrigation equipment, tools)

Houston Daylily Gardens
    P.O. Box 7008
    The Woodlands, TX 77387
    (Daylilies)

J. L. Hudson, Seedsman
    P.O. Box 1058
    Redwood City, CA 94064
    (Seeds)

Klehm Nursery
    Route 5, Box 197
    South Barrington, IL 60010
    (Daylilies, peonies, hostas)

Logee's Greenhouses
    55 North Street
    Danielson, CT 06239
    (Flowering vines, begonias)

Louisiana Nursery
 Route 7, Box 43
 Opelousas, LA 70570
 (Trees, shrubs, vines)

Mellinger's Nursery
 2310 W. South Range Road
 North Lima, OH 44452
 (Trees, shrubs, vines, tools)

Musser Forests
 P.O. Box 340 M
 Indiana, PA 15701
 (Trees, shrubs, hedge plants)

Pacific Tree Farms
 4301 Lynnwood Drive
 Chula Vista, CA 92010
 (Zone 10 ornamentals)

Rex Bulb Farms
 P.O. Box 774
 Port Townsend, WA 98368
 (Lilies)

Roses of Yesterday and Today
 802 Brown's Valley Road
 Watsonville, CA 95076
 (Roses)

Smith & Hawken
 25 Corte Madera
 Mill Valley, CA 94941
 (Tools, books, furniture)

Thompson & Morgan
 P.O. Box 1308
 Jackson, NJ 08527
 (Annual flower seeds)

W. Atlee Burpee Co.
 Warminster, PA 18974
 (Flower seeds)

Wayside Gardens
 Hodges, SC 29695
 (Trees, shrubs, vines, perennials, ground
  covers, conifers)

White Flower Farm
 Route 63
 Litchfield, CT 06759
 (Perennials)

Woodlanders, Inc.
 1128 Colleton Avenue
 Aiken, SC 29801
 (Trees, shrubs, vines)

Hardiness Zone Map

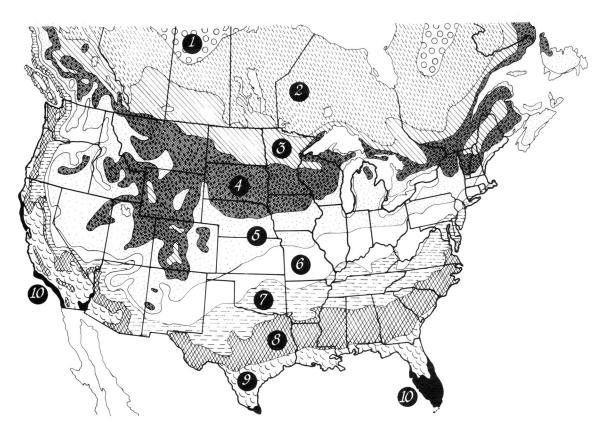

Average Minimum Temperatures for Each Zone

Zone 1	below -50°F	Zone 6 -10° to 0°
Zone 2	-50° to -40°	Zone 7 0° to 10°
Zone 3	-40° to -30°	Zone 8 10° to 20°
Zone 4	-30° to -20°	Zone 9 20° to 30°
Zone 5	-20° to -10°	Zone 10 30° to 40°

Photography Credits

Candace Billman: photo 41
Richard Brown: photos 30, 40
David Cavagnaro: photos 2, 3, 7, 8, 9, 10, 11, 12, 13, 14, 15, 17, 18, 19, 20, 23, 26, 45, 53, 54, 55, 56, 62, 63, 65, 67, 69, 70, 73, 75, 76, 77, 78, 79
Marilyn Cox: photos 5, 6, 31, 37, 49, 51, 58, 59, 64, 68
Brian Davis: photo 71
Derek Fell: photo 66
T. L. Gettings: photos 21, 28, 29, 34, 60
Heather Hafleigh: photos 25, 27, 42
J. Michael Kanouff: photo 47
Alison Miksch: photos 16, 32, 33, 38, 57
Joanne Pavia: photo 24
Rodale Press Photography Department: photos 1, 4, 46, 50, 74
Margaret Skrovanek: photo 43
Marilyn Stouffer: photos 22, 35, 36, 39, 44, 48, 52, 61
M. Hamilton Whitman: photo 72 (Ladew Topiary Gardens)

Index

Page references in italic indicate charts and tables. Boldface references indicate illustrations and photographs.